ETHICS
MATTERS

How to Implement
Values-Driven
Management

ETHICS MATTERS

How to Implement Values-Driven Management

Dawn-Marie **Driscoll**

AND

W. Michael **Hoffman**

CENTER FOR BUSINESS ETHICS

BENTLEY COLLEGE • WALTHAM, MASSACHUSETTS

LIBRARY OF CONGRESS CATALOGING-IN-PUBLICATION DATA

Driscoll, Dawn-Marie.
    Ethics matters : how to implement values-driven management / Dawn-Marie Driscoll and W. Michael Hoffman.
      p.cm.
    Includes bibliographical references and index.
    ISBN 0-9675514-0-4 (pbk. : alk. paper)

    1. Business ethics. 2. Industrial management—Moral and ethical aspects. I. Hoffman, W. Michael. II. Title.

HF5387.D75 1999
658.4'08—dc21   99-052887

For Norman Marcus, who lives his values every day and for Sister Thérèse Higgins, who made this, and everything, possible.

DMD

For my family who continues to support me and for my colleagues who also toil in the ethics field who continue to inspire me.

WMH

For all those ethics practitioners to whom it matters that business be values-driven.

DMD and *WMH*

CONTENTS

Acknowledgements

Some authors describe the writing process as a lonely endeavor. We are fortunate that our experience in writing this book was exactly the opposite. We have been blessed with a wide circle of colleagues and friends in the business ethics field who were generous with their time and opinions and who contributed to the ideas, stories and facts in this volume. Obviously, ethics matters as much to all of them as it does to us.

A heartfelt "thank you" only begins to describe the debt we owe them. The meetings and telephone calls, the debates and dialogues, the invitations to participate in their most senior level councils of ethics oversight, the papers, speeches, and reference materials and resources — all were invaluable. The quotations in this book are taken from personal interviews with all of them, unless otherwise cited.

While we in no way can list everyone who has assisted us in this project, special acknowledgement must go to Megan Barry, Mary Ann Bowman Beil, John Boatright, Harry Britt, Jack Casey, Glenn Coleman, Steve Cohen, Carol Conway, Randy Corgan, Frank Daly, Bill Davis, Craig Dreilinger, Joan Dubinsky, Tony Earley, John Ferraro, Ray Forster, Dana Freyer, Sylvia Ann Garcia, Jacqui Gates, Bob Gebing, Bill Giffin, Jerry Guthrie, Liz Gusich, Phil Hertz, John Howell, Steve Kasloff, Douglas Lint, Ian Jones, Ben Kincannon, Bobby Kipp, Faith Leavitt, Ira Lipman, Diane McDaniel, Angie McPhail, Nick Moore, Joe Murphy, Chris Nolan, John O'Byrne, Vin O'Reilly, Carrie Penman, Shirley Peterson, Ed Petry, Vic Pompa, Jay Resnick, Michael Robinson, Ivan Seidenberg, Carl Skoogland, Win Swenson, Cathleen Sullivan, Dick Syron, Lynn Tetrault, Frank Walker, Dave Walsh, Steve Wassersug, Pat Werhane and Graydon Wood. In addition, there are several individuals who assisted us with crucial sections in the book who wished to remain anonymous. They may be unnamed but they should know how much we appreciate their willingness to share their information and perspective. Time and time again, they helped us get the story right.

Ideas in a book such as this take time to percolate and develop. Our research laboratory to test and try these concepts was the invitation by Professor Ian Jones of Oxford University to participate in a special edition of a journal he was editing devoted to the subject of putting values into action. The process of writing that article and our subsequent participation at a conference devoted to the subject at Robinson College at the University of Cambridge gave us an ideal opportunity to formulate our concepts and discuss them with colleagues in the international business ethics field. Professor Jones subsequently told us that our insights had been most valuable, as Europe is struggling with what to import from the business ethics movement in United States and how much to alter it. He saw our ideas as an excellent source of best practice and thanked us for our contributions to the conference. It is now our turn to thank him. Without his idea for the special journal and the conference, *Ethics Matters* might not have come to fruition.

Similarly, Pat Werhane and Al Gini invited us to think and write for a special issue of *Business Ethics Quarterly* about the challenges facing the business ethics movement as the next millenium approaches. Many of the ideas we first considered for their project subsequently made their way into *Ethics Matters* as well.

As we have mentioned in the book, less than a decade ago, the Ethics Officer Association was but a gleam in the eye of a handful of ethics practitioners at the Center for Business Ethics and in many companies across the country. After its birth and incubation at the center, the EOA has flown the nest and matured into a vibrant, respected national organization of over 600 members, ably led by Ed Petry and his staff. Many of the individuals we have cited in the book are members and leaders of the EOA. In great measure it is their candor and cooperation, both at their conferences and at the semiannual *Managing Ethics in Organizations* course, taught at Bentley College, that has helped form our experiences as well. We are privileged to advise and work with the EOA.

Ethics Matters would not have seen the light of day without the support, encouragement and assistance of so many of our colleagues at the Center for Business Ethics. The center is a lively place. Its scholars, advisory board, executive fellows, foreign and domestic visitors, researchers, faculty and staff have contributed to making it a hotbed of ideas, articles, books, conferences, lectures and papers. We owe special thanks to all of them, but particularly to Mary Chiasson and Kelly LeBlanc, the center's able staff.

Occasionally we take pen to legal-size paper and write, but more often than not we convey our thoughts by desk computer or laptop. To our cyberspace hand-holders and fixers, Neil Moir at the center in Waltham and Christopher Marcus in Florida, we strew rose-colored microchips in your path and bow low to your expertise. Many thanks for rescuing us when we needed it.

Ethics Matters is a publication of the Center for Business Ethics at Bentley College. President Joseph Morone and the college administration have generously supported this project, understanding our decision to politely refuse offers from other publishers and to keep it in-house. We made this decision greatly aided by the expertise and professionalism of Maureen Lauran, our book designer and publishing guru. We have been guided by her great sense of style and clarity and are grateful for all her assistance.

Finally, to the many students, companies, organizations, boards, councils and managers we have consulted and worked with over the years, we owe a special debt of gratitude. All of our ideas have been sharpened and refined by those experiences, by listening to others' thoughts and concepts, by participating in their debates and dialogues and by responding to their challenges.

In past books and articles we have thanked our patient family members, whose time and companionship we appropriated to produce a finished product. *Ethics Matters* is no different, except that we must give special bouquets to both Norman Marcus and Bliss Hoffman. Not only were they patient, encouraging and accommodating, but their sharp editing skills and conversations at home made this a much better book. Our love to both of them.

Dawn-Marie Driscoll, *Florida*
W. Michael Hoffman, *Massachusetts*
September 1999

AUTHORS' NOTE

One of our colleagues asked us, "What's new? Why this book, now?"

Not bad questions. After all, we had written *The Ethical Edge: Tales of Organizations That Have Faced Moral Crises* (with Edward S. Petry)[1] and outlined how organizations were putting infrastructures in place for ethics and compliance programs. In that book, we told a few horror stories (such as Bath Iron Works and Nynex, which is now BellAtlantic) about what led companies to find ethical religion. In a sense our colleague was right. In the four years since *The Ethical Edge* was published, there isn't much that is new today. There are still moral crises and ethical conversions.

But we had a few reasons to fire up the computer again. First, we're almost out of copies of *The Ethical Edge*. Second, there are ideas we want to state differently and more clearly. There are new stories to tell, with new lessons to learn.

In truth, however, the most important reason to write again is that some of our ideas have changed. The catalyst to write this book was a paper we were invited to write for *Long Range Planning* (the journal of the British Strategic Planning Society and of the European Strategic Planning Federation).[2] This article outlined how organizations should implement values-based management. Our task was not to suggest what values organizations should adopt — that was left for other authors and other papers to recommend. We were the pragmatists instead of the philosophers, outlining ten steps toward building an effective

---

[1] Dawn-Marie Driscoll, W. Michael Hoffman and Edward S. Petry, *The Ethical Edge: Tales of Organizations That Have Faced Moral Crises*, NY: MasterMedia, Ltd., 1995.

[2] Dawn-Marie Driscoll and W. Michael Hoffman, "Gaining the Ethical Edge: Procedures for Delivering Values-driven Management," *Long Range Planning*, Vol. 32, No. 2., 1999, pp. 179-189.

program. It was a recipe that gave managers the ingredients they needed.

We presented the paper at Robinson College at the University of Cambridge and were gratified by the reaction from participants. "Very practical — just what we were looking for," said one.

Since that conference we have had other conversations and inquiries from managers and executives, asking how to go about implementing a values-driven organizational culture. "I understand why companies are moving from compliance to values," said one corporate executive at a conference. "But what are they actually doing? What works?"

An ethics officer, new in his job, asked us if we knew of any written material that explained the basic elements of a good values-based program. He was frustrated that there seemed to be no benchmark other than the seven elements of the US Federal Sentencing Guidelines. We had to ask him to wait, but promised we'd include the basic ingredients in our book.

Thinking about the recipe for *Ethics Matters* forced us to revisit the "compliance" versus "ethics" debate, learn new cooking techniques and, of course, tell a few more stories to illustrate our points. That is the stuff of this new book, describing how and why managers are concentrating on the matters of core values first, the bottom line second.

We hope you like the results.

Let's start at the beginning and agree that ethics and values are no longer merely personal issues. They are organizational issues as well, as Professor Lynn Sharp Paine argued in the *Harvard Business Review*, explaining that managers need to institute systems that encourage ethical conduct. [1] Such procedures will not prevent all illegalities or improprieties but they can help to influence the character of an organization and its employees.

Not just rotten apples

There's a need for systems not because business people are inherently less ethical than others, but rather because these procedures are critical for developing a moral corporate culture within which individuals can act ethically. We have found that the root of unethical behavior is quite often systemic and not simply the result of rotten apples in the corporate barrel. Ethical people can be brought down by serving in a bad organization, just as people with questionable integrity can be uplifted, or at least neutralized, by serving in an organization with clear values. For that reason, managers should carefully examine their organizational cultures to see if the structures and procedures, which systematically bind and move their employees, encourage or inhibit ethical behavior. If they do not, they must act to change or supplement them. This book provides the how-to.

Two personal stories will illustrate our point about the importance of corporate culture. When Mike Hoffman was sixteen, he worked in the meat department of Kroger's supermarket during the summer. His job was to package cuts of meat in trays

---

[1] Lynn Sharp Paine, "Managing for Organizational Integrity," *Harvard Business Review*, March-April 1994, pp. 106-117.

and seal and label them. His supervisor was explicit about how to do this. "Put the fat side down in the tray," he said, "and show the best side of the meat. We want it to look as attractive as possible." Mike did as he was told. Was the point of the instruction to put the supermarket's best face forward to customers or to cheat? The company's values were unclear.

The following summer Mike worked at A&P supermarket, again in the meat department. He was no longer a novice and showed his manager that he knew how to package meat. "Who taught you to do it like that?" his manager asked with indignation. "You do it that way again and you're fired. Make sure if there's fat in the cut of meat, it's visible in the package for the customer. We don't want her taking it home, discovering it and then complaining."

Two different supermarkets, two different cultures. Mike learned that honesty was an important value at A&P and, from that point on, it was easy for him to make ethical choices without being told. The fat side went up.

Dawn-Marie Driscoll has her own story of a rotten barrel. As vice president and general counsel of a large retailing chain, she knew she had to be accessible to help employees who had difficulties. She had an open door policy and her telephone rang off the hook; that's how she found out what was going on in the company. She also operated with what she thought was a sensible approach — training her people well and then backing them up.

Among her responsibilities was the security force for all the stores, a very secretive group. To gain their confidence, she needed their trust in the fact that she would not shoot a messenger who brought bad news. They would apprehend customers and employees for shoplifting, and she had an ironclad rule. No exceptions. The store prosecuted everyone, including a priest who was apprehended on Christmas Eve for stealing a pair of gloves.

One evening she was working late and answered her phone. She found herself listening to the husband of a customer who had been apprehended. He proclaimed his wife's innocence, despite the fact that she had already received a guilty verdict in district court. Why was he bothering her, Dawn-Marie wondered? But he had caught her late in the office, so she listened politely and told him that the best she could do would be to reexamine the matter and get back to him. She had already decided, of course, that it would be a perfunctory look; the wife was guilty, that was that. She always backed her security forces. But the husband didn't sound like a crank and she figured a little due diligence on one case would probably be a good idea.

To make a long story short, Dawn-Marie uncovered massive fraud in the security department of one store — and the caller's wife was probably innocent. The security manager, whom she had decorated, awarded and promoted, was falsifying cases, manufacturing evidence and lying in court. Perhaps higher than normal turnover among his young security operators might have been a clue, a red flag she hadn't noticed. In retrospect, she had to admit the whole scandal wasn't the case of a bad apple, a rogue security manager gone wrong. The problem belonged at her desk, because of the performance appraisal system she had approved, which rewarded security managers for the *number* of apprehensions they made. What did she think would happen? She had built in the incentives to cheat. If asked, security managers would probably say that "making cases" was more important to the company than honesty.

This, and other cases, brought Dawn-Marie to a realization and an important lesson from an ethical challenge: it's not always bad people that cause problems, sometimes it's bad infrastructure, bad incentives, and bad systems that tempt basically good people to do the wrong thing. And in most cases, the line of blame goes right up to senior management. Values and systems go hand in hand. Unfortunately, stories like this one are common, as Sears discovered with its commission-based automotive center fraud in 1992. Likewise, the Internal Revenue Service admitted in 1997 that its incentive systems led to taxpayer harassment.

Mike and Dawn-Marie's stories are admittedly old. Today everyone from the White House to the playground is talking about ethics, morals and values. Why should the business world be an exception? Even religious leaders, who generally limit their sermons to personal values, are making a connection to the world of work. The National Conference of Catholic Bishops, for example, recently issued a plainspoken pastoral reflection on values at work. "How do we connect worship on Sunday to work on Monday?" the document questions, echoing what many parishioners have been struggling with their entire lives. [2]

The bishops lay out the hard choices. "Decisions about the use of capital have moral implications: Are they creating and preserving quality jobs at living wages? Are they building up community through the goods and services they provide?"

The bishops were talking about matters of ethics.

Word choices

It's become fashionable to toss around words like ethics and values in the workplace but we shouldn't forget that old standby, compliance.

It's often regarded as "that department over there," the province of the lawyers or sometimes the auditors. It's developed a reputation as nothing more than mechanical checklists and papers that insure everyone has signed an acknowledgment indicating they attended the antitrust training seminar, for example. Compliance is the lowest common denominator, the ground floor of ethics. It's obeying laws and policies, which are necessary to proscribe the conduct of bad leaders or wayward employees. We believe that compliance deserves a few more words in the next chapter, although we stress that compliance programs should not be confused with values-based management.

What then, are values and ethics? According to Shirley Peterson, former ethics officer at Northrop Grumman, values are important beliefs that shape attitudes and motivate actions. Values are how you act if no one is around and no one would know the difference. "Values" itself is a morally neutral term, because of course individuals can hold negative values. But for our purposes, we assume that chosen values are positive. Words like "honesty," "accountability," "fairness" and "loyalty" all embody values. Values become the box, or framework, within which we make decisions.

Sometimes the values of a company are so clear that they become the company's mission. For example, ServiceMaster, the

---

[2] Gustav Niebuhr, "Leaders Offer Advice on Life at Large," *The New York Times*, November 21, 1998, p. A10.

Illinois-based franchiser of cleaning services, states its primary objective is "to honor God in all we do," and its company name choice reflects that. From its origins in 1947 with a handful of employees to its present status as a global company with over $6 billion in revenues, ServiceMaster has operated by its consistent value of servant leadership. Every employee has dignity, every job has worth.

Ethics and values, while often used interchangeably, are not quite the same. Ethics is the thought process that comes into play when we are deciding between right and wrong, or more typically, about weighing two rights. It's establishing the process of using appropriate principles of decision-making, when differing values come into conflict with each other.

Ethics and values go hand-in-hand because they work together, but they are not the same. For example, people from different cultures or backgrounds may have the same values but because their ethics are different, they may reason through to an opposite conclusion. Here's a stark example. Two businessmen may both say they respect women. To one, this means offering women every chance at the same work experiences and opportunities for advancement as their male peers. To the other, respect may mean never placing his spouse in an economic position that would force her to work. The source of ethics, therefore, is varied — from different cultures, religions, education, and family background. Some believe that as businesses strive to agree on a global ethic, they may now become the institutions that set the standard.[3] That's a heady assignment, but as logical a starting place as any.

Values alone, without ethical decision-making, are empty abstractions. Ethical decision-making without values to guide the decisions is like operating with blindfolds. Having values makes us understand the importance of ethical decision-making; being ethical helps us choose the right values. In this way, values and ethics are reciprocal.

Here are two, albeit simple, examples. Susan is the office manager at a small company. Her boss sends her to the office

---

[3] John Dalla Costa, *The Ethical Imperative: Why Moral Leadership is Good Business*, Reading, MA: Perseus Books, 1998.

supply store to pick up several notepads and binders for an upcoming meeting. As Susan is going through the checkout line, the cashier hands her a coupon for ten percent off her next purchase. Susan's brother, a writer, has a birthday next week. Does she keep the coupon?

If Susan understands that one of the core values of her company is loyalty, she doesn't need a complicated and lengthy manual of procedures to tell her that a coupon like the one she received rightly belongs to the company. She can make her own ethical decision that her first duty of loyalty is to the company, including the actual use and related benefits accruing from company assets — assets which she just bought at the store.

Of course, the interplay of values and ethics is not always this simple. Let's change our example slightly. Susan, a manager of human resources, knows that her company is soon planning layoffs. A friend from another department asks Susan's advice about her career prospects at the company because she is planning to sign a contract for the purchase of her first house. Susan is loyal to her company, but also feels care and concern about her friend. Two values are now conflicting. What ethical process will she apply in reasoning to a decision about what to tell her friend?

Not apple pie

Introducing the concept of values to an organization and its management processes is not without danger. Before reading further, two cautions are in order.

First, the process is open-ended, and in a real sense, never satisfied. As Frank Daly, corporate director of ethics and business conduct at Northrop Grumman Corporation has explained, "Once introduced, you either 'go with the flow' or eventually your program will wither. With respect to content first, companies that begin a serious discussion about ethics soon find that the 'genie is out of the bottle.' When ethics is introduced as serious and articulated in a company, efforts to limit it to one or other area of concern quickly become futile."[4] In other words, don't stick your toe in the water unless you plan to swim.

---

[4] Francis J. Daly, "The Ethics Dynamic," *Business and Society Review*, Vol. 102/103, pp. 37-42.

A TEN-POINT PROGRAM
for Implementing Values-Driven Management

1 Self-assessment

2 Commitment from the Top

3 Codes of Ethics

4 Communication

5 Training

6 Resources

7 Organizational Ownership

8 Consistent Standards and Enforcement

9 Audits and Evaluations

10 Revision and Reform

Second, adding values to an organization implies a culture change. Mere policies and procedures alone will not bring about change. Just as the individual ingredients of a cake, lined upon a counter, do not constitute an edible dessert, policies and procedures that are devoid of values constituting an organizational vision will not achieve the desired outcome. So although we lay out a ten-point program that we believe is a good description of how to get from here to there, it is not enough. The values come first.

Chapter 1

The Drivers

The fact that global managers are now exchanging ideas about values programs, rather than just compliance programs, did not happen overnight. Awareness has been slow to develop, but is now accelerated by global communications that make a business scandal in one country headline news in another. Prescient organizations today realize that many of the world's best companies have made a commitment to ethical business conduct. Others do not want to be left behind, particularly if they want to become customers, suppliers or strategic partners with these global leaders.

In the United States, six factors have brought us to where we are today. [1]

The carrot and the stick

The first was the adoption in November 1991 of the Federal Sentencing Guidelines for Organizations, which imposed a mandatory system of heavy fines and rigorous probation conditions for organizations convicted of federal crimes. [2] These Sentencing Guidelines might have gone relatively unnoticed except that regulators were increasingly using financial penalties and even jail time for executives to punish all types of corporate wrongdoing.

These Sentencing Guidelines act as a hard stick. Organizations convicted of federal crimes face a mandatory system of stiff fines and tough probation conditions. Rather than rely on the discretion

---

[1] For a more complete discussion, see Dawn-Marie Driscoll, W. Michael Hoffman and Joseph E. Murphy, "Business Ethics and Compliance: What Management is Doing and Why," *Business and Society Review*, No. 99, July 1998, pp. 35-51.

[2] United States Sentencing Guidelines, Chapter 8, Sentencing of Organizations, Washington DC, 1991.

Federal sentencing guidelines for organizations

SEVEN STEPS

1. Establish compliance standards and procedures

2. Assign high level individuals to oversee compliance

3. Exercise due care in delegating discretionary authority

4. Communicate and train

5. Monitor, audit and provide safe reporting systems

6. Enforce appropriate discipline with consistency

7. Respond to offenses and prevent reoccurrences

of individual trial judges, this new system put forth a mathematical formula which assigned points to various factors, such as having senior managers involved in an offense. Companies caught in this formula could face fines in the millions of dollars, in some cases inviting bankruptcy.

But the Sentencing Guidelines also contain a carrot. A company is allowed to reduce its penalties dramatically if it had an effective system in place to prevent and detect violations before the offense occurred. Companies could reduce fines, avoid criminal prosecution and use the establishment of such ethics and compliance programs as a defense in civil charges. This idea of escaping liability by showing that management tried to prevent misconduct has proven beneficial in other cases. For example, a company program to prevent and react to allegations of sexual harassment can be invoked as a defense in hostile work environment cases.

Prior to the Sentencing Guidelines, some companies had adopted codes of conduct and established programs to disseminate them, with little effort to measure their impact. In specific areas, such as environmental hazards, antitrust or safety compliance, programs to educate and monitor employees gradually began to include such elements as audits and monitoring.

The Sentencing Guidelines' suggested elements of an effective program broke new ground, however. While the seven steps outlined were specific, they were just the minimum. Companies were expected to design their own programs based on industry practice, their individual problems, and new developments. The job of complying with what the guidelines required to earn credit for a program was not completed if managers checked off the seven elements and said, "finished." Continuing diligence and flexibility were required. On the one hand, they mandated that having an "effective program" will make a big difference. On the other hand, they were somewhat vague about how to meet the standard.

The Federal Sentencing Guidelines for Organizations, now almost ten years old, were a good impetus to make corporations pay attention to ethics programs, but many companies have gone far beyond what the Sentencing Guidelines may have envisioned.

Caremark, a household word

A due diligence defense, which has been part of the legal system in a number of countries, has offered a reward to companies that are diligent in preventing misconduct, including protecting members of the board of directors from individual liability. While the Sentencing Guidelines may have caught the attention of company lawyers, a second major factor in shaping corporate ethics programs was the *In Re Caremark* case, decided in 1996, which caught the attention of senior managers and boards of directors.[3] The *Caremark* opinion, written by Delaware's influential chancery court, long a leader in the development of corporate law, was a case of good news/bad news.

Caremark, a medical services company, had been subjected to government investigations and eventually paid $250 million in fines, reimbursements and penalties. Shareholders alleged that the board of directors breached its fiduciary duty of care to Caremark by failing to supervise the conduct of its employees and to take corrective action.

The good news was that the court exonerated the board of directors, finding that the members had acted diligently. The board and company had established ethics and compliance

---

[3] *In Re Caremark International Inc. Derivative Litigation*, 1996 WL 549894 (Del. Chancery C.A. 13670, 1991).

reporting systems before the problems began and during the government's investigation of the company. The bad news was that the court issued a stern warning to other boards, stressing that directors could, at least in theory, face liability for failure to insure such a program if improprieties later developed.

If the standard for directors was once to pay attention and to take action only when they had knowledge of a problem, now the criterion has changed. The flow of information is a two-way street and directors can no longer claim ignorance as a defense. *Caremark* has made it clear that directors have an affirmative obligation to find out what is going on.

Nothing catches the attention of directors more than the word "liable." With the development of the Sentencing Guidelines (acting as a quasi-best practices model) and the *Caremark* edict, directors are now affirmatively required to probe, ask questions and establish procedures that will allow them to find out what is going on in the company. If the prior standard was a one-way street of information flowing up to the board, now the flow was two-way and the board was affirmatively required to probe and ask questions.

Chancellor William T. Allen, author of the *Caremark* opinion, may not have anticipated that it would become a household word among ethics and compliance experts. As he said to a gathering of corporate directors, "Advisors go to boards and they say, 'Look at this opinion. You'd better have a special session. You'd better do this, you'd better do that.' Frankly, I think lawyers (and I don't mean to be a traitor to my profession) have a little bit of an interest in whipping up excitement about these things."[4]

Yet even Allen was forced to admit the rules of the game had changed. He warned directors that they must recognize the moment when action is called for, often in opposition to their former loyalty to management. "It's a moment that some structural protections can help you with," he said. "That is, being informed, having the right kind of information."[5]

---

[4] "Independence, Integrity and the Governance of Institutions," *Director's Monthly*, January 1998, p. 14.

[5] Ibid. p. 15.

Not just Caremark

America is a litigious society. In the last few years we have seen evidence that despite efforts at tort reform, companies and organizations are still vulnerable to lawsuits, investigations and class action litigation. The steady stream of litigation against companies and organizations has one silver lining, however — it has provided an impetus for companies to pay attention to how they conduct their business practices. Could they explain them to a jury?

There is perhaps no sorrier example of massive litigation than the case of Dow Corning and the silicone breast implant controversy. [6] Dow Corning, a company once ranked in the top 250 for sales and in the top 100 for profits, was forced to file for protection under the bankruptcy laws — thanks to a product that represented one percent of its sales. When all the thousands of claims were totaled up for allegations of injury and illness caused by the company's silicone breast implants, a settlement fund of more than $4 billion was not enough to satisfy them.

The worst part of the Dow Corning story, however, is that the company did not lose because it was shown to have manufactured a dangerous product. Subsequent scientific studies have indicated that Dow Corning may have been right all along on the science. Dow Corning lost in the larger court of public opinion and in the smaller courts of individual juries, which concluded that Dow Corning should be punished. For what? Most likely for acting unethically, although to us, the jury is also still out on that issue.

Dow Corning's is not an isolated case. The instinct to punish is alive and well in American jurisprudence, as evidenced by the stunning $4.9 billion verdict announced against General Motors in July 1999 in a case of an exploding fuel tank in a car crash. The jurors wanted to send a message. "We're just like numbers, I feel, to them," one juror said. "Statistics." [7]

---

[6] See Dawn-Marie Driscoll, "The Dow Corning Case: First, Kill All the Lawyers," *Business and Society Review*, Nos. 100/101, 1998, pp.57-63, based in part on material in Dawn-Marie Driscoll, W. Michael Hoffman and Edward S. Petry, *The Ethical Edge: Tales of Organizations That Have Faced Moral Crises*, MasterMedia, Ltd., 1995.

[7] William Glaberson, "Looking for Attention With a Billion-Dollar Message," *The New York Times*, July 18, 1999, p. 3.

General Motors had a different view. "To suggest that General Motors would sacrifice safety to make the selling price of the vehicle $8.59 less is just absurd," said one of the lawyers representing General Motors.[8]

One could argue about the evidence allowed before juries or the guidelines they are given in setting damages, but those are not the issues at hand. An ordinary citizen's perception of whether a company acted ethically is of critical importance today. We have had runaway juries and staggering verdicts for years. What is new, however, is the fact that business ethicists are now examining court documents, giving depositions, writing opinions and testifying in cases involving the conduct of company managers. We have been involved with many such cases and can state that the best defense is a good offense. This means clear values-driven programs that integrate ethical considerations in all spheres of a company's operation.

Power to the people

It's not just individuals on juries who are taking notice of what organizations are doing and sending a message. Companies are embracing ethics and values initiatives because they believe — with or without hard factual evidence — that they will have a competitive advantage if they do so. We think they are right. Consumers are more educated, more inquisitive and more demanding than ever. Rightly or wrongly, they form impressions about an organization's brand image — whether it be the United Way or Exxon — from a myriad of impressions they read, see and hear about the company's culture.

Frank D. Walker, chairman of Walker Information, Inc., has tracked the relationship between corporate character and customer loyalty and believes the two are interconnected. Managers may believe that price, product quality and customer service are the major factors that drive their success. They are not entirely wrong, but Walker warns that the firm's general reputation for ethics and integrity, what he calls "business prac-

---

[8] Jeffrey Ball and Milo Geyelin, "GM Ordered by Jury to Pay $4.9 Billion," *The Wall Street Journal*, July 12, 1999, p. A3.

"If you look at the dominant economic development in the last quarter century in the American economy, and increasingly in economies around the world, there is a decisive shift in power away from the producer to the consumer. Some of this is aided by technology and some has to do with more open markets in every good and service. Increasingly, you can't stay in business unless you are doing, every day, what is ultimately good for your customer. What is ultimately good for your customer, in many cases, has to do with making ethical judgements. This is getting to be a tougher and tougher issue."

Richard F. Syron
former chairman and chief executive officer, American Stock Exchange,
and president and chief executive officer, Thermo Electron Corporation,
from his *Sears Lecture in Business Ethics* at Bentley College, February 8, 1999

tices," is fast becoming a major indicator of both customer and employee loyalty.

In the keynote address before the 1999 annual meeting of the Society for Business Ethics, Walker explained the results of a wide-ranging study his firm conducted. "Rating the business practices category along with the other eight traditional and non-traditional measurable drivers using a point allocation system clearly indicated the importance of this factor. In terms of measuring a firm's overall or general reputation, business practices was ranked second to quality. In terms of how people choose where to work, business practices were second only to the treatment of employee category. And, when we asked the more than three-fourths of the total sample who said they were currently refusing to buy some product or service from a particular company, business practices, second only to service in this case, was given as the reason for their purchasing boycott. We also found a connection with investment decisions." [9]

---

[9] This keynote speech before the Society for Business Ethics (August 1999) is forthcoming in *Business and Society Review*, a publication of the Center for Business Ethics at Bentley College.

Organizations that ignore the impact of consumer perception of their business practices do so at their peril. The increase in households with internet access, the number of web sites that monitor companies, and the proliferation of information and news outlets all contribute to the fact that one's reputation can be lost in the blink of an eye. As Johnson & Johnson demonstrated in its famous Tylenol recall, perhaps only an imbedded and longstanding reputation for integrity will protect a company in the case of wrongdoing or sudden crisis.

Togetherness

Fifth, with the spotlights of the financial press, activist shareholders, regulators and the public shining on corporate misdeeds, many industry groups have decided to drive values and ethics throughout their member companies. These coalitions are now taking the lead in designing programs of ethical behavior, believing that a model crafted by industry is preferable to government regulation.

One of the first major efforts came in the mid-1980s when major companies in the defense industry united in response to the Packard Commission Report which investigated high-profile instances of fraud, waste and abuse in the defense industry. The resulting 1986 industry initiative called the Defense Industry Initiative on Business Ethics and Conduct (DII), contained six necessary principles that all signatory defense companies had to take to build effective ethics and compliance programs. Approximately sixty companies have joined the initiative and developed programs, which have served as models for companies in other industries.

The DII model of industry cooperation has spawned other efforts. For example, in the wake of allegations of personal trading by mutual fund portfolio managers and the firing of John Kaweske by Invesco Funds Group, the press, Congress, the SEC and the rest of the industry took notice. Fund advisers manage nearly approximately seven trillion dollars for more than sixty-five million shareholders. Therefore, trust and integrity are key ingredients in the success of the American mutual fund industry. The SEC invited the Investment Company Institute (ICI), the national mutual fund association, to convene a special task force to study the issue of portfolio manager trading. The panel rec-

Defense industry initiative on business ethics and conduct

SIX PRINCIPLES

1. Provide a written code of business ethics and conduct

2. Train employees regarding their responsibilities

3. Provide a free and open atmosphere

4. Adopt procedures for voluntary disclosure

5. Be responsible to other companies in the industry

6. Have public accountability

ommended a series of clear and vigorous steps that all fund companies should take to implement more stringent fund codes of ethics and compliance, a best practice model for the industry. Two years later, a majority of fund complexes reported that they had implemented the panel's recommendations.[10] That model of industry cooperation worked so effectively that in 1999 the ICI again undertook to raise the bar for voluntary adherence to a code of best practices. This time, the subject was corporate governance. In June 1999 its Advisory Group on Best Practices for Fund Directors released its recommendations, *Enhancing a Culture of Independence and Effectiveness*.[11] Chairman Arthur Leavitt of the SEC called the report "an important step forward."[12]

Further examples emerge as new crises appear. We expect that industry-wide initiatives will continue as companies come together to set their own values and ethical standards. This development reminds us of the old story about the owner of a paper company, one of the first converts to the cause of environmental protection. He spent millions to prevent his paper mill from polluting nearby rivers but by doing so, could no longer compete with the firms that did not follow his example. The company closed, 500 workers lost their jobs and the river remained polluted. But the business owner still believed that government regulation of paper mills was not the answer. He preferred that

---

[10] Investment Company Institute, *Report of the Advisory Group on Personal Investing*, Washington DC, 1994.

[11] Investment Company Institute, *Enhancing a Culture of Independence and Effectiveness*, Washington DC, 1999.

[12] "Mutual Fund Group Calls for Stronger Independent Directors," *Bloomberg*, June 24,1999.

government not intervene in business activity. It's too bad he didn't consider an industry-wide conference of his fellow paper mill owners and convince them of the need for voluntary standards that they would all pledge to follow.

Today the paper owner might be pleased to see that industry initiatives are becoming more common. For example, the National Automobile Auction Association, whose members handled $70 billion worth of vehicles in 1997, has adopted a comprehensive code of ethics for all its members, and suspends or dismisses auctions if there are violations of the code. After prominent scandals in the life insurance industry, the American Council of Life Insurance formulated a voluntary program of ethical principles and an industry code of conduct. The Insurance Marketing Standards Association, which confers membership on companies that have complied with the program, began in 1996.The Chemical Manufacturers Association's Responsible Care initiative, now ten years old, is a voluntary environmental, health and safety performance improvement effort. Member companies, who account for 90% of the country's basic chemical production, pledge to manage their businesses according to the principles set out in the program, including independent verification.

The apparel industry response to widespread criticism about labor rights violations in overseas plants may be a model for other industries. In partnership with nongovernmental organizations, labor unions and watchdog groups, corporations such as Nike took part in new efforts to promote global codes of conduct and to monitor such codes. President Clinton's White House Apparel Industry Partnership (Partnership) and the Council on Economic Priorities' Social Accountability 8000 (SA-8000), a measurable benchmark for international labor workplace standards, were two programs that emerged from the public scrutiny of apparel industry practices. The Partnership created a Fair Labor Standards Association, an organization to oversee compliance with the voluntary manufacturing and labor standards. [13] In general, initiatives and programs that are drafted and championed by the industry groups affected will have a better chance of success

---

[13] See Thomas A. Hemphill, "The White House Apparel Industry Agreement: Will Self-Regulation Be Successful?" *Business and Society Review*, Vol. 104, No. 2, Summer 1999, pp. 121-137.

than those which are created by outside organizations that might not have the experience to know what will work.

A new profession

While industry-wide ethics initiatives are particularly helpful in addressing specific problems, many companies and organizations are not waiting for their peers to "get religion." A sixth major factor that has hastened the implementation of comprehensive ethics programs is the growth of the business ethics movement in general and the creation of the new position of ethics officer.

As a result of the DII effort, several large corporations appointed individuals to oversee their compliance efforts. In 1991, the Center for Business Ethics (CBE) at Bentley College in Waltham, Massachusetts hosted a gathering of approximately forty ethics and compliance managers to share information and common concerns. This meeting led to the formation of the national Ethics Officer Association (EOA) in 1992. By 1999 its membership had grown to over 600 professionals who serve as managers of internal ethics and compliance programs. The EOA sponsors annual national conferences and, in partnership with CBE, offers executive education and certification programs for ethics officers. Most importantly, the EOA operates as a forum for members to exchange and review hundreds of corporate ethics materials, to attend skill enhancement seminars, to share problems via the EOA's website and to keep current with new developments in the field.

Other associations have also formed to help ethics professionals, including The Ombuds Association, the Healthcare Compliance Association and the Office of Government Ethics (OGE), which oversees hundreds of ethics and compliance directors within government agencies. The networking that takes place in and among such organizations will help insure that best practices in the business ethics field continue to be promulgated to anyone who is interested in learning about them.

Ethics and compliance

The Ethics Officer Association is open to managers who are responsible for ethics, compliance and business conduct pro-

"Employees need to be motivated, inspired if you will, to levels of integrity and virtue beyond the minimum set out in a specific rule or law. I would argue that one of the values we want to motivate is a pattern of regard for law and rules as essential for mutual respect and the success of common process. A certain disdain for compliance and a sense that compliance is something you move beyond rather than incorporate into a new and developing perspective, is shortsighted in day-to-day practice. It removes an important element that offers a basic and helpful clarity and direction to even the most motivated employees."

Francis J. Daly
corporate director, ethics and business conduct, Northrop Grumman
and executive fellow, Center for Business Ethics, "Rules and Values
are Ethical Allies," *CBE News*, Vol. 6, No. 2, Summer 1998, p. 7

grams. While these three may sound similar, some practitioners believe there is a big difference between programs that concentrate on compliance and those that focus on values.

Compliance, they say, tells employees about the law and tries to prevent violations. Employees are motivated to do the right thing by the fear of being caught, if not by their desire to be law-abiding. Compliance is about obedience to rules and authority. Programs that concentrate only on compliance rarely help employees resolve situations that aren't covered by law and regulation. Such programs can not expect to develop employees' ethical autonomy and individual responsibility.

In defending compliance-based programs, its managers state that words like "ethics" are too vague and hint of instructing individuals on moral issues. In the face of business imperatives, employees will forget what they learned in an ethics training course and will do what they have to do to get the job done. What is important, some compliance managers emphasize, is teaching employees how to meet their legal requirements and documenting that the company has complied.

The argument about the difference between compliance and ethics programs could go on all day, but in truth it begs the wrong question. They are not divergent program approaches, but rather are complementary program components. As Frank Daly from Northrop Grumman says, "Rules and values are ethical allies." [14]

Historically, especially in heavily regulated industries, companies have begun programs in response to a violation of law and have understandably started with a compliance approach. Daly explains that in many such companies, the decision model taught to employees begins with the question, "Is it legal?" If the answer is no, that's the end of the story. An employee needn't proceed further.

But it doesn't take long, Daly says, for employees to raise issues and questions that aren't decided neatly by referring to a code of regulations. Furthermore, if the proposed action is legal, that doesn't mean it's necessarily right. Therefore guidance beyond obeying law and policy should be provided.

"Yes!" answer the ethics advocates. That's why the best programs concentrate on teaching employees how to make decisions for themselves when the answer to their question is not necessarily spelled out. Freedom of ethical choice is always better than a bunch of "shall nots."

Daly agrees but stresses that the ethics champions should not leave compliance in the dust. "Emphasizing ethics and values without stressing the necessity of rules and laws leaves employees and the company vulnerable," he says.

"In a large organization especially, there is a vast difference among people's abilities. They learn at different stages, they read at different levels, and their moral sensibilities develop at different rates. Consider too, that some rules and laws are counterintuitive and that some employees may have come from a more freewheeling environment than others. Thus, it is important that clear guidelines exist for those who might need them."

We agree with Frank. Compliance is necessary and we'll assume that most organizations have good compliance programs in place. The goal is to then incorporate it into a new val-

---

[14] Francis J. Daly, "Rules and Values are Ethical Allies," *CBE News*, Vol. 2, Issue 2, Summer 1998.

ues-based management culture. In short, compliance and ethics programs are interdependent. Neither can be fully successful without the other.

Chapter 2

Why Values?

Talking about values has become an industry. Best selling books promote earthly virtues for living and spiritual values for reflecting. Conventional wisdom — and opinion leaders such as the Dalai Lama and the late Basil Cardinal Hume — believe that the decade of greed is evolving into an era in which many people are seeking the meaning of life. "The interest toward inner values is increasing," the Dalai Lama said. "People begin to realize that material facility alone is not the full answer for life." [1]

Even baby boomers have come full circle, it appears, from championing causes larger than themselves to cocooning inward, concentrating on career and family. Now they are finally looking outward again, espousing a way of living that, if not guaranteed to leave a legacy, at least will make their grandchildren proud.

That's all fine. But the last time we looked, the business world was still engaged in delivering goods and services and making a profit. Does that mean that business ethics is still an oxymoron?

No. Values have a pragmatic place in the business world precisely because of society's shifting sands. Name any of the currents that are buffeting organizations today and you'll find a rationale for values-driven management. Here are a few:

Diversity   Individuals of different ages, religions and gender clearly have distinct and perhaps contrasting ideas about appropriate ways to behave in an organization, depending upon their perspective and life's experiences. Their interpretations of the same set of facts may differ widely, as well as their response to them.

---

[1] Gustav Niebuhr, "For the Discontented, A Message of Hope," *The New York Times*, August 14, 1999, p. A12.

Globalization   Individuals raised in diverse cultures may have different reactions to various questions or issues. Instead of describing some actions as ethical and others unethical, some prefer to say they are dealing with cultural sensitivities. But that doesn't help companies or their employees understand what is expected of them.

Cost pressures   Often eliminated in rounds of cost-cutting are the compliance police and structural backups designed to prevent misdeeds. Individuals are increasingly left on their own to make decisions.

Virtual work   With so many employees out in the field, working from home or at other diverse locations, a common organizational standard of behavior is difficult to assimilate from afar.

Strategic alliances   The individuals you work with on a daily basis may not be fellow employees. They may be customers, suppliers or even competitors, who are not even a part of your own organizational culture and business goal framework.

Teamwork   Hierarchical management structures are being replaced by teams, with leadership earned by personal skill rather than title. This eliminates the "because I told you so" standard of decision-making.

Entrepreneurship and intrapreneurship   Many companies are encouraging employees at the lowest possible level to take risks, innovate and even spend company resources, acting like owners of the business. With responsibility for major decisions comes the necessity to act responsibly. [2]

Downsized, deregulated government   As regulation is replaced by voluntary industry and company codes, government laws and enforcement are no longer the only or the complete resources for those looking for answers or limitations. Of

---

[2] Studies have suggested that many entrepreneurs employ personal values within their businesses to a greater extent than do managers and that entrepreneurs appear to be more sensitive to societal expectations, more critical of their own performance, and place more emphasis on ethical behavior. Robert D. Hisrich, "Ethics of Business Managers v. Entrepreneurs," *Research Institute for Small & Emerging Business*, Working Paper Series 98-03, 1998.

course, they really never were but, more often than not, business acted as if they were.

Competitive, 24-hour media   Few organizations have the luxury of time to figure out what the right response should be to an ethical crisis, particularly if the crisis is public rather than private. When a crisis occurs in the public eye, the aggressive competitiveness of a multiplicity of 24-hour media outlets makes it imperative that the manager's first response be the right one.

Talking about "values" is hard work because the meaning is subject to interpretation. Values is a word like "motherhood," seemingly benign and positive. Yet a vociferous, extroverted Italian mama is very different than a white-gloved, soft spoken, reserved New England Episcopalian mother. The word "motherhood" conjures up a kaleidoscope of images, as does values.

You've got mail

Let's take a simple example and try to apply the idea of values (rather than compliance) to the issue of employee use of e-mail. Several ethics officers recently debated about what the appropriate corporate policy for the use of e-mail should be. They concluded it was difficult to draft one. Prohibiting the use of e-mail at work for an employee's personal use seemed not only too restrictive, but also unworkable. But they felt the company should make it clear that improper use of e-mail (and internet access) would be disciplined. So the ethics officers began to debate the values they would apply to frame the issue.

One of the ethics officers, who was from the United Kingdom, strongly disagreed with any restrictions or discipline. The "right to privacy" was an important value in his organization and the thought that an employer would read or oversee an employee's private e-mail was unthinkable.

"But we're talking about corporate property and corporate time," another ethics officer argued. "What about the value of loyalty? When at work, you owe the company your time and attention." Here the European emphasis on the value of individual privacy had clashed with the American value of respect for private property, suggesting future arguments in global business endeavors.

The debate continued. Surely employees should not be viewing pornography over the internet, but how about sports or investment web sites? Where do you draw the line? Forwarding jokes to personal friends may be allowed, but what about disseminating internal company communications or those that criticize the company? If trust is a more important value than accountability, then the monitoring and disciplining of e-mail usage may differ from organization to organization.

As that example shows, before implementing values, it's necessary to start by being clear about what you mean.

What values?

Agreement on values is not easy. Even William J. Bennett, the Republican values czar, admits to being confused about what the American public thinks is important today. "Values, schmalues, I don't get it, " he said.[3] He may have been trying to draw too fine a line. Let's start at the beginning, with the Golden Rule or the Ten Commandments.

"Do Unto Others As You Would Have Others Do Unto You." That's not a bad starting place, except that it doesn't provide much guidance for the competitive business environment. If I'm trying to make my monthly quota of life insurance policy sales in order to qualify for my commission draw, and I've just sold a policy to a young man who doesn't completely understand what he bought, I may need a bit more advice from my company about its values. Is my company focused on making its profit projections and believes "*caveat emptor*?" If I gave the customer a brochure with all our disclosures, perhaps it is not my job to tell him he really would be better off with a simpler, cheaper policy.

If my company's chief value is customer satisfaction, and my president refuses to sell inappropriate products to naïve buyers, that's a different story. I understand what I have to do at the risk of losing my commission. (The company should also understand that it needs to rethink its commission policy, but that's a different story.)

---

[3] Melinda Henneberger, "Most Conservatives See Clinton Ouster as Dream," *The New York Times*, December 3, 1998, p. A22.

"Thou Shall Not Kill, Lie, Cheat or Steal." That's an abbreviated version of some of the Ten Commandments, but they are helpful to illustrate how they work in a business setting. To paraphrase political strategist James Carville, "It's the application, stupid."

Surely no company would suggest it has a right to kill others. But the Union Carbide disaster in Bhopal, India provides an example of a difficult decision about implementing safety standards in order to prevent death and illness. The plant in Bhopal was in complete compliance with India's safety standards, but we have heard the suggestion made that if Union Carbide applied the same measures in India that it does in the United States, the human toll from the accident would have been much less. This point of view is expressed in hindsight, of course. Prior to the accident Union Carbide managers had to balance expenses and profitability on the one hand with their obligation to implement uniform safety standards worldwide on the other. This is a difficult choice for any company when its foreign competitors do not follow United States standards. Here the answer may be global, industry-wide standards, a far-reaching goal to be sure, and one that has yet to be implemented.

Consider another example related to the prohibition against stealing. Does asking, lobbying and currying favor with elected officials for the purpose of obtaining large tax breaks for your company meet the definition of stealing? The Cato Institute has estimated that because of federal protection of the domestic sugar industry, ethanol subsidies, subsidized grain exports and other programs, the Archer Daniels Midland Corporation has cost the American economy forty billion dollars since 1980.[4] This did not happen by accident. ADM and its chairman Dwayne Andreas donated millions of dollars to both political parties. The return on these contributions has been great; at least 43 percent of ADM's annual profits are from products heavily subsidized or protected by the American government. Moreover, every dollar of profits earned by ADM's corn sweetener operation costs consumers $10 and every dollar of profits earned by its ethanol operation costs taxpayers $30.

---

[4] James Bovard, "Archer Daniels Midland: A Case Study in Corporate Welfare," Cato Policy Analysis No. 241, September 26, 1995. Reports of the Cato Institute can be found at www.cato.org.

ADM is not the only example of corporate welfare.[5] Seaboard Corporation officials announced that they would reopen a shuttered pork-processing plant in Albert Lea, Minnesota. Seaboard had been the town's largest employer. The reopening came at a cost: the town agreed to fund a $2.9 million low-interest loan, a special deal on the company's sewer bill and grading and paving parking lots for employees. But four years later, Seaboard phased out the plant and moved its operations eight hundred miles away. Albert Lea has debt, higher utility bills, an abandoned plant and no jobs. Is that stealing?

Some companies, industries and nonprofit organizations are attempting to fathom these difficult questions by considering the adoption of universal values upon which all can agree. Ideas such as justice, human dignity, honesty, fairness and freedom might be considered for such a short list. These are overriding values that apply to everyone and, by extension, to every company operating in every country.

Whose values?

We suggest that companies start by considering a few basic values, appropriate to the economic structure of the company, the community and the industry. The lowest common denominator is the law. "Obeying the law" is usually a logical place to begin. (We say "usually" because as past segregation laws have shown, what's legal is not always the same as what's moral.) Glenn Coleman, director of communications & training in the office of ethics and business conduct at EDS, proposes that companies first make a list of laws, regulations and procedures that apply to them. It might be a short list, but it will remind managers of obvious prohibitions (e.g., no sexual harassment).

These legal prohibitions may lead to the next level and suggest ideas about what's moral, ethical and valued in the organization. A discussion of values implies agreement that a company will do more than just what is legally required. However, narrow-

---

[5] For information about corporate welfare, see www.enviroweb.org/enviroissues/ corporate/welfare, as well as www.commoncause.org. See also *The Boston Globe*'s three part series on corporate welfare first published on July 7, 1996. A similar seven part series in *The Philadelphia Inquirer* was first published on June 4, 1995. *Time Magazine*'s four part series on corporate welfare began on November 9, 1998.

ing down a long list of other values that will apply to work is not easy. Managers may want to start with the obvious ones, such as a moral obligation not to cause harm, steal, and lie. How do these play out in a work situation? For example, if we agree we have an obligation not to cause harm, how will that work in our corporate culture? The Thiokol engineers who were hesitant about the safety of the O-ring in cold temperatures no doubt could point to how the attitude of the Challenger space managers inhibited their ability to push their concerns up to the final decision-makers. After all seven astronauts were killed in the resulting explosion, investigations suggested that NASA officials were operating in a "get-this-launched-at-all-costs" culture rather than one in which "safety first" was the predominant value.

Organization values can't be selected by three top managers brainstorming in a conference room for an hour. Selection of the core values for an organization should be guided by three words: test, test and test. If employees at all level of the organization don't respond positively to the values emphasized, chances are that the effort will be fruitless. In the following chapters, we lay out a program by which values-based management can be integrated into the organization, but none of the procedures will be useful if the values themselves don't "match" and aren't "bought by" the organization.

Professor Patricia H. Werhane, Ruffin professor of business ethics at The Darden School, University of Virginia, has argued that individuals need to take a broad view in perceiving their situation if moral principles are to have any effect (she calls this "moral imagination"). [6] She uses the example of General Electric, a highly regarded company, led by Jack Welch, often honored as one of the best chief executive officers in the country. Yet GE has been plagued by scandal, from accusations of criminal price-fixing in the diamond market to defense industry fraud and fraudulent trading in the bond market at Kidder Peabody.

What's going on here? GE has a values statement and has put its employees through ethics training. One possible assumption is that the declaration of what ought to be valued does not

---

[6] Patricia H. Werhane, "Moral Imagination and the Search for Ethical Decision Making in Management," *Business Ethics Quarterly*, The Ruffin Series: Special Issue No. 1, 1998, pp.75-98.

match what is actually valued. According to Werhane, Jack Welch's motto is "Be #1 or #2 or get out." To take the Kidder Peabody example, bond trader Joseph Jett and his superiors were undoubtedly under pressure to succeed. Whether Jett knew he was inflating his trading profits or not, with Welch's overriding cry for success at all costs, it would take an extraordinary amount of moral imagination for Jett to step back from his situation, see it from all sides and admit that things didn't look right. His superiors would have had to look hard to see what they did not want to see (how was Jett getting those extraordinary returns?). [7]

But for now, change the slogan at GE. Assume for a moment that Welch's motto was "integrity at all costs." Further assume that the three chief values at General Electric were "integrity," "accountability" and "responsibility," and that these values were well known and subscribed to by everyone from the corner office to the mailroom and warehouse.

With this change we think these scandals might have been prevented. Rather than being a poster child for unethical behavior, General Electric might have a reputation more like that of Johnson & Johnson, hailed as a leader in ethics. It all starts with the values that not only are articulated, but also are believed to be real by the organization. To assure this belief Johnson & Johnson over the years has tested its famous Credo values statement by having its employees, especially its top executives, question the relevance and importance of the values constituting The Credo. The company does this to make sure those values are still believed in by J&J employees, and if not, then The Credo should be revised or even taken down from the walls on which it is hung throughout the organization. After much serious debate, The Credo has remained on the walls relatively unchanged, but with a deeper awareness and commitment from all employees. This is why when the Tylenol poisoning crisis hit the company's employees all over the world acted as one to insure the safety of J&J consumers. The company's values drove its actions.

Here we must insert a cautionary note. Some organizations go to great lengths to arrive at their "core" values. They do the right thing by continually testing them against real-life examples

---

[7] We return to the Jett story in chapter 20.

Johnson & Johnson Credo

We believe our first responsibility is to the doctors, nurses and patients, to mothers and fathers and all others who use our products and services.

In meeting their need everything we do must be of high quality.

We must constantly strive to reduce our costs in order to maintain reasonable prices.

Customers' orders must be serviced promptly and accurately.

Our suppliers and distributors must have an opportunity to make a fair profit.

We are responsible to our employees, the men and women who work with us throughout the world.

Everyone must be considered as an individual.

We must respect their dignity and recognize their merit.

They must have a sense of security in their jobs.

Compensation must be fair and adequate, and working conditions clean, orderly and safe.

We must be mindful of ways to help our employees fulfill their family responsibilities.

Employees must feel free to make suggestions and complaints.

There must be equal opportunity for employment, development and advancement for those qualified.

We must provide competent management, and their actions must be just and ethical.

We are responsible to the communities in which we live and work and to the world community as well.

We must be good citizens — support good works and charities and bear our fair share of taxes.

We must encourage civic improvements and better health and education.

We must maintain in good order the property we are privileged to use, protecting the environment and natural resources.

Our final responsibility is to our stockholders.

Business must make a sound profit.

We must experiment with new ideas.

Research must be carried on, innovative programs developed and mistakes paid for.

New equipment must be purchased, new facilities provided and new products launched.

Reserves must be created to provide for adverse times.

When we operate according to these principles, the stockholders should realize a fair return.

drawn from their experiences. When they settle on the primary values, they announce them with fanfare and incorporate them in a wide range of material. There's nothing wrong with that, as long as the values are flexible and are allowed to change as the environment changes.

Too often we have seen organizations which become paralyzed, afraid to change, edit, delete or add to a list of values, because somehow they believe these values, once articulated, are immutable. Nothing could be further from reality. Only when values become a guide for decision-making in many situations do organizations really know if they are useful as a guide. Industries change, competitors change, company direction changes, the regulatory environment changes, internal processes change, and so it is likely that conflicts among values may arise, or managers will face situations that may not have been envisioned when the values were adopted.

It is not a mortal sin to revisit values and test whether they are still appropriate and to change them if required.

Why values?

Business — no, make that ordinary life — has become so complex these days that conduct which was taken for granted years ago is now suddenly criminal. Make up symptoms so that your insurance company will pay for a doctor's visit? Say the loan from your parents was a gift when filling out a mortgage application? What might be considered minor ethical infractions could land you 5-10 years in jail if a prosecutor wanted to make a point.

Statutory and regulatory penalties are increasing and employees — along with the company — are more and more vulnerable to doing the wrong thing and paying for it dearly. The financial penalties on companies for employees' misdeeds are steep, but the use of nonfinancial penalties such as probation can be equally punishing, requiring court monitors to supervise every aspect of the business, or barring companies from certain activities. But we can't run our businesses with a compliance manual that is as thick as the tax code. We all have to do the right thing, and if we're not sure what that is, we have to know and feel free to ask. The encouragement of consultation through-out the organization is, we think, a key value to a corporate ethi-cal culture.

There are other reasons why businesses without values are businesses at risk. Their reputation suffers in the marketplace, depressing stock prices and eroding consumer confidence. Recruitment of talented personnel is more difficult, as Prudential Securities discovered after its $2 billion fraud scandal. Many companies now perform due diligence on companies they are considering as partners or suppliers, and are passing on those that don't meet their ethical standards.

Employee morale is higher in a company that has well-devel-oped values and lives by them. Nicholas G. Moore, chairman of PricewaterhouseCoopers, the global accounting firm, calls this personnel benefit key in explaining his commitment to values. "Ethics values are the glue that holds widespread organizations together," he said.

Corporate executives like Moore are not the only ones who have noticed that a values orientation provides real benefits. A commitment to shared values, rather than a culture that is based on distrust of employees (and resulting rules and penal-ties), encourages employees to aspire to success. A study done by Professors Gary Weaver and Linda Trevino suggested that there were several benefits to a values-based culture, including increased awareness of ethical issues, commitment to the organization (and less conflict between organizational and extra-organizational roles), employee integrity, willingness to communi-cate openly about problems, willingness to report an ethics violation to management, improved decision-making, willingness to seek advice about ethical issues, and reduced unethical con-duct. [8] Those are all good outcomes!

We like to cite such bottom-line oriented practical reasons when we argue for values-based management. But we admit that the best reason we have heard comes from our Center for Business Ethics colleague, Executive Fellow Emeritus John Casey, who capped his career in the investment services world by writ-

---

[8] Gary R. Weaver and Linda Klebe Trevino, "Compliance and Values Oriented Ethics Programs: Influences on Employees' Attitudes and Behavior," *Business Ethics Quarterly,* Volume 9, No. 2, April 1999, pp. 315-335.

ing *Values Added: Making Ethical Decisions in the Financial Marketplace.*

Casey wrote, "Laws alone are a poor substitute for morality. The greatest blessing of living in a free society is that we have the ability to steer ourselves. Once we give up that ability, that privilege, we risk losing sight of the ethical spirit and the law becomes a cage. We'll do, as so many others have done in this century, just what we're told to do. The world can no longer afford that kind of obedience."[9]

---

[9] John L. Casey with Bruce McCandless III, contributing editor, *Values Added: Making Ethical Decisions in the Financial Marketplace*, Lanham, MD: University Press of America, 1997, p. 5.

Chapter 3

Texas Instruments
FROM VOLUMES TO
THREE WORDS

Some companies start with a mission statement and a
few core values, and as the company grows, add detailed
policies and procedures. Texas Instruments, the global
semiconductor company, followed that pattern but then
did an astounding thing. It reexamined what it stood for
and ended up with just three words. How it discovered its
contemporary values is a story of corporate leadership and
soul-searching.

Texas origins, Texas principles

The "old" Texas Instruments began in the 1930s with a smarter
way to find oil deposits in the boom towns of East Texas. As
Geophysical Services Inc., the company was built on its
founders' principles of honesty, integrity and service.

As the company expanded into the world of advanced elec-
tronics, it won U.S. Navy contracts during wartime. After the war
it developed a range of technological firsts, including the integrated circuit. As the company grew and the modern world became
more complex, TI published in 1961, *Ethics in the Business of TI*, its
first formal code of ethics, codifying what had been the company's
long-time legacy of integrity.

Business ethics leadership

Throughout the 1970s and 80s, TI became a global powerhouse,
with employees operating in more than 30 countries on five con-

> **"T**he corporation will ultimately be judged by society
> on the basis of its ability to meet the world's material
> needs. We must do so with the highest standard of
> ethics, with a deep sense of obligation to the societies in
> which we operate, and with a willingness to stand before
> the public and defend our commitments as well as our
> capacity to carry them through."
>
> Mark Shepherd, Jr.
> former chairman, Texas Instruments, 1976

tinents. Along with TI's growth came more laws, more regulations, and more oversight. TI, an early leader in the business ethics movement, established its ethics office in 1987. In 1991 the company won the David C. Lincoln Ethics and Excellence in Business Award and in 1994 won the American Business Ethics Award and the Bentley College Center for Business Ethics Award.

TI's ethics apparatus was far-reaching and sophisticated. Led by Carl Skooglund, the TI ethics director, the office updated *Ethics in the Business of TI* and created several supplemental communication resources— the "Cornerstone" series, a set of glossy publications that featured real questions on ethics from TI employees worldwide, concentrating on specific subjects; more than 400 weekly electronic news articles on current subjects of interest, which were compiled into a resource library called "Instant Experience;" and ethics helplines comprising a secure message system, toll-free phone lines and a U.S post office box separate from the TI internal mail system. The office produced handy pocket guides, informative posters, training materials and an on-line, menu-driven web site linked to all TI Ethics Office materials and resources.

So what was wrong? According to Glenn Coleman, former TI manager of ethics communication and education, the material was beginning to look like the United States tax code. Too much, too confusing. Not only that, but Texas Instruments was suddenly jolted by a series of events that forced it to become a "new company."

Change happens fast

First, in 1996, its popular chairman, Jerry Junkins, died suddenly of a heart attack while traveling in Europe. Revered by all, his death brought into focus other major organizational and policy changes that actually had been in the works prior to the sad event. But now there was a sense of urgency on the part of the new leadership to complete Junkins' plans for reformulating the global semiconductor company into a fast-paced, focused designer and supplier of digital signal processing solutions.

TI sold its defense business to Raytheon, the largest of nearly twenty divestitures and acquisitions over a two-year period. It competed aggressively for the most talented people, dramatically changing its benefits and compensation policies to provide more individual choice and flexibility. The Dallas-based company was shedding its paternalistic, command-and-control ways and emerging into a global leader providing products to serve a networked society. For the first time, TI had more employees outside the United States than inside.

The new chairman, president and chief executive officer, Tom Engibous, was determined that TI reward its shareholders by increasing its value as a market leader. To do this, they would provide stable financial performance and grow in markets with potential. He placed a strong emphasis on quality strategies, improved profit margins and insisted that every employee define a personal plan for individual development.

Engibous's favorite phrase became "a passion for winning." He wanted TIers to be fast, creative and collaborative, and this superb communicator lost little time in repeating the message to everyone.

Skooglund was concerned. "TI had a long history of ethical emphasis right from its founders," he said. "It was ingrained in the culture and made my job easier.

"But I wasn't sure how ethics would fit in this new TI, with its passion for winning. The heightened emphasis on financial results could have been interpreted to mean doing whatever it takes to get the job done. That could have been a recipe for disaster if we didn't clearly explain how ethics and values were a part of it."

Skooglund met with Engibous to discuss these concerns to develop a plan to assure that the company would not lose its focus on integrity in the face of increased pressure for performance.

New model, new approach to ethics

Engibous was clear. He was proud of the ethical history of TI and insisted that ethics be a foundation of the new TI. But he was also clear that the company must operate on a values and principles approach, rather than a rules-based approach. Engibous did not want to lose the transformation from TI's old hierarchical model to a new one of empowerment and responsibility.

Skooglund wanted to make sure that he understood. "If we're successful, what's the end state going to look like?" he asked.

Engibous's response couldn't have been clearer. The TI core values would be understood and owned worldwide. TIers' behavior would be consistent with the core values, which would give the company a competitive advantage. Decisions would be made according to the company values, not its rules. Bureaucracy would be minimal, as would barriers to productivity, innovation and collaboration. Policies would be few, simple and easy to understand. TIers would have the flexibility to manage their work and their personal lives. They would be trusted and responsible.

Skooglund understood. Now he just had to translate the marching orders into action. He participated on a cross-functional team to examine all the human resource policies of the company to see which of them could be eliminated.

The process of change

"We challenged each policy by asking five questions," Skooglund recalled. "Why do we have it? What is the business reason for having it? Is it a legal requirement? What is the worst thing that can happen if we don't have it? Should it be local or corporate?

"We started off with 46 policies. We scrapped 9, recognized that 24 were actually how-tos, or procedures, and we kept 13. The ones we kept we rewrote and significantly shortened. That process took us over a year."

As the process of eliminating policies and other barriers continued, the importance of reassessing the company's basic values took on increased urgency. Skooglund recalled, "We realized that we were taking away a security blanket from many who had become very comfortable in referring day-to-day decisions to the policy book. We were asking TIers to face a future defined by enormous changes, increased complexity and intense competition. The only way we could expect them to make good decisions and choices, and to do it quickly in that environment, was to provide value-based resources and to put them in everyone's hands. Those values had to be crystal clear, directly aligned with TI's business objectives and relevant to every employee worldwide. We launched a year-long process to define those values."

A task force set out to define the TI values in a single document. The first draft was three pages, single-spaced and contained fourteen values. Three drafts and several international reviews later, the feedback was consistent: shorter is better! Keep them simple, concise and easy to remember.

Skooglund admitted they were rewriting the Constitution when their constituents only wanted soundbites. By the summer of 1997, all the company's human resource directors had reviewed a new draft. It was time to try it out on 19 separate worldwide employee focus groups.

"At that point we knew what we wanted to say," Skooglund said," but we needed to know what employees were hearing. As a result of the focus groups, the draft changed quite a bit."

Just three words

The three core TI values in the draft were integrity, innovation and commitment. Each value was illustrated by two descriptive phrases, which could be called principles. For example, integrity was linked with "respect and value people" and "be honest."

Skooglund admits that the definitions of values and principles are imprecise and to make matters worse, the final document booklet was entitled "The values *and ethics* of TI."

"Several of our operations, particularly those in Asia, wanted to know precisely why we used these words. What did "values" mean? What did "principles" mean? Is "innovation" really a value? What's the difference between principles and ethics? In hindsight, perhaps we didn't need all those words, but to me,

The values and ethics of Texas Instruments

INTEGRITY
Respect and Value People   Be Honest

INNOVATION
Learn & Create   Act Boldly

COMMITMENT
Take Responsibility   Commit to Win

values are deeply seated universal concepts that give us guidance. Principles are more prescriptive and directed towards conduct."

While it is interesting to see the final three words that TI settled on to represent its corporate values, it is more interesting to learn what words and concepts did not make the final document.

The TI Mission Statement, "Leadership in Digital Solutions for the Networked Society," was highlighted in the initial draft. Following the focus group discussions it was left on the cutting room floor. While inspiring, many felt that it had no place in a values document.

Engibous's favorite phrase, "a passion for winning" was interpreted by many focus groups to mean, do whatever it takes, a perspective that surprised and concerned Engibous. "It became clear," Skooglund said, "that we had to put that objective in ethical perspective. But at the same time, Tom and the rest of the leadership team were adamant that a commitment to making TI a winner had to remain an essential principle."

The original draft contained a concept that work should be fun. Asian employees reacted strongly. In their view, the concept of setting fun and humor as a workplace objective was weird. Business is business and should remain so.

The notion that TIers would "respect local customs" was also eliminated, after Europeans complained that the concept was too vague and would open up potential justification for abuses.

One word that Skooglund thought was appropriate evoked a sharp negative reaction, particularly in Europe. The drafters had extolled the virtue of collaboration and teamwork. To some employees, however, collaboration meant collusion. Combine "collaboration" with "world leadership" and "passion for winning" and you have a recipe for world war.

Well if you can't collaborate, how about "nurture informal relationships," in order to reinforce candor and communications? No. Informal doesn't work everywhere, particularly in places where formal relationships indicate respect for one's superiors.

Early drafts frequently contained the words "do not," or "never." Focus groups in Asia thought those words were too negative and suggested that drafters minimize their use, writing the same message but in a positive way. "Bureaucracy" was viewed as a negative and unclear word that didn't make the final draft.

Skooglund was surprised by two concepts that engendered negative responses. "In past documents, we had stressed that TI has an open door process, meaning that any employee could take a concern up the ladder to anyone in the company. But our employee focus groups thought we should leave it out. While some had good experiences with the open door process, evidently enough employees felt they been burned by it that the concept had taken on a negative aura. We were told that it might create a credibility issue. So we didn't repeat it.

"We also had drafted a principle stating that because one's activities and behavior outside of work could have an impact on the company's reputation, we could have a legitimate reason to take corrective action. While we understood this in the United States, Europeans did not like this idea, believing that one's work and personal life should be kept quite separate. So we left it out."

Through this entire process there was a constant drumbeat of criticism and advice regarding the document—too many words, people won't read it. Keep it simple and straightforward.

All these subtractions made a better document in the end, as each reviewing group urged brevity and clarity. The basic values should be so clear and distinct that employees could keep them in their heads.

After the drafting group reviewed the input from the focus groups, it met with the four top human resource directors, who then met with their regional business teams to approve a final draft.

But the process still wasn't complete. The drafters met individually with the top 9 executives in the company (the Strategy Leadership Team) to review the final draft. In October 1997 the SLT approved it.

One more step remained. The stockholder relations and public policy committee of the board of directors approved the final version, and in December 1997 it was officially introduced at the annual TI Leadership Conference.

The fourteen-page booklet was striking in design, its graphics and typeface reflecting a fast-paced global technology company. Those looking for rules would not find any, but the last page contained a list of information resources, including TI's values web-site, where specific information could be obtained.

If employees agreed with the notion of decision-making through values, rather than rules, they'd find that TI's new booklet worked. Illustrative bullet sentences under each value and principle help lead to the right decision.

Did it work?

We decided to test TI's new approach to see if we could find the answer to a common ethical dilemma by referencing TI's values. Using the example of employees' use of company computers to access web sites and e-mail, one might first look under Integrity. The value of Integrity is paired with two principles, one of which is "Treat others as we want to be treated." Illustrative bullet points include:

- Recognize and avoid behaviors that others may find offensive, including the manner in which we speak and relate to one another and the material we bring in to the workplace, both printed and electronically.

- Understand that even though TI has the obligation to monitor its business information systems activity, we will respect privacy by prohibiting random searches of individual TIer's communications.

Under the value Commitment, and the principle that TIers "take responsibility," bullet points include:

• Use company assets for personal purposes strictly on an infrequent basis with negligible expense to TI.

Inquiring employees now understand the answer. They shouldn't use their computers to download pornography, but if they want to check the net asset value on their mutual funds or tomorrow's weather, or perhaps send personal e-mails, the company probably wouldn't mind. And if they're unclear about whether such a use of the computer adds expense to TI, they have places to ask. If they're still in doubt, they could take the TI Ethics Quick Test in the back of the booklet.

Suggestions for next time

Skooglund, now retired from TI, is happy with the process and the final product that resulted in the three TI values. He admits, however, that with the benefit of hindsight his team would have done a few things differently.

"We drafted the document in English and then translated it into 12 languages. To make sure we translated it right, we retranslated the translation back into English. We wanted to make sure that the document read in a conversational manner. That step proved to be very important but extremely challenging.

"The process worked all right, but what we should have done was postpone the final printing in English until we had finished all the translations, because there were words and phrases we

Ethics quick test from Texas Instruments

• **Is the action legal?**
• **Does it comply with our values?**
• **If you do it, will you feel bad?**
• **How will it look in the newspaper?**
• **If you know it's wrong, don't do it!**
• **If you're not sure, ask.**
• **Keep asking until you get an answer.**

would have changed, based on the feedback from the other parts of the world. We would have been more sensitive to the fact that every word has meaning.

"For example, we have a phrase in the document that insures that every employee can resolve ethics questions without 'retribution and retaliation.' The Japanese wanted to know what's the difference between retribution on the one hand and retaliation on the other. Well the answer is that there's not a big difference, and when that was brought to our attention, we might have changed the English version if we had the time."

Skooglund would also have orchestrated the timing of the booklet's release a little more precisely. "We wanted to get it out early, so we put it out in a bit of a naked fashion, without really explaining where it fits into the scheme of the new TI and our business objectives. Our web site, which was our primary resource link for more prescriptive information, was late. We conducted company-wide training in values and decision-making, but that didn't happen until later. It would have been better had all pieces been coordinated together."

If that's the worst criticism that Skooglund can muster about a mammoth process on behalf of a global $9 billion company of 44,000 employees, that's not too bad. He and his team deserve a great deal of credit for continuing to be the pioneers that TI has always been in the business ethics movement.

TI may have boiled its volumes of rules and regulations into just three words: integrity, innovation, commitment; but the reason remains the same as it has been since the company's founding. Chairman Tom Engibous said it well in his introductory letter to the new TI values document:

"If TIers are going to continue to be successful in this highly competitive global marketplace, we must be creative, fast to act, and we must work together effectively. We must make our choices in an informed manner - in the field and on the factory and office floor. We cannot do this by referring every decision to a book of rules or policies, but rather from having an understanding of an appreciation for the company's values and principles."[1]

---

[1] Tom Engibous, *The Values and Ethics of TI*, Texas Instruments, 1998.

Chapter 4

Self-assessment

You can't plot a course without knowing where you're starting from. Therefore a diagnostic assessment, self-assessment or liability inventory, is a first step in determining what, if any, cultural assets and organizational risks may be present and require attention.

The initial impetus for an assessment can come from any direction. Senior managers may have attended a conference where they heard a speech about the newest developments in compliance and business conduct programs and wondered, "Where are we?" A new senior executive from another company or industry may have had experience in an organization in which values were well integrated and sees an opportunity to make his mark on his new employer. A savvy member of the board of directors may ask for a report about the status of the company's ethics initiatives. Or, an ethical crisis or government investigation may precipitate an in-depth review of the company's programs (or lack thereof).

It may well be that there is nothing in particular to trigger the need for self-assessment. The company is doing nicely, employees are seemingly content and growth is steady. This is an opportune time to take stock of how the company measures up.

We suggest that a diagnostic assessment be conducted by asking who, what, how and why.

Who

Managers can conduct an in-depth examination themselves, although many prefer — and we advise — having outside consultants perform the assessment and analyze the results, much like an auditor's report and letter of recommendation. Such services are generally preferable because employees and external stakeholders often perceive the efforts to be more objective and the results to be more credible. Consultants bring specific expertise to the assessment process and to interpreting the results in a way that insiders may not. This is particularly important during a first ever assessment since the findings will most often be used as a benchmark for future comparisons. Credibility or lack thereof will therefore revisit the scene. And, if employees do not feel they can speak freely (i.e. because they fear being candid with members of their own organization), true risks will not be identified and distrust will emerge instead.

As Mary Ann Bowman Beil, corporate ethics and compliance officer at Memorial Health in Savannah, said, an effective assessment should "beat the bushes in search of risks and flush them out into the open." Can company insiders find those hidden risks as well as a "private investigator?" Probably not.

What

Randall J. Corgan, former manager of business practices at GE Engine Services, suggests that companies begin by compiling a comprehensive list of "whats" that should be on any assessment list. First,

- Know the marketplace in which you are operating, both domestic and global. Is it highly regulated? Highly competitive? Volatile? Shrinking? Then use this knowledge to inform the specific questions the assessment asks.
- Assess your customers. Risk assessments too often focus on internal surveys of employees and neglect the company's customer base, and customers' perceptions of the organization's behavior shape their realities.
- Assess the competition. What are the parameters of acceptable behavior of both your domestic and global competition? How might that form a benchmark later for what your organization chooses to do — or not do?
- Understand what constitutes violations of the laws that govern your company, both in the United States and globally. Ask

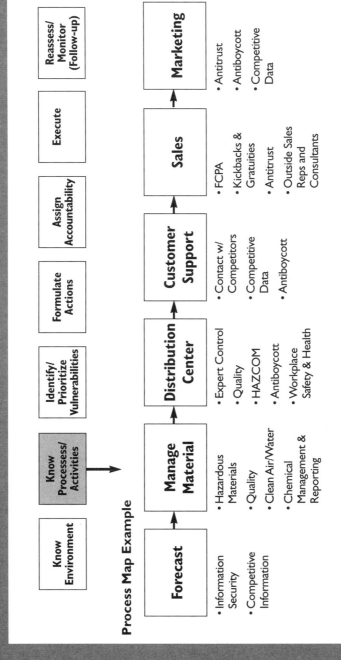

Risk assessment and abatement

| Know Environment | Know Processess/ Activities | Identify/ Prioritize Vulnerabilities | Formulate Actions | Assign Accountability | Execute | Reassess/ Monitor (Follow-up) |

Process Map Example

Forecast → **Manage Material** → **Distribution Center** → **Customer Support** → **Sales** → **Marketing**

Forecast
- Information Security
- Competitive Information

Manage Material
- Hazardous Materials
- Quality
- Clean Air/Water
- Chemical Management & Reporting

Distribution Center
- Expert Control
- Quality
- HAZCOM
- Antiboycott
- Workplace Safety & Health

Customer Support
- Contact w/ Competitors
- Competitive Data
- Antiboycott

Sales
- FCPA
- Kickbacks & Gratuities
- Antitrust
- Outside Sales Reps and Consultants

Marketing
- Antitrust
- Antiboycott
- Competitive Data

questions which assess whether violations may exist or, equally as important, whether conditions which tend to promote violations exist.

- Know which regulatory agencies apply to your business. For example, companies governed by the Securities and Exchange Commission may develop a values program that is different than companies governed by the Environmental Protection Agency or the Food and Drug Administration.

- Examine carefully your existing policies that govern organizational behavior, no matter how decentralized they may be. What policies do employees think are in force and apply to them? You may find you have no policies where you thought you did or where you should. You may find you have out-of-date policies that need updating.

The second step that Corgan recommends is an in-depth look at the company's processes and activities. Unless you map out exactly what the organization does, as Corgan suggests, it is difficult to present a comprehensive picture of all the risks that need to be understood and addressed. In Corgan's example of a process map he includes material management (with its attendant responsibilities for clean air and water, chemical reporting and handling of hazardous materials), customer support (competitive issues) and sales (antitrust, issues about gifts and gratuities, and the use of outside sales representatives).

The third step in the "what" process is to identify the risks and vulnerabilities facing the company, after understanding how and where it operates. These are not just legal risks, but may include cultural ones as well. Does the company have a history of problems? Are there risks posed by the company's organizational structure, its compensation structure, and its corporate personality?

Dana Freyer, a partner in the international law firm of Skadden, Arps, Slate, Meagher & Flom, poses several cultural questions she asks when performing a risk assessment for a company:

- To what extent is communication candid or covert?

- To what extent does the culture support or discourage employees from raising sensitive issues?

- Is it centralized or decentralized? To what extent does the organizational structure influence employee behavior and communication?

- To what extent are there turf battles? What are they usually about?

- Has it acquired or merged with other companies? If so, what were the cultural integration issues that were or were not addressed?

- Do the divisions operate as separate business fiefdoms? If so, what are the cultural norms that inform acceptable behavior in each?

Freyer focuses on the issue of understanding corporate culture because she has seen the risks of a poor one. She notes that companies will never be able to totally prevent wrongdoing by employees, but the culture that a company has created will go a long way to determining whether government prosecutors will bring criminal charges against it and its executives when wrongdoing occurs and is investigated. The culture will also have a bearing on the amount of penalties a company will receive from sentencing judges. Consider just two excerpts from judicial opinions in cases in which companies were given stiff fines and court-imposed restrictions:

One of the things I found disturbing here was the sense that there are people at Con Edison, who testified at the trial, who clearly knew and who should have been jumping up and down saying there is asbestos there, we know it. It was obvious they didn't say it because they were intimidated from saying it, because they didn't think that was the corporate culture.

Another:

This is a case in which a pervasive and powerful corporate culture exalted the value of profit above the value of human life. No one in the company felt he or she could go to anybody at Bard to attempt to stop the deliberate scheme to subvert the FDA process intended to assure the safety and effectiveness of its catheters . . . . The officers and directors of Bard. . . are morally responsible for a corporate culture which placed potential profit above the values of human life.[1]

---

[1] See Dana H. Freyer, "Corporate Compliance Programs for FDA-Regulated Companies: Incentives for Their Development and the Impact of the Federal Sentencing Guidelines for Organizations," *Food and Drug Law Journal*, Vol. 51, No. 2, 1996, pp.226-242.

The assessment should not only help answer the question, "In what specific ways does our corporate culture contribute or detract from appropriate business conduct?" but it should also look at vulnerabilities the industry, competitors, suppliers and customers often face. The results also should be factored into the review.

Corgan reminds those doing assessments that not all risks are equal. Some business units, processes or products may have greater risks than others. The consequences of various risks should therefore also be noted so that companies can spend their resources, time and attention effectively. Obviously there will be costs of litigation and perhaps immeasurable costs to company reputation. In some cases of government contractors, there may be disbarment, a serious issue for the long-term viability of a company.

One need only recall Dow Corning, the highly profitably company which endured bankruptcy and thousands of tort claims due to allegations against its silicone breast implants, to understand the consequences of risk.[2] When the controversy erupted, silicone breast implants represented only a small portion of Dow Corning's sales. A risk assessment at the time might have resulted in the conclusion that the consequences of pulling the implants off the market would be less than the risk of continuing to sell them.

However, risk assessments involving ethics often result in complex and sometimes conflicting findings. So, for example, Dow Corning might have considered that it had a continuing obligation to continue to provide the implants for women who had breast surgery, as it was one of a few companies that manufactured them. On the other hand, the assessment would have also pointed out that the company had an ethical obligation to its shareholders and employees to remain viable and profitable.

How

Do the diagnostic assessment well or not at all. First, consider the number of locations and ensure the assessment samples all

---

[2] See Dawn-Marie Driscoll, "The Dow Corning Case: First, Kill All the Lawyers," *Business and Society Review,* Vol. 100/101, pp. 57-63.

stakeholders. The issues and cultural differences usually vary greatly from location to location, even within the same state. For example, in a one-location company headquarters employees usually have different opinions than those of field employees.

There are several methods of conducting an assessment and in most cases, all should be used to paint a complete picture.

One-on-one and focus group interviews require a high degree of structure and expertise. They are also time-consuming and costly. Nonetheless, their benefits are significant and unique. The advantage of such interviews is that they allow for follow-up questions and provide a forum in which issues that the survey failed to consider may be identified and addressed. More importantly, they not only answer the "What are your perceptions?" question but also, "Why do we perceive things this way?" Focus groups are best conducted by trained outside facilitators because some employees are naturally shy when asked to speak frankly in groups.

The professional services firm of PricewaterhouseCoopers conducted focus group interviews with over 200 employees to identify issues that impacted them and reviewed all existing policies before crafting a new policy statement and publishing its code of conduct book, *The Way We Do Business.* Harry Britt, the firm's global manager of ethics & business conduct, pointed out that this was one part of a longer risk assessment which was essential in helping him and his colleagues frame an ethics initiative responsive to his firm's needs.

Employee surveys are the most efficient way of reaching many employees and are often the most reliable. The results can be quantified and tracked and can address specific areas of risk. And they help answer the critical question, "What is the 'state-of-the-state' as regards acceptable business conduct within this organization?"

Consultants for diagnostic assessments should be closely interviewed and carefully chosen. They should not only be able to describe the process they employ, but explain the benefits of their approach. They should be able to discuss their use of both interviews and surveys — i.e. both the features and the outcomes.

They should demonstrate that they understand and will honor cultural differences. So, for example, they should convey the importance of translating the survey they construct for you in a way that ensures that the questions have the same meaning in another language.

The consultant should not only be skilled at assessing the ethical climate, but also be experienced at assessing and understanding organizational and managerial practices and in showing you how they impact the ethical climate.

But, perhaps most importantly, they should be able to tell you convincingly how their approach will specifically help you solve the problem you seek to solve — i.e. how their approach will provide you with the information you can really use.

Finally, it is a plus if the consultant is familiar with your industry. Many professions or industries are unique. Therefore consultants who have specific subject matter experience in your type of industry may have an advantage in doing a complete analysis of the results of the assessment, because they understand the context for the results.

Why

It is critical to communicate the bottom-line benefits of a good diagnostic assessment. Here are several reasons:

- Avoiding future risks requires the organization to know the places where they might arise.
- Pinpointing areas that need further attention is "targeted prevention."
- Providing a definitive baseline enables the organization to measure future improvement.
- Demonstrating to employees, customers, vendors and others that the company is serious about strengthening its ethical culture is automatically beneficial to morale and trust.
- Helping to retain valued employees is a practical benefit. Talented people like to work in a company that shows it values integrity and asks their opinion.
- Addressing critical issues early, before they become crises, is less costly and more credible than addressing them later.
- Shielding senior management and the board from liability for not having asked probing questions about risk assessment

and remedial measures is a benefit that rarely is articulated but is a reality.

Finally, we want to stress a point that we will repeat later in the book. A diagnostic assessment is best conducted with the full support of senior management. Getting the support of all the key management team, and not just the CEO and a few others, is worth some concentrated effort at the beginning, and in fact can actually be a part of the assessment itself. Begin the individual interviews with the senior leadership in order to get their buy-in as well as crucial assessment information.

We have found that most enlightened managers today understand that their greatest liability is in not knowing where their risks are. An effective assessment will tell them.

Chapter 5

Pacific Bell
A DIAGNOSTIC ASSESSMENT
DONE RIGHT

Dr. Craig Dreilinger, former president of The Dreiford Group, does not hesitate when asked to describe an effective assessment process. An organizational change management consultant, Dreilinger has conducted hundreds of assessments for more than twenty years. During this time, he says that Pacific Bell, the telecommunications company,[1] wins the prize hands down.

In recalling his experiences with Pac Bell, Dreilinger said, "Their assessment process worked because it was— and became seen by everyone as being — an ongoing process rather than an isolated event. It wasn't 'today we'll do our self-assessment.' It became like taking the temperature of a person being administered to in real time. We could watch the assessment change before our eyes, as we were introducing change, and the credibility of the effort increased in degrees over time."

Crisis compels change

Pacific Bell did not necessarily set out to achieve such distinction. Its president, Philip Quigley, asked Dreilinger to help the company develop and implement a broad-based ethics initiative after the company had been embroiled in two legal and ethical scandals in the late 1980s.

---

[1] Pacific Bell is a subsidiary of SBC Communications Inc., a global telecommunications company. Information about SBC can be found at www.sbc.com.

"These were major, public, documented gaffes," recalls Dreilinger. "Worse, they were caused — or at least enabled — by senior management. One was called the Sales Practices Case, and the other was angrily referred to as 'Croning.'" The two terms came to have their own meaning in the company.

Dreilinger and his team faced an opportunity and a challenge. Pac Bell's new ethics initiative was launched by senior managers but, by and large, most employees distrusted them. It appeared that the effort would be dead at the start.

"We explained that if the ethics initiative stood a chance of succeeding, it had to be a process rather than an event. We needed to do an intervention that included assessment, code development, training and building a broad-based sense of ownership as part of the rollout," Dreilinger recalled.

"To succeed we needed not only ongoing 'skin-in-the-game' commitment from senior managers, but action research so we could measure our progress over time. We had to find out what line managers thought about the new code that was developed as part of the initiative as we developed it, because ultimately they'd be the trainers and communicators about the initiative for the rest of the 50,000 employees."

Dreilinger and his team found out loud and clear. As 875 district level managers convened for two-day "training" sessions, Dreilinger's team posed open-ended questions to try to get a sense of the "state of the state" at Pac Bell and how they reacted to the newly developed code. Dreilinger's plan was to obtain feedback for Pac Bell's officers at the outset of the initiative so changes could be made to it as it was rolled out.

Dreilinger laughed as he recalled the response. "The managers," he said, "were not shy. They didn't believe the ethics initiative and thought the only motivation for it was that senior management had been caught in an unpleasant situation. They were convinced the only unethical people were the sponsors of the initiative. They were certain the initiative was insincere.

"I went back and told Pac Bell's executives that they had no currency with their employees. In fact, employees' trust in them was largely less than zero. It was at a zero minus. Furthermore, the district managers said that the new code was full of platitudes, provided no guidance and demonstrated that the drafters didn't have a clue about the real live issues facing them."

But this seemingly dismal situation was an opportunity, said Dreilinger, for Pac Bell officers to convincingly demonstrate that the company was critically listening. At every training session (all of which were limited to less than twenty managers) he and his colleagues summarized line managers' views and promised confidentiality in exchange for candor.

"We had a rule of three. I'd only report back to senior management what we heard more than three times or from three or more people in a session," he said. The rule of three allowed consensus to develop, without attaching names to the opinions. "It also meant that the committee of senior managers who had advocated the ethics initiative had to listen.

"I'd go back to the committee and say, 'the good news is that we are doing the self-assessment, and removing some resistance to the initiative by listening and reporting feedback. The bad news is their views.'"

Dreilinger told Pac Bell's executive team that they should publicly address their lack of credibility at the same time as the workshops were being held. They needed to state publicly what they had heard about the overall initiative and acknowledge what their line managers were saying. The code had to change in response to the comments from the training sessions, so those participants would begin to believe that management was listening and responding.

"The code ended up being radically different at the end of the process than at the beginning," Dreilinger said. "People actually saw it change. For example, managers immediately saw the code had no teeth. There was no language in it that said who it was applied to, so no one believed that senior managers would be held accountable. As a result, Pac Bell's officers made sure that the code grew teeth and made it clear that it applied to everyone, including the officers themselves."

Rolling out the process

The company training sessions, called "Managing Ethical Issues," were divided into two parts so that participants could see the results of their discussions. The first part was two days long. Six weeks later, managers came together for another day-and-a-half. That six-week break gave the senior manager committee and Dreilinger's team a chance to analyze the results of the assessment and interview process, suggest and make changes in the code and the overall ethics initiative, and present it again to the participants.

"This process, although time consuming, was essential if we were to successfully energize the line managers to help us roll it out to the rest of the organization," Dreilinger explained. "The managers were the messengers. They had to believe the ethics initiative was for real or they could never communicate that belief to the lower level employees they would ultimately be training. The messages that people trust the most are from their immediate supervisors. We had to make the supervisors credible.

"We taught the manager/participants how to be trainers and coaches as part of our first workshop. Then we gave them a forum during the second workshop to share what worked and what didn't. By doing that, we also made them accountable for the results. They had a chance to change the program and express their opinions.

"As the managers rolled out the program to their employees, they brought back more assessment and feedback from all parts of the company. As credibility grew we could measure the changes through the ongoing assessment. The number of people who believed in the sincerity of the effort increased. The contents of the code and the overall ethics initiative also changed slightly, but less than in the first round.

"This turned out to be a very effective process of corporate self-assessment. It was up front and personal, two-way and two-day, and we could continually build on it. That's why it worked."

Advice for others

Not all companies have Pacific Bell's commitment to implement a comprehensive effort. But Dreilinger tries to steer them in the right direction. In most cases where Dreilinger has been asked to conduct a self-assessment for an organization, it has begun with: "What prompted you to do this self-assessment now, and what conditions do you want to exist two years from now that don't exist now?"

Dreilinger feels it is insufficient for senior managers to just articulate the problem they are trying to solve. They must also become clear about the outcomes they are trying to achieve. From this he can recommend a process that makes sense, one that usually includes focus groups with a stratified random sample of employees in the organization, a structured interview protocol, and a statistical survey that provides benchmarks.

"The focus groups answer the whys and wherefore questions, and the surveys answer the whats," he said. "Particularly in the surveys, it is important to take into account the realities and the profile of the employee base. For example, some may not read or write or speak English. All of these factors must be accounted for in the design of the survey and its implementation."

So what was the ultimate result of Dreilinger's effort and of Pac Bell's initiative?

"Clearly, the initiative didn't solve all of the company's trust-based issues. But we knew it wouldn't. But it did rebuild trust — trust among employees, trust by customers and trust by its regulator, the Public Utilities Commission. And perhaps most importantly, it created an article of faith among employees that said, 'Maybe ethics really does matter here. And maybe we should play.'"

Chapter 6

Commitment from the Top

No values initiative should begin without the most senior levels of management making an explicit commitment to its long-term success.

We could give you a lot of fancy reasons but the best one is that, in most cases, it's the top executives who make the decisions about priorities in an organization. Ideally, these top executives would be what Professor John Boatright, the Raymond C. Baumhart, S.J., Professor of Business Ethics at Loyola University Chicago, calls "moral managers," those who incorporate ethical considerations into their decision-making (along with such factors as the law, profit-making, organizational design, marketing strategies, and the like).[1]

Boatright suggests that the traditional goal of business ethics — to influence these moral managers — is both paternalistic and narrow. He reminds us that in most organizations there are many more Indians than chiefs, and the objective should be to get everyone to act and think morally and make decisions that help turn the marketplace into a center for moral behavior.

There is truth that this should be the ultimate goal of business ethics, but the last time we looked, the Indians are very aware of what their chiefs are doing. The values and actions of top executives filter down and influence the rest of the tribe. If they don't practice what they preach, they can expect little exemplary behavior from their underlings. On the other hand, if the boss happens to bend over to pick up a scrap of paper from the floor or makes it a point to learn the name of his secretary's

---

[1] John R. Boatright, "Does Business Ethics Rest on a Mistake?" Presidential Address to The Society for Business Ethics, August 6, 1998.

grandchild, then it is amazing how fast others in the company begin to adopt the same habits. We've seen this imitation phenomenon work too often to discount the impact that behavior of those at the top can have. It's probably not surprising, then, that a 1997 survey of the Ethics Officer Association revealed that the predominant factor influencing an organization's commitment to ethics was because the chief executive officer had initiated it.[2]

The notion that form and substance are intertwined at the top is no doubt one of the reasons why the Federal Sentencing Guidelines include a requirement that a senior officer be in charge of compliance and ethics programs. Those drafting the guidelines knew the importance of the role of top executives in carrying out any company-wide initiatives. But in our opinion, senior managers are not the only top-level individuals who have an important part to play in reinforcing the values of an organization.

Boards of directors

We often say, "The ethical buck stops with the board of directors." It is difficult, if not impossible, to implement values-driven management if the board itself is unethical, uncaring or dismissive of senior manager's commitment to developing such an organizational culture.

Directors who are aware of the importance of ethical values in an organization (sometimes it is those who are new to the board) can change an existing culture quickly, even when senior managers are oblivious. All they have to do is mention the subject and request a briefing on the program's progress at the next meeting.

It should be axiomatic that the board itself be ethical and its members be individuals with a reputation for integrity. Unfortunately that is not always the case. An ethical board more likely exists in instances where directors are nominated by their fellow independent directors, the board sets the agenda for the meetings, the directors meet in executive session, directors have established their own code of conduct to deal with such

---

[2] Ethics Officer Association 1997 Member Survey, p. 9; see also www.eoa.org.

"There is compelling evidence that shareholders care deeply about the ethics of the companies in which they invest. This evidence inspired us — in 1995 — to be the first major corporation in America to post our Code of Ethics and Business Conduct on the World Wide Web.

Lockheed Martin is comprised of a score of diverse corporate cultures and heritages. Through all this rich diversity, we draw our strength and cohesiveness from our vision as a company known for highly ethical people, working together with integrity, as a team, with a "can-do" attitude and a commitment to achieving excellence. Our collective dedication to ethics is truly the glue that unites us."

Peter B. Teets
president and chief operating officer,
Lockheed Martin Corporation, acceptance remarks
upon receiving the 1998 American Business Ethics Award

issues as conflict of interest and board procedure, and directors regularly evaluate themselves.

Ideally, boards should specifically authorize ethics and values programs and formally appoint a senior officer to oversee them. Many boards require this officer to report to them regularly, usually through the board's audit committee, regarding the progress in implementing the program. Some boards have established a separate ethics committee of and for the board in addition to its audit committee.

Furthermore, boards of directors such as the Michigan Physicians Mutual Liability Company use time at board meetings or retreats to undergo their own customized ethics training, in which they focus on ethical issues at their level. Consensus about standards of business ethics and the values by which the organization operates is critical for board members to understand. A board may not make the right decision in an ethical crisis unless it has discussed ethical concerns and addressed hypothetical ethical issues many times as a group.

Ethics officers

Why is a "senior officer" appointed by the board to direct its business conduct program? While adhering to company standards and values is every employee's responsibility, this does not mean than an overseer is unnecessary. There is an apt analogy here to a company's internal auditing function. Every employee in a company is responsible for financial integrity, but a separate internal auditing group is needed to give focus and direction to this function and to serve as a check on the process. So too, ethics managers serve a similar purpose.

Ethics officers are a varied group. In the EOA's 1997 survey of ethics officers, 23% listed human resources as their area of professional expertise; 23% operations/administration, 19% legal, 12% internal audit and 11% finance/accounting. The average age was 49 years and 72% were male.

Some ethics officers have had an outstanding track record within the company in other areas of responsibility. If the person

Titles held by senior executives in charge of values programs

Sr. VP, Organizational Effectiveness & Ethics Officer

VP, Office of Corporate Compliance

VP, Business Practices

VP, Ethics & Business Conduct

VP, Compliance & Integrity

VP, Corporate Ethics

VP, Market Conduct

VP, Ethics & Business Policy

VP, Ethics & Employee Relations

VP, Environmental, Safety and Ethics

Ethics Officer

Director, Business Ethics & Integrity

is well-known and respected for qualities of independence and personal integrity, he or she can lend great credibility to any values-based program.

In companies where there has been an ethical scandal, an outsider, someone of stature, may be the best choice to bring objectivity to the organization. These individuals may have been ethics officers at other companies or be well known in the business or civic community. This approach works well if there is strong commitment from all areas of management to insure that the ethics and values programs will be effective and ongoing no matter who implements them.

According to Graydon Wood, the former ethics officer of Nynex's award-winning ethics program, the ideal qualifications for an ethics officer are that he or she:

- holds a high level position within the company
- operates with unrestricted access to the chief executive officer and the board of directors, or a committee of the board
- maintains a high degree of trust and respect among members of the senior management team
- can assemble resources for affecting internal procedural changes and carrying out investigations
- has access to information and support mechanisms that provide monitoring, measuring, early warning and detection
- offers incentives and rewards for productively carrying out the compliance role
- has the skill to operate effectively with the media, public forums and the legal process[3]

While some companies have appointed full-time ethics officers, other companies underscore the importance of ethical values by giving its top executive the responsibility. Some do both. For example, at USAA, the diversified financial services company, Chief Executive Officer Robert T. Herres is the chief ethics officer and Sylvia Ann Garcia, who oversees the program,

---

[3] For more information on ethics officers see Dawn-Marie Driscoll, W. Michael Hoffman, Edward S. Petry, *The Ethical Edge: Tales of Organizations That Have Faced Moral Crises*, MasterMedia, Ltd., 1995, pp. 105-117.

is ethics coordinator. At Bell Atlantic, a telecommunications company with 140,000 employees and 22 million customers, the chief compliance officer is the chief executive officer — perhaps the only corporation in the United States that has so designated its CEO. The vice president of ethics, compliance, diversity and organizational development reports to the board of directors' audit committee as well as the management audit committee and the CEO.

BellSouth's approach

Jerry Guthrie, corporate director of ethics and business conduct for BellSouth, describes his program as one having the commitment of top management, a requirement he demanded before setting up the telecommunications company's ethics program.

Guthrie and his boss, the senior vice president, corporate compliance and corporate secretary, have dotted line reporting authority directly to the board of directors' audit committee, and Guthrie meets regularly with the audit committee to provide updates on what his staff has been doing and what they are hearing.

BellSouth's chairman and chief executive officer, Duane Ackerman, chairs the company's ethics committee, which Guthrie uses to champion ethics, to provide oversight and feedback and to implement policy changes. But Guthrie says the board's audit committee has the ultimate oversight role and he enjoys unusual access to board members. "My boss expects me to meet alone with the audit committee and I have the freedom to tell them anything I want. That's the way it should work," Guthrie says.

Business leadership and moral leadership

Interest from the board of directors and the appointment of an ethics officer is not sufficient to establish an effective values-based program. Senior managers must lead the effort.

In trying to understand ethical leadership and the process of how values flow from the top down through management ranks,

"Technology today has given people added choice and power, whether they're individuals or individual corporations. This additional choice means everyone has more responsibility to exercise that choice in a fashion that's consistent with doing 'the right thing.' This is the significant change that technology has wrought, and it's why we need to pay more attention to the ethics process than ever before."

Ivan Seidenberg
chief executive officer, Bell Atlantic Corporation,
from his *Sears Lecture in Business Ethics*
at Bentley College, April 13, 1998

it is useful to first understand "good" leadership.[4] Getting things done is often regarded as a trait of an effective leader, until we remind ourselves that Mussolini and Hitler got things done. Yet just being an ethical leader is often not good enough. Former President Jimmy Carter might be regarded by many as an ethical leader but a relatively ineffective one. So obviously both effectiveness and a reputation for integrity and ethics are important to leadership.

Ethical leadership is comprised of three essential elements:

First, it is ***relational.*** Leadership requires followers and a commitment to values from senior managers is meaningless without a similar commitment from those around them — employees, customers, suppliers, and members of the community. Therefore leaders must evoke and elicit consensus about values in their constituencies, and their followers, by their responses, will influence the leaders. To become

---

[4] Some of the ideas on ethical leadership in this chapter come from or have been greatly influenced by Al Gini's article, "Moral Leadership and Business Ethics" and Robert Solomon's article, "Ethical Leadership, Emotions and Trust: Beyond 'Charisma,'" both of which appear in *Ethics, the Heart of Leadership*, edited by Joanne B. Ciulla (Westport, CT: Praeger Publishers, 1998). This influence also extends to Joanne Ciulla's article, "The Importance of Leadership in Shaping Business Values," *Long Range Planning: International Journal of Strategic Management*, Vol. 32, No. 2 (April 1999), pp. 166-172.

> **"T**he signs of outstanding leadership appear primarily among the followers."
>
> Max DePree
> former chief executive officer, Herman Miller Corporation
> from *Leadership is an Art*

leaders who demonstrate a commitment to values, senior managers must recognize the interests of those they are trying to influence. They must seek to empower those around them, to create opportunities for their followers to embrace and adopt the organization's values as their own.

The second element is ***emotion.*** A demonstrated commitment to values involves more than a signature on a piece of paper that is distributed to every employee. It involves passion and an emotional response to situations that call for action. At the same time, followers will respond emotionally to leaders who exemplify and champion values. They will believe in them and be inspired and motivated by them.

The third element is one of ***choice.*** This may seem misplaced, in an argument for leaders to demonstrate clear commitment to values by their every action and deed. But to be truly effective, followers need to be able to debate, disagree and choose to adopt the organization's values by their own free will. The alternative is compliance, with its "shall not's" and punishments. Commitment to values must be freely given, not coerced. Only then will it be sincere. Ethics — including ethical leadership — without freedom is no ethics at all.

Trust and appropriate values

Senior managers can only demonstrate their commitment to values in a framework of trust. Leaders earn the trust of followers by their words and deeds, and followers give trust to leaders; it is reciprocal. Without trust, values-based management will not succeed. Using an earlier example, Hitler may have inspired and moved his followers. He may have had their trust, at least for a time. But he had the wrong values and betrayed his followers' trust. The leader we admire does the right thing in the right way for the right reasons. This leader is guided by appropriate values and inspires and motivates others to be guided by the same values. This leader is a teacher, empowering people with new information, a values-centered environment, and a culture that encourages followers to come to their own conclusions. These leaders develop followers who then can morally lead themselves, demonstrating a commitment to appropriate values themselves.

Ethical leadership failure

Not all stories are positive. We know of board members who have quietly resigned from public companies because senior management was acting unethically and the director could not find a way to change the culture or to suggest a different set of values to other board members.

We know senior managers who have professed to believe in a code of conduct and then gone out and behaved in a diametrically opposite way.

We know senior managers who, as part of a values-based management program, have attempted to draft codes of conduct that applied to all employees. Unfortunately, they did so without talking to any employees at lower levels. The values statement talked of "our responsibility" and then every sentence thereafter began with "you" instead of "we" The code of conduct proscribed one policy for gifts and contributions for one part of the company and a different policy for another part. The sins go on, albeit in most cases unintentionally.

Ethical leadership is a voluntary, emotional relationship between leaders and followers based on trust and driven by appropriate values.

As we all know, professing a commitment to values doesn't always mean that senior managers act on those values. We have identified seven symptoms of ethical leadership failure.

Ethical Blindness

Leaders are unable to see an ethical issue when he or she should — perhaps because of not paying attention. Or maybe they're not wearing "moral glasses" at all.

Ethical Muteness

These leaders don't have or don't use ethical concepts and language. They may say they have a commitment to values but they don't talk about them or stress their importance.

Ethical Incoherence

These leaders are unable or don't try to recognize the inconsistency among values they may espouse. For example, they may say they value integrity in business but they base performance evaluations solely on reaching numerical goals. Or they aren't able to think through possible actions to appropriate conclusions.

Ethical Paralysis

These leaders are unable to put their values into action because either they don't know how or they are frozen because they fear the consequences.

Ethical Hypocrisy

These leaders aren't really committed to the values they say they have. They say one thing but do another, or tell people to do things that they are unwilling to do themselves.

Ethical Schizophrenia

These leaders don't have a unified set of values, but for example, act out different values at work than they do at home.

Ethical Complacency

These leaders believe that they could never do anything wrong because of who they are. Perhaps because they think they are good people they think they are therefore immune to being unethical. As soon as they think this way, a personal or organizational ethical crisis often results.

An important element

"Commitment from the top" sounds easy to achieve. But in fact it does not automatically happen. Often senior management just "doesn't get it" and efforts from below fall on deaf ears. The Center for Business Ethics receives many calls asking how to gain senior management support. Strategies are suggested, but these ultimately must fall on receptive ears to be successful. And to get a professed commitment from senior management is not enough unless this commitment is continually demonstrated.

One of the most respected senior managers we know was a chief executive officer with an uncanny ability to laugh at himself, admit mistakes, and to praise others who did the right thing, even as he confessed to falling short. He endeared himself to every employee and his reputation spread throughout the company. By his everyday actions and words, he encouraged others to strive to higher standards, to continue to do the right thing. His values were a part of his persona and they quickly became part of the company's personality, remaining there long after he left for another assignment.

This particular executive exemplified "commitment from the top" and we shall keep his identity anonymous in the hope that every manager who reads this book might check the mirror to see if this description fits him or her.

Chapter 7

Computer Rescue Squad
A "SIZZLING-HOT"
ENTREPRENEUR SPEAKS

> In large organizations, the board of directors and senior
> management take the lead jointly in developing a
> commitment to values-based management, which
> includes overseeing ethics programs and, in most cases,
> appointing a senior ethics officer.
>
> But where does that leave small companies that don't
> have a board or an ethics officer? They have the same
> needs but not the same resources.

The example that the president of a small firm sets establishes
the tone for the actions of its employees. In fact, a sincere commitment from the top is perhaps even more necessary for a small
company to develop an ethical corporate culture than it is for a
large one.

Granted, a commitment to values is not necessarily easy in a
small company in which cash flow is generally tight and
resources stretched. Often there is just one senior officer who
alone has to bear all the pressures of running a business. It's
lonely at the top, and small businesses are notoriously fragile. If
making the sale is critical, values can often take a back seat to
profit.

Nothing tests management's commitment to a company's
values more than a financial downturn. Everyone knows that

"walking the talk" (a popular ethics-management expression) is easier done when times are good than when they're bad. Big companies have an advantage in this regard. Senior executives of large firms usually can afford to allow the core values defining a company's culture to remain inviolate, despite the vagaries of the quarter's bottom line. The president and chief executive officer usually understand they are stewards of the organization's long-term culture and continue to recite the company's values creed like a mantra, knowing that they have the financial resources to endure.

For companies to be successful in the long term, basic values must be enduring. But what about an entrepreneur who has just bought a small business and is forced to mortgage her house, sell her car and cash in her retirement savings to keep it going? In such a situation, financial survival could easily — and perhaps understandably — take precedence over values-based management. Managers must have extraordinary strength of character to make and keep a commitment to values, no matter what the marketplace throws at them. It worked for one young Florida entrepreneur.

Values, no matter what else

Carol Conway believes that creating and adhering to a values-based culture, even in tough times, was what catapulted her small business to stunning growth, profitability and national recognition.

Conway bought Computer Rescue Squad, a 3-person computer-fix-it company, in June 1993. The company had no market presence in its home base of southwest Florida and a mediocre reputation in the community. "It really had no culture," Conway recalled, "and brought in just over two hundred thousand dollars in annual revenues."

By 1999 Conway had transformed Computer Rescue Squad into a sophisticated local area network technical support organization with twenty-one employees, revenues that exceeded two million dollars, branch offices, national recognition as Florida's Small Business of the Year and distinction as one of four national Blue Chip Enterprise Initiative winners, honored by the United

States Chamber of Commerce. Kiplinger's Magazine described her as president of a "sizzling-hot business." [1]

When Conway moved to Florida, she had given a lot of thought to the values she inherited from her big company experiences in a big city environment. "My business beliefs were shaped by my experiences at IBM and Herman Miller," she said. "IBM believed in doing what's right for the customer. Herman Miller, the furniture company, was noted for its culture of valuing employees. I worked with furniture distributors and dealers instead of customers. They had to be innovative and adaptable. Through their work, my eyes were opened to the excitement of the entrepreneurial world with its daily challenge to excel."

When Conway bought Computer Rescue Squad, she knew she had to make her mark by transforming the sleepy little outfit into a firm that would reflect her own exuberance and high standards. Two of the stated values of Herman Miller obviously had an impact on Conway (the value of "ownership, participation and teamwork" and the value of "excellence") because she wasted no time in adapting them to the atmosphere she would produce at her own company.

A new culture

"Creating an environment of accountability and purpose is what I do every day," Conway explained. "The biggest thing we did at Computer Rescue Squad was to create a culture where none had existed before."

"We run the company based on three core values:
- pride of ownership and excellence;
- accountability;
- doing what's right for the customer."

Because the company is small, Conway believes she doesn't need a written code of conduct or a formal ethics training program yet (although the Federal Sentencing Guidelines would suggest she reconsider that soon). She prefers to keep her corporate

---

[1] Melynda Dovel Wilcox, "Keep Your Fingers Crossed," *Kiplinger's Personal Finance Magazine*, January 1999, p. 93.

culture simple, leading by example and by relating anecdotes. In that sense she echoes Herman Miller Chairman Max DePree, who often reinforced his values and priorities with stories.

"We have a fighter-pilot mentality here," Conway says. "Although I am the owner and bear the financial risk for the company, we all consider ourselves responsible for the business. It's as though we are all part of a squadron, going out every day saying 'We're the best. Go ahead and test us and we'll prove it.'

"We are always pushing forward. Computer Rescue Squad pays for the technical certifications for our employees and we celebrate each award. Everyone gains confidence from his or her own professional development and by solving problems out in the field. Every award the company has been given is really earned by its employees. In five years, no one has left to compete with us. Employees have either washed out or they like the high performance culture.

"I call this going outside our comfort zone and we operate the same way. The business has really built up now so that we could hum along quite nicely and profitably doing what we're doing. But I want to push us more, to see what else we can do. It

"'This is really a great business, a vibrant industry, and we're in the right place at the right time,' Conway says with abject confidence. 'But I cannot stress enough how important our employees are to our success. They are this business. I give it direction and momentum, but my employees are the business.'

That powerhouse combination earned Computer Rescue Squad the Blue Chip Enterprise Initiative in November, awarded by the U.S. Chamber of Commerce and Massachusetts Mutual Insurance, created to recognize and reward the entrepreneurial spirit in small business.**"**

Patricia J. Hewitt
"Computer Rescue Squad Knows the Lay of the LAN,"
Southwest Florida Business People, January 1997

seems that every time the company starts to make real money, I put it back in the business and expand, instead of taking it home."

Conway cited a recent example. "We started three new projects or divisions: a document imaging service, contract services and information project consulting. All of these were expensive, time consuming and fell outside our regular day-to-day business. But I think they are important for us as a company, both to service our customers and to stay fresh.

"I discussed these with my employees and I think initially they were overwhelmed. It must seem that just as they get their heads above water, I sink them again. But I told them, 'I could do these as a separate company, but then it would be my money and not ours.' They didn't understand that at first. However, I reminded them that because we had pushed the envelope in the past and had grown, they are all making good salaries, driving leased cars, flying to distant cities to take additional classes and enjoying company-funded retirement plans. If these new opportunities have profit potential, they are going to want a piece of it.

"One of my employees finally spoke for the group when he said, 'If it weren't for you, we'd be sitting here with three employees, fixing PCs.' They understand that our mission is never to let ourselves get soft or comfortable, or even too profitable, for that matter."

Conway's "fighter pilots" are given a great deal of autonomy in the field but are also accountable to her and to each other. "We make mistakes every day. This is an imperfect business," Conway said. "Owning up to mistakes and problems is critical. It's about as basic as the commandments against lying, cheating and stealing."

Will values endure?

Conway's commitment to the value of accountability was severely tested when she accepted the resignation of her most senior employee, her operations manager, who had covered up mistakes in the field and had lied to customers about the status of their service engagements.

"This was the toughest management decision I've ever made," Conway admitted. "She was my right arm, my first hire.

She was a key employee in the firm and we became good friends. She did a lot of my job for me and made my life easier."

At first, Conway did not want to see or believe hints that her valued employee was not telling the truth about client complaints. "I wrote off a lot of the early information to petty jealousy. Everyone wanted to be close to mama, and I thought maybe they were just envious of our close working relationship.

"But my field engineers and support staff were dropping bread crumbs, hoping I'd pick up the trail of deceit. After a while I couldn't ignore the rumblings, particularly when I received calls from clients asking me if I was aware of certain situations. When I confronted my employee, she finally admitted she had covered up, thinking she was protecting the business.

"I was shocked and disappointed. I offered to redesign her position, giving her fewer responsibilities. I was willing to think that she had done this because she was overwhelmed by the press of business, but I was not willing to compromise our value of accountability. We have to be straight with each other if we are going to solve complex problems for clients. We can't make up excuses for our shortcomings.

"She declined to work under a new reporting structure and resigned. In hindsight, the other employees felt liberated. I proved to them that I practiced what I preached and wouldn't protect even my closest friend. I exercised leadership by demonstrating our core value of accountability. The rest of the employees picked up additional responsibilities and felt more trusted and more important in the scheme of things. It was the right thing to do."

Conway had ushered a key employee out the door, in part because the employee had compromised the company's relationships with its customers, and in large measure because she had violated Conway's trust in her and the trust that employees place in each other. Computer Rescue Squad is committed to customer service, whatever that entails. To deliver customer service every employee has to trust each other to provide truthful information and to be accountable. There is no confusion about this value among the firm's employees.

"'Empowerment' is such an overused word," Conway said, "but I don't know a better way to express it. Everyone knows they have the full authority to do what's right for the customer, no matter what the cost. It's such an integral way that we do business, we don't even discuss it. If we lose money, we figure out what we can learn from it and go on."

Conway still shakes her head over another particularly chilling example. "The worst thing for a business customer is to have a new computer system installed, have it crash and have no backup. That is a nightmare beyond belief. Yet that is what happened to one of our customers.

"We had installed a new system. When we finished the job, it was working fine, as was the backup system. But about a month later, the new system crashed and the customer discovered its tape backup system had also failed. The client thought it was our fault; our field engineers believed the client had done something wrong.

"In truth, it didn't matter. Even though our contract specifically says that we are not responsible for data loss, I felt the client had hired us to be their technical eyes and ears. They loved the new system. They trusted us. We could have argued with them all day long that it worked when we left, but that's not the point. We had to go beyond the call of duty.

"We spent a week at the client site, helping them recreate files from their PCs and putting them back in business, at our cost. We also discounted their bill.

"Through that experience — and others like it — our company reinforces its core value of customer satisfaction. But we also learned accountability from it. Now, before we leave a job site, we don't assume that customers are backing up their files or that they know how to test the validity of backup files. We don't just test them ourselves, we make the customer show us that they can do it too. Every incident like that makes us a better company in the long run."

The glue that works

Small company, dedicated owner. Three core values. No fancy programs or catchy phrases. Just commitment from the top, communicated over and over again in every possible way, reinforcing a values-based management culture that breeds entrepreneurial success.

Chapter 8

Codes of Ethics

A blueprint for building a values-based culture within an organization must include a written ethics code that contains at least a sufficient level of guidance for employees and others who may read it. These written codes perform many functions and therefore should be drafted as carefully as an important letter to shareholders. These documents are communication vehicles and reflect the covenant that an organization has made to uphold its most important values, dealing with such matters as its commitment to employees, its standards for doing business and its relationship with the community.

Most managers assume that the audience for its code of conduct is the employee base. While that's true, the authors should assume that shareholders, regulators, suppliers, customers, business media and competitors will also read the code. It should reflect an organization's best face and be an open disclosure of the way it does business.

Large companies are not the only ones who need a written code. Nonprofits, government agencies, private companies, partnerships, and small organizations should all have a document they can point to with pride when asked, "What do you stand for?" Most organizations now have a publication that serves this function.

Form and content

These corporate codes of ethics vary in quality and substance. Some consist only of a set of specific rules, a list of do's and don'ts (usually corresponding to clearly illegal or unethical actions such as bribery, price-fixing, conflicts of interest, improper accounting practices and acceptance of gifts). Other codes consist largely of general statements that put forth corporate goals and responsibilities, a credo expressing the company's philosophy and values. The more substantive codes consist of both. Rules of conduct without a general values statement lack a framework of meaning and purpose. Credos without rules of conduct lack specific content.

In addition, codes of conduct should not imply that whatever has not been strictly prohibited is thereby allowed. There is no way that all ethical or unethical conduct can be exhaustively listed and mandated through a code, nor should there be. Business ethics, like all areas of ethics, has gray areas that require individual discretion and thought. A good corporate code of values should include certain managerial and employee guidelines for making ethical decisions, including the principles and factors that one ought to consider before arriving at a decision.

We're not fussy about the name of this written instrument. Whatever words in the title communicate its content most clearly should be used. Some are called a "Code of Values." Others are known as "Code of Business Practices," "Code of Conduct," "Compliance Code," or "Code of Ethics." Some have a single value as a title, such as "Integrity." One of the titles we like best is called *The Way We Do Business*, from PricewaterhouseCoopers.

Commitment from the top

We recommend that any written document begin with a short introductory letter or message from the chief executive or board of directors, explaining and transmitting the document. This message should contain more than standard blathering narrative, bland language that will be perceived as just pure boilerplate ("This code of conduct contains guidance to ensure that our work is done in an ethical and legal manner." "It's up to all of us to conduct our business in a way that promotes the highest principles of integrity and ethical behavior."). While these words aren't bad, they don't convey the impact and urgency that explains why *this* company, in *this* industry, is focused on *these* particular values or principles.

Columbia/HCA Healthcare Corporation, for example, had an unfortunate scandal resulting from allegations of medical billing fraud. Its top executives resigned and the company faced long and difficult government investigations and fraud prosecutions. New managers brought in an experienced ethics and compliance officer and the company published a glossy booklet titled *One Clear Voice*, its code of conduct. The introductory letter from Chairman Thomas F. Frist, Jr. and President Jack O. Bovender, Jr., clearly states the company's core value: "The true foundation of Columbia/HCA has always been its commitment to provide quality care to our patients. As part of this, we strive to ensure an ethical and compassionate approach to healthcare delivery and management."[1] Inexplicably, the letter makes no reference to the company's past ethical problems, well known to all. We think this was a missed opportunity to be straightforward about the reason for *One Clear Voice*.

By contrast, Wesley W. von Schack, chairman and president of New York State Electric & Gas Corporation, was more specific in his opening letter to NYSEG's *Principles of Business Conduct*: "NYSEG's Principles of Business Conduct have been revised to address emerging areas of compliance created by the industry's shift to competition. These include our business relationships with other Energy East Corporation companies (affiliates) as well as information about NYSEG's Corporation Compliance Program and its employee Assistline."[2]

Such a statement gives a much clearer picture to employees as to why they received this September 1998 book!

Reinforce values

If you are writing a code of conduct without an opening explanation of the company's values, start again. To plunge right in and make the written document a compilation of laws and regulations is to lose a perfect chance to reinforce the values that the company views as important. (If the company has not identified its primary values, reread chapters 2 and 3.)

---

[1] Columbia/HCA Healthcare Corporation, *One Clear Voice*, 1998, p. 2.
[2] New York State Electric & Gas Corporation, *Principles of Business Conduct*, 1998, p. 1.

Sir Adrian Cadbury, former chairman of Cadbury Schweppes and chairman of the "Cadbury Committee," is a respected authority on voluntary codes of conduct and best practices. In his view, how and why codes are drawn up may well determine how effective they will be in influencing behavior.[3] If a code is introduced as window-dressing or viewed as simply legal protection for management ("see here, Mr. Regulator, it says right in our code that . . .") employees may ignore it and keep on doing what they have been doing right along. If the words are not helpful to those out in the field, it will also be ignored. ("It says in our code we are not to pay bribes, but how do I account for the fact that in order to get this shipment to my biggest customer, I must deal with the local 'customs broker?'")

Finally, Cadbury cautions that codes are just the first step. What individuals do every day in the running of an organization can't be covered in a code. Codes can't contemplate every subject, and they can be easily ignored. You have to be able to trust the people in the field and have confidence in their judgment. In the end, business transactions are built on trust, not on regulation, standards, or even contract law with a system of justice to enforce it. This is where values come into play, according to Cadbury, and we agree.

Chrysler Corporation has five core beliefs and values and includes them in its quizzes on ethics to ensure that employees know all five of them. They are:

- Customer focus
- Inspired people
- Continuous improvement
- Our reputation
- Financial success

These are certainly admirable values, but Chrysler's written document, *Integrity: The Chrysler Code*, merely lists them in the inside cover and in no place in the code are the five values explained. We see this as an overlooked possibility to reinforce

---

[3] Adrian Cadbury, "The Role of Voluntary Codes of Practice in Setting Ethics," in *The Role of Business Ethics in Economic Performance*, Ian Jones and Michael Pollitt, eds., St. Martin's Press, Inc., 1998, pp. 68-84.

Core values: A guide to ethical business practice

"New ways of organizing people and work within the corporation are giving each of us more decision-making responsibility. Given the complexity and constantly changing nature of our work and our world, no book of hard-and-fast rules — however long and detailed — could ever adequately cover all the dilemmas people face. In this context, every Nortel employee is asked to take leadership in ethical decision making."

Acting With Integrity
Nortel Networks, p. 4

the importance and meaning of these five concepts which, presumably, were chosen with care.

Nortel Network's code of conduct is called *Acting With Integrity* and its inside cover also lists Nortel Network's "core values."

- We create superior value for our customers.
- We work to provide shareholder value.
- Our people are our strength.
- We share one vision. We are one team.
- We have only one standard — excellence.
- We embrace change and reward innovation.
- We fulfill our commitments and act with integrity.

Inside the document the section called "Core Values: A Guide to Ethical Business Practice" explains the statements as a series of commitments, presumably all tied up in the concept of "acting with integrity," although it is subtitled "A Shared Responsibility." The ensuing sections talk of ethical commitments and global leadership. Some might argue that these are too many concepts that don't quite hang together as succinctly as Texas Instrument's three core values (see chapter 3). But there is some wonderfully clear language in the book that more than makes up for the possible confusion among various values.

On the opening page, next to a quote from Nortel Network's Vice Chairman and CEO, John Roth, the text states: "In our working lives, we often experience situations where the 'right thing to do' is not immediately apparent. Loyalties — to our fellow employees, to managers, customer and supplier, to our families, our communities, the environment, the corporation as a whole, and to ourselves — may seem to conflict. When we're faced with a complicated situation, it can be difficult to decide where the ethical path lies."[4]

We believe this couldn't have been said any better. And in perhaps the best statement we have seen, Nortel Networks erases the distinction between the worker and the corporate entity: "Remember that the ethical conduct of 'the corporation' is really the collective conduct of its employees, officers, and members of its board of directors."[5]

According to Megan Barry, Nortel Network's former ethics officer, the language inside the book was chosen with care. "The former code was drafted by the legal office," recalled Barry, "and it read like a legal document. We wanted to be more aspirational in this version. We based our code on our responsibilities to our five basic stakeholders: employees, shareholders, customers, suppliers and the community. Everything else flowed from that overall concept of responsibility."

Here's another example. NYSEG's Introduction to its *Principles of Business Conduct* says right up front what its shared values are, with short explanations of each:

- Excellence
- Innovation
- Integrity
- Teamwork
- Caring
- Accountability

NYSEG also gets credit for clear, conversational language that not only tells the reader exactly what he or she needs to

---

[4] Nortel Networks, *Acting with Integrity*, 1998, p. 1.
[5] Ibid, p. 7.

Accountability

"We are responsible for our actions and results. Our accountability encompasses the success of other departments, divisions, units and the entire company."

Principles of Business Conduct
New York State Electric & Gas Corporation, p. 3

know, but expresses what the reader may very well be feeling: "It would be nice if every business conduct decision were cut and dried, with no exceptions or compromises. A lot of them are, but some are not. Some decisions are in the gray areas and can present us with real dilemmas. You can best protect yourself and NYSEG if you ask for guidance before acting."[6]

This is a wonderful example not only of an important insight, but also of how to write a corporate code of conduct.

Give us a clue

While we stress that organizations should reinforce their values-based management goals with a written code, we also know that many employees don't read — even when the document is put in front of them. Francis J. Daly, corporate director of ethics and business conduct at Northrop Grumman, has a good suggestion: "Codes of conduct should be policies that are easy to read and easily understood by people who don't like to read, can't read or respond much better to visual information." For that reason, the document should be easy to follow.

Most codes contain tables of contents at the front, such as those at Columbia/HCA, NYSEG and Chrysler. Nortel Networks spreads the information over two pages, with the heading "What You'll Find Inside . . ." and provides sufficient white space to break up the content. Its booklet also contains a "quick reference" guide to key issues on the back cover. Chrysler's codes contains a lot of white space, graphics worthy of the most user-

[6] New York State Electric & Gas Corporation, p 3.

"Face difficulties as they arise and resolve them before the customer brings them to your attention. You are a professional, and you must review your service to the customer on a regular basis to ensure that it meets company standards, regardless of whether the customer asks you to do so."

Code of Ethics
Guardsmark, 1998, p. 4

friendly owner's manual, and boxed problems with the question ("situation") expressed as a short anecdote and the answer ("what's right") immediately following it.

Guardsmark, one of the world's largest security services firms, issues its annual Code of Ethics in an eight-page booklet, appropriate to the Company's purpose, which is to strike a balance between a brief statement of values and what other companies might consider a business conduct manual.

Guardsmark has some exceptional language in its document. It emphasizes that it is every employee's responsibility to "review not just the results of subordinates' work, but how those results were obtained."[7] When was the last time you've seen that caution, the source of more than one ethical scandal? Employees are also urged to "actively seek the suggestions of subordinates, acknowledge their value and strive to implement all practical ideas."[8]

Innovation through ideas is obviously a Guardsmark value. For example, in the section on customer relationships, employees are told to "be courageous and suggest ways a customer can innovate and improve his or her product or service."[9] That's a novel responsibility that we haven't seen in many codes.

---

[7] Guardsmark, *Code of Ethics*, 1998, p. 2.

[8] Ibid.

[9] Guardsmark, p. 4.

Guardsmark's Code of Ethics carries the Company's handsome crest on the cover and inside the booklet. The look of the Code is straightforward rather than ornate, unlike documents some other companies produce. According to Stephen Kasloff, Guardsmark's ethics officer, the format was chosen deliberately. "We want this to be read by security officers on their posts. The Code is printed with a matte finish to improve readability, and is printed in all capital letters for the very reason that this Code *is* important to the company. It is meant to be shouted out. It is also meant to be a working document. I can fold it up and put it in my pocket."

Perhaps the most important reason for the form of Guardsmark's code is the fact that all 14,000 employees are asked to help change the document *every year*. We were so impressed with this process that we decided it deserves its own story, in chapter 23.

A look at content

There is no doubt that most contemporary codes reflect a trend towards brevity. Some companies with mature ethics programs have reduced voluminous codes of conduct to just a few key values, trusting that their employees will do the right thing when confronted with a situation for which there is no easy answer. For example, the Sears employee booklet, *Freedoms and Obligations*, combines both: the folder contains two inserts, "My Code of Business Conduct" and "My Leadership Principles."

Ivan Seidenberg, chief executive officer of Bell Atlantic, recalled that several years ago company executives thought they should update the code of conduct. Rather than add more rules and regulations, however, they focused on the value of "responsibility," implying that the company and its employees know how to behave. Each employee now has the responsibility to do the right thing. Presumably if they aren't clear on what the right thing is, they know where to ask.

Even within the notion of brevity, however, most codes contain at least a mention of several universal topics, such as environment, discrimination, competitive intelligence, insider trading, conflict of interest, gifts and invitations, outside employment and use of company property. Depending on the industry, codes might contain information on political contributions, copyright, intellectual property and records management.

We can spot the codes drafted or influenced by lawyers. Employees looking for guidance must wade among "Antitrust," "Foreign Corrupt Practices Act" and "Equal Employment Opportunity." The better codes talk about "Competitor Relations," "Bribes, Kickbacks and Gifts" and "Discrimination and Harassment."

Balancing the objectives of usability with comprehensive content is a tough task. Many companies now cover subjects in the code with a brief statement, a question and answer and then a reference to a more complete resource, such as a web site.

Consider the common problem of the use of internet access, computers and copiers by employees and see how various codes address it.

Nortel Networks covers the subject under the heading "Protecting Assets," a positive statement. The section begins with a general statement of principle ("We have a responsibility to protect the corporation's assets and ensure their efficient use. Theft, carelessness and unnecessary waste have direct impact on the corporation's profitability, and, ultimately, on all of our jobs." [10]) Then the rule follows ("Supplies and equipment purchased by the corporation are intended to be used for Nortel Network business purposes only. Any other use — for after-hours charitable work, for example — must receive prior approval from your manager."[11]) A highlighted question and answer conveys the same message. Left unaddressed is the use of Nortel Network's computer to send personal e-mail or download web sites during work, but perhaps Nortel Networks didn't want to get into that level of detail in a general code. The reinforced suggestion to check with your manager or ethics office works in all cases.

Columbia/HCA's code, with 19 single-spaced pages, has the luxury of a bit more information. Colleagues are told that e-mail, internet access and voicemail are company property, but "highly

---

[10] Nortel Networks, p. 16.

[11] Ibid.

[12] Columbia/HCA Healthcare Corporation, p. 9.

limited reasonable personal use" [12] is permitted, although such communications are not private. Colleagues are told that the company might monitor such use, and that anyone who abuses the communications systems or uses them excessively for non-business purposes may be subject to discipline. In the question and answer section, two specific questions related to typing a spouse's resume on the computer and copying fundraising leaflets are answered with the directive to check with supervisors.

NYSEG's code handles the issue under a brief section called "Electronic Communications." After defining the term, the code states "occasional personal use is permissible as long as such use is authorized by your manager or supervisor."[13]

Good question, glad you asked

Most codes reflect the understanding that above all, employees want their questions answered. For that reason some insert questions and answers throughout the code to break up the page and provide a point of interest. Others place the questions and answers at the end of the code. While many questions are standard (What do I do if one of my co-workers is telling offensive jokes? Can I accept a box of chocolates from one of my suppliers?), we especially like the thought given to nonspecific questions that candidly express what employees might not dare ask their managers.

From Nortel Networks: "Do people really get dismissed for violating Nortel's ethical standards?"[14] Megan Barry recalled a humorous incident regarding that question. "When we were drafting the code, we conducted focus groups with employees all over the world to get their feedback. The process allowed us to spot some serious 'North Americanisms' right away. For example, we had drafted a question that asked whether employees would get 'terminated' for violations of the code. Our employees from the United Kingdom reacted with horror. They thought killing employees for an ethical infraction was a little harsh. So we changed the word."

Chrysler's *Integrity* booklet contains a question we rarely see, but like. "I am a loyal, hardworking employee and always consider

---

[13] New York State Electric & Gas Corporation, p. 36.

[14] Nortel Networks, p. 24.

SITUATION

I am a loyal, hardworking employee and always consider the consequences that my actions may have on Chrysler. I do not understand why Chrysler is interested in what I do in my spare time.

WHAT'S RIGHT

Chrysler expects a fair day of work from all of its employees, but full support of our core beliefs and values requires one additional step. Even outside of work, when you are technically not on Chrysler time, you still have a stake in our reputation. People may associate you with Chrysler because of your employment. Each of us informally acts as a representative for our company and each of us should uphold Chrysler's reputation.

Integrity
Chrysler Corporation, 1998, p. 2

the consequences that my actions may have on Chrysler. I do not understand why Chrysler is interested in what I do in my spare time."[15]

Finally, from Columbia/HCA: "How do I know if I am on ethical 'thin ice?'"[16]

Ask, ask, ask

Whether brief or comprehensive, all codes should include appropriate sources both inside and outside the corporation through which advice and counsel could be offered. Ready reference lists, 1-800 telephone numbers, e-mail and web sites, wallet cards, refrigerator magnets and the like are all techniques that companies use to reach the employee Frank Daly described, who doesn't like to read, can't read or responds better to visual information. Nortel Networks rolled out its advice line at the same

---

[15] Chrysler Corporation, *Integrity*, 1998, p. 2.
[16] Columbia/HCA Healthcare Corporation, p. 18.

time as its revised code and found that call volumes have been steadily growing. Megan Barry sees that as a positive indicator that the code is being read and more questions are being asked.

Summing up

Whatever content a code of values includes, the language should make a person aware that there may well be difficult ethical judgments to make based on the values inherent in the code, rather than on the letter of the law. Employees should also know that they will be accountable for their behavior. This will place a greater sense of personal ethical responsibility on employees and send a clear message that corporate integrity is dependent on individual integrity.

Here are some final guidelines for writing an ethics or values code:

- Be clear about the objectives that the code is intended to accomplish.
- Get support and ideas for the code from all levels of the organization.
- Be aware of the latest developments in the laws and regulations that affect your industry.
- Write as simply and clearly as possible. Avoid legal jargon and empty generalities.
- Respond to real-life questions and situations.
- Provide resources for further information and guidance.
- In all its forms, make it user-friendly because ultimately a code fails if not used.

Chapter 9

Boston University and Hawaii's Bishop Estate
BOARDS NEED CODES OF CONDUCT TOO

It's easy to neglect the nonprofit world in discussing values-based management and the procedures, programs and codes of conduct that are an integral part of any management culture. One would assume that nonprofits, dedicated to doing good, are more likely to have solid values than profit-driven companies and therefore are less in need of strict codes.

That type of reasoning demonstrates one of our favorite subjects — ethical complacency. It's exactly the moment when you relax and assume that everyone is doing the right thing for the right reasons that a scandal erupts. In the nonprofit world, where trust and donor commitment to a mission are an organization's most important assets, the costs of an ethical misstep can be high. But sadly, few nonprofit organizations see the need for a strict code of conduct, even at the highest level, the board of trustees. This is also true for boards of directors of for-profit corporations. What we have to say about boards of trustees in this chapter, for the most part, can also be said about boards of directors of for-profits.

The nonprofit world

The nonprofit sector is a name given to the wide range of organizations that are neither government agencies nor businesses.

Outside the United States nonprofits are often referred to as NGOs or nongovernmental organizations. They can be as large as the International Red Cross or as small as a local church. They encompass hospitals, colleges and universities, social service agencies and voluntary organizations. About one in fifteen Americans works for a nonprofit. Perhaps surprisingly, nonprofits can charge fees and make a profit, even though they themselves are tax-exempt. The distinguishing characteristic about nonprofits is that they do not generate returns for their owners or investors.

While there are governmental agencies that provide oversight and checks and balances that protect against abuse in the government and business worlds, there are few monitors in the nonprofit sector. Nonprofits aren't required to hold public meetings; they file few reports and generally escape the scrutiny of the press. Therefore, boards of trustees of nonprofits are the frontline defense to make sure that the organization upholds its mission, operates with financial accountability and operates to serve the public interest.

According to the National Center for Nonprofit Boards (NCNB),[1] a board has responsibility for ensuring that the organization meets legal requirements. Its members represent the community, which has granted it the advantages of nonprofit status, to make sure that its assets are safeguarded and that it is well run.

But what does that mean? Unlike directors of public companies, who have a myriad of financial objectives to attain and standards by which to measure the performance of its executives, trustees of nonprofits have less well-defined scorecards. They also have no shareholders or Securities and Exchange Commission looking over their shoulder to provide incentives for diligence.

The NCNB suggests ten basic responsibilities of nonprofit boards:

- Determine the organization's mission and purpose
- Select the executive

---

[1] The National Center for Nonprofit Boards produces an extensive collection of materials on nonprofit governance. Its material and information can be accessed at www.ncnb.org.

- Support the executive carefully
- Ensure effective organizational planning
- Ensure adequate resources
- Manage resources effectively
- Determine and monitor the organization's programs and services
- Enhance the organization's public image
- Serve as a court of appeal
- Assess its own performance

That's a comprehensive list, but it is the rare board that has been briefed on how to approach such an inventory of responsibilities.

Board members have three general legal responsibilities in carrying out their duties and, as with any organization, their legal duties are a good place to start in formulating a code of business behavior.

The first is the duty of due care. According to the NCNB, a board member owes the duty to exercise reasonable care when he or she makes a decision as a steward of the organization. A board member must be competent, well prepared and attentive to his or her responsibilities. Diligence requires the same level of scrutiny and careful consideration as if the organization were a for-profit concern. A board member cannot check his or her expertise at the door.

The second duty is loyalty. It sounds simple: a board member must act in the best interest of the organization and not for personal gain. Yet this is the area that seems to cause the most problems, perhaps because of the lack of attention this concept receives in either board training or in written codes of conduct.

The third legal duty is that of obedience to the organization's mission. The public, and particularly donors, have entrusted board members with money, assets, volunteer time and goodwill because they support the mission of the organization.

If trustees of nonprofits are men and women of good will, diligence, intelligence, and perhaps even some standing in the community, committed to the vision and goals of the organization, why do nonprofits get in ethical trouble?

The reason often rests with the absence of a code of conduct, drafted, discussed and enforced by the board, to govern their decision-making and procedures. In this situation, an educated trustee may feel like the "skunk at the garden party," suggesting to his colleagues that such a code is needed and implying that the way others have been operating for years may somehow have been deficient.

To provide ammunition for any "skunk" trustee, consider two stories about one element that should be contained in any such code, conflict of interest. The stories are about Boston University's Board of Trustees and the Trustees of Hawaii's famed Bishop Estate. First, some necessary background.

Conflict of interest

Conflict of interest usually arises when the personal objectives or benefits of a board member affect, or appear to influence, his or her ability to put the welfare of the organization above any other consideration. Conflict of interest may occur not just with regard to legal issues, but in almost every other aspect of over-sight and decision-making.

Conflict of interest is best described through examples. Assume a board member performs professional services for the organization. While such an arrangement may seem to be per-fectly acceptable if the board member's firm is the most qualified and the fees are competitive, the very fact that such a transaction occurs raises questions about competitive bidding, undue influ-ence, a board member using his position to enhance his profes-sional compensation, a board member's unspoken obligation to return the favor by approving or ignoring issues of concern to the director or other trustees of the organization, the inability of other firms to seek and win bids from the organization, and so on. Even if such arrangements were legal, it does not mean they are ethical. They give the appearance of impropriety and call into question the entire board's due diligence in exercising objective fiduciary responsibility over the organization.

Conflict of interest is a good example of an issue that should be included in a code of conduct for board members of nonprof-its, precisely because it cannot be adequately addressed by a law or regulation alone. It rests in that gray area where making difficult choices, balancing competing benefits and preserving favorable public perception are critical.

Because a nonprofit can suffer incalculable injuries from a loss of public confidence and damaged reputation, boards should take deliberate and distinct steps to spell out guidelines against conflict of interest, knowing that such guidelines will not cover every eventuality.

These guidelines might include prohibitions against any business transactions between board members and the organization, thereby making it clear that board members volunteer to further the mission of the nonprofit, not to seek personal gain. In addition, board members should be required to disclose potential conflicts, such as if a business partner or family member of a board member has a business relationship with the organization or will benefit by a particular transaction or decision.

Board members might be required to fill out extensive disclosure forms prior to joining the board, so that those voting on him or her will be well aware of any conflicts. All members should complete such forms annually. Board members should not be allowed to participate or vote in any decision that presents a potential conflict. The organization should have carefully documented procedures for making such decisions that demonstrate that the board carefully and objectively considered all factors and made sure the organization benefited from the transaction.

Conflict of interest is not the only subject that should be included in a nonprofit board code of conduct. While it may be the most obvious indication that board members are too cozy with the organization, other indices of independence should also be spelled out. How board members are selected, who acts as chairman, how the agenda is set, who serves on committees and whether committee membership is rotated, whether there are term and age limits, whether the board meets in executive session and whether the board hires its own outside counsel, auditors or other professionals are all issues for boards to discuss and adopt.

Boston University — a banana republic?

Dr. John Silber took over as president of Boston University in 1971 and, according to his critics, the magnetic, pugnacious leader ran the institution his way right from the beginning, rewarding allies and punishing those who disagreed with him. Silber might have argued that this was the only way to transform a mediocre urban school into a world class university, by attracting thousands of applicants and top scholars, and building a new campus through smart real estate deals and increased donations. Silber accomplished so much at Boston University that, by 1990, he was a candidate for governor of Massachusetts, a political office that he may have thought would be a way-station on a run for the presidency of the United States.

Silber's ambitions might have materialized if he had allowed his board of trustees to act as true fiduciaries, demonstrating their independence to guarantee decision-making processes of due diligence. Instead, by 1993, Silber and Boston University were embroiled in a state investigation that allowed the media to characterize BU "a banana republic of lavish perks, insider deals and sweetheart contracts." [2]

Silber and his trustees were brought down by Seragen, a promising biotechnology company founded in 1979, that was developing a new class of drugs that might prove effective in treating cancer.[3] When one of Seragen's founders, Dr. John R. Murphy, joined the BU faculty, Silber took notice of his work. From 1980 to 1985, Boston University invested $1.2 million in Seragen through its venture capital fund, a modest investment. But in 1987, Boston University bought a majority interest in Seragen for $25 million.

There were two problems with that investment. First, the university's total endowment at that time was $175 million, raising the question of the fiduciary nature of the trustees' decision to put so many eggs in one high-risk basket. Worse, however, was the fact that ten trustees invested their own funds in Seragen at the same time.

Now the trustees could not let Seragen fail. In 1989, the university began spending about $1.1 million a month to finance

---

[2] Anthony Flint, "John Silber's Endgame," *The Boston Sunday Globe Magazine*, May 9, 1993.

[3] See David Barboza, "Loving a Stock, Not Wisely But Too Well," *The New York Times*, September 20, 1998, Section 3, p. 1.

Seragen's operations. Critics claimed the university was throwing money down a rathole to protect its trustees' investments.

The trustees came under scrutiny when the public furor over Boston University's corporate governance hit a fever pitch. According to some reports, Silber was instrumental in picking the 58 trustees.[4] They were treated lavishly, both at their board retreat in Scottsdale, Arizona and in Boston. Silber had become a national celebrity, and his dinner parties at the 25-room president's mansion were a hot ticket, legendary for stimulating conversations with Nobel Prize winners, heads of states and elected officials. Trustees were feted at the university's sites in Europe, were given opportunities to make private investments in companies such as Seragen, encouraged to do business with the university and some served as paid directors of Seragen. Any trustees who had urged caution or disagreed with Silber's ways had long since quietly resigned from the board, refusing to act as rubber stamps or yes-men.

The Massachusetts attorney general's office, overseer of public charities, commenced an investigation of BU's investment in Seragen, which by 1992 had reached $85 million. It questioned whether it was prudent for a private nonprofit university to bet so much of its donor funds on a single company. In addition, BU had guaranteed a $10 million loan to Seragen from First National Bank of Chicago, and five of the fifteen Seragen board members had connections to BU. The university agreed to reduce its ownership in the company from 92% to 69% by forcing a public offering of the biotech company. Seragen went public and in the next two years Silber invested about $1.7 million of his own money.

But the attorney general was not through with Boston University. Threatening a civil suit, the state's chief legal officer said he was ready to take legal steps "to remedy a range of governance and trustee stewardship practices"[5] at the university. Specifically he criticized the fact that trustees were not selected through a process independent of the president, that business transactions between the university and individual trustees had

---

[4] Alice Dembner, "BU trustees agree to increase control," *The Boston Globe*, December 15, 1993, p. 33.

[5] "BU's tarnished Silber," *The Boston Globe*, March 18, 1993, p. 18. See also John H. Kennedy, "AG puts plans for BU lawsuit on hold," *The Boston Globe*, March 18, 1993, p. 29.

proliferated, that the trustees did not use adequate safeguards to assure that the compensation paid to the university's top executives was in the best interest of the university, and that BU's annual financial reports contained substantial omissions.

The attorney general was well aware that Silber had earlier made a $2 million personal profit by buying stock in an electronic company owned by a BU trustee, that various trustees held business contracts with the university or were paid for sitting on the boards of BU-related entities, and that Silber often held the distinction of being the highest-paid university president in the nation ($414,715 in 1992, with $1.25 million in deferred compensation). These and other dealings raised questions about whether the board of trustees was exercising arms-length oversight over Silber and the university, or whether the university was being run by and for the benefit of Silber and the trustees.

The trustees decided to hire Coopers & Lybrand to perform an audit and make recommendations to the board. The recommendations included changes in the way trustees are selected, requiring the full 58-member board to approve Silber's compensation, and provisions for the board to disclose and discuss conflicts of interest between the board and the university.

Meanwhile, the Seragen saga continued. Its cash needs were unabated, and in November 1995, Silber helped facilitate a $23.8 million loan backed by the university, one of its trustees and the university's lobbyist. The university then invested another $5 million in the company. In December Seragen's board (including Silber, the university's treasurer and a trustee) voted to raise

> **"B**oston University will continue to take great pride in having fostered Seragen and kept it alive long enough to assure development of medicines of profound humanitarian potential. In this, as elsewhere, no good deed goes unpunished."
>
> John Silber
> Letter to the Editor, *The New York Times*,
> November 1, 1998, p. 32

the number of authorized shares, diluting present shareholder value.

Predictably, minority shareholder suits followed, accusing Silber and others of self-dealing and conflicts of interest. By 1998 Seragen's shares were worth 45 cents and the company was acquired by Ligand Pharmaceuticals. Boston University lost 90% of its investment. According to one financial reporter, for just the $50 million that the school had put into the company as of 1989 it could have had $175 million by 1998 if the money had been invested in a Standard and Poor's 500 Index fund.[6]

The lesson of the Boston University trustees story is not about avoiding risky investments. On the contrary, not all decisions will bring good results and sometimes, even in the nonprofit world, taking a risk is sometimes necessary for high return. But bad results, particularly like those in the Seragen situation, inevitably raise the question of trustee negligence, lack of oversight and conflict of interest. The legal concept of due diligence protects trustees from the consequences of bad results if they are able to show that their decisions were made with the university's best interests in mind, after careful consideration of all the factors.

When conflicts of interest are so obvious that they call into question whose interest was being protected, everyone suffers. The entire Boston University saga was avoidable if the trustees, from the beginning, established a clear and effective code of conduct for all its members. The trustees did not have to reinvent the wheel; they only had to inquire about codes drafted by other boards of nonprofit organizations that had previously examined best practices in corporate governance.

Bishop Estate — broken trust

The story of Hawaii's Bishop Estate reads like a cheap mystery novel, but fortunately for the 4000 Hawaiian students it educates at the Kamehameha Schools, the heroes win in the end.[7]

It begins with a display of courage by Nona Beamer, a prominent alumna and former teacher, who wrote the state Supreme

---

[6] Barboza, p. 13.

[7] The entire saga, including court reports and other documents, has been preserved and segregated by the *Honolulu Star-Bulletin* at www.starbulletin.com/specials/bishop.

Court in May 1997 about her concerns with the low morale at the school. She was particularly concerned with the behavior of the school's trustees and their demotion of the school's president. (The trustees are appointed by the state's high court justices, clearly a conflict of interest should there be litigation regarding Bishop Estate.) Her letter sparked a public protest and march by frustrated alumni, parents and teachers.

The Kamehameha Schools are no ordinary private institutions. Funded through the 1884 will of Princess Bernice Pauahi Bishop, the schools and their students are the beneficiaries of an estate worth an estimated $10 billion. Trustees of Bishop Estate, Hawaii's largest landowner, have perhaps the most desirable post in the state, receiving as much as $1 million each per year for their oversight duties. It is no wonder that among the trustees are a former senate president and former speaker of the house of representatives.

As public leaders they should expect scrutiny, but they were unprepared for the next salvo, a carefully-crafted document entitled "Broken Trust" which appeared in the *Honolulu Star-Bulletin* on August 9, 1997, written by five prominent Hawaiians, including a trust law expert, a priest and a former appellate judge.[8]

The essay outlined excessive compensation, political favoritism and conflict of interest in the trustee selection process, as well as in contracting and hiring; conflicts with regard to investments made both by Bishop Estate and trustees personally; lack of accountability; investment losses; and interference in school administration. It sparked a bonfire that took almost two years to extinguish.

Governor Benjamin J. Cayetano immediately asked his Attorney General Margery Bronster to investigate and respond to him. (The attorney general in Hawaii is appointed by the governor and confirmed by the senate.) In November 1997, five educators wrote their own "Broken Trust" treatise, outlining educational abuses by the trustees, including intimidation, firings, favoritism and micromanagement.[9] The Hawaii Supreme Court, perhaps sensing where

---

[8] Samuel King, Msgr. Charles Kekumano, Walter Heen, Gladys Brandt and Randall Roth, "Broken Trust," *Honolulu Star-Bulletin*, August 9, 1997.

[9] Isabella Aiona Abbott, Winona K.D. Beamer, Gladys A. Brandt, Roderick F. McPhee, Winona Ellis Rubin, "Schools' gross mismanagement must stop now," *Honolulu Star-Bulletin*, November 27, 1997.

"The evaluation team found little evidence of the Hawaiian values of *pono* (to be moral and proper), *laulima* (to work cooperatively), *na'au pono* (to possess a deep sense of justice), and *malama* (to care for each other) stated in the school's mission statement in the governance and decision-making of the trustees."

Rod Ohira
"Report says trustees create fearful climate,"
Honolulu Star-Bulletin, March 19, 1998

the controversy was leading, disqualified itself from hearing any matters relating to the removal of Bishop Estate trustees.

After extensive review, court-appointed masters' reports found extensive financial mismanagement. The attorney general concluded in September 1998 that the rights of the beneficiaries were at risk and asked state courts to remove three trustees for engaging in a widespread pattern of self-dealing and using a labyrinthine maze to shield financial information from the beneficiaries.

The process was long and contentious. Criminal courts indicted two of the trustees and two others began legal proceedings to remove the fifth for breach of fiduciary duties. Finally in May 1999, a state probate court removed four trustees and accepted the resignation of the fifth, amid Internal Revenue Service hints that it would revoke Bishop Estate's tax-exempt status if any of the trustees remained in power.

By that time, Hawaiians had learned that trustee Lokelani Lindsey billed Bishop Estate for thousands of dollars of personal charges, including trips to Las Vegas. She also accepted trips to sporting events from vendors seeking to do business with Bishop Estate and used Estate employees for personal work.

Trustees Henry Peters and Richard "Dickie" Wong allegedly received kickbacks in real estate deals Bishop Estate conducted with Wong's brother-in-law. Peters received director's fees and options at a company in which Bishop Estate had extensive holdings. Trustee Gerard Jervis overdosed on sleeping pills a week after the suicide of Bishop Estate lawyer Rene Kitaoka, who had been found with Jervis in a compromising position in a hotel restroom.

In addition to annual stipends ranging from $800,000 to $1 million, trustees received free country club memberships and personal credit cards. Financial reports indicated the trustees withheld $350 million they should have spent on the schools, cutting programs instead; awarded no-bid contracts to golfing partners; allowed former politicians to run up casino and strip club charges on Estate credit cards; and spent trust money to lobby against federal legislation prohibiting excessive salaries for charity trustees. Furthermore, the trustees used Estate funds to defend themselves in court.

The attorney general, who waged the battle against the trustees and implicated several powerful politicians in the course of her investigation, was a casualty. The senate rejected her nomination to a second term in April 1999.

As the *Star-Bulletin* said, "Is this the way to run a multibillion-dollar charitable organization?"[10] The answer is no. Like the Boston University trustees, had Bishop Estate trustees sought to learn more about codes of conduct that might guide their actions, they had many resources for guidance.

Nonprofit governance — a recent example

The mission of the nonprofit National Association of Corporate Directors is to enhance the governance and performance of business entities.[11] Through its many conferences, publications and Blue Ribbon Commission Reports on Director Professionalism, the NACD has developed a reputation as a leader in promulgating best practices for boards.

Interestingly enough, however, the NACD, like some other nonprofits, had not focused attention on the conduct of its volunteer board of directors. So in 1997 the NACD board appointed a special committee to prepare a set of governance guidelines

---

[10] Rick Daysog, "Bishop's 'bizarre' scandal deepens," *Honolulu Star-Bulletin*, March 13, 1999.

[11] For further information see www.nacdonline.org.

> **"T**he school is wealthy but not at all healthy. We're a very sad and sick place after years of abuse. They've kept us on our knees for years now, and my sense is that we're standing tall today. Whether we can move forward now, I don't know ... I think we're exhausted, but the energy is starting to flow back and we'll be all right."
>
> Kawika Eyre
> Kamehameha Schools Hawaiian language teacher,
> in Rod Ohira, "Trustees no more,"
> *Honolulu Star-Bulletin*, May 8, 1999

for its own board. Among the subjects included in the recommended guidelines were:

- Standards for legal and ethical conduct
- Annual formal evaluation of the CEO
- Review of the goals and accomplishments of senior managers
- Decisions on the compensation of the CEO and senior managers
- Establishment of the agenda for board meetings
- Requirements for advance distribution of agenda materials
- Provisions for executive sessions of board members
- Establishment, assignment and rotation of committee members
- Conduct of committee business
- Self-assessment of the board
- Requirement of attendance at board meetings
- Provisions for disclosing and resolving conflicts of interest
- Provisions for the selection of directors, including criteria, term limits and orientation
- Board compensation policies

The NACD's committee on board guidelines offered them as a useful starting point for other organizations, particularly nonprofits, but added a caveat. "We emphasize *starting point*," the committee said, "because an important benefit of board guidelines comes from the discussions involved in developing them."[12]

As Boston University and Hawaii's Bishop Estate discovered, such discussions are better held before a scandal occurs than after.

---

[12] "The NACD Board Guidelines," *Director's Monthly*, Vol. 22, No. 12, December 1998, p. 1.

Chapter 10

Communication Vehicles

It may seem obvious that it makes little sense to establish a values program and then not reinforce it with constant communication, but it happens. The best program in the world is worth little if it is not communicated well, often and in various forms. The biggest challenge for any management is to keep the concepts of the company's core values out in front of the organization at all times.

How to do it

According to Vincent O'Reilly, former vice chairman of the global accounting firm Coopers & Lybrand (now Pricewaterhouse Coopers), an organization's values mission cannot be overemphasized. He stressed that all discourse, every decision, every meeting, in fact every way the firm did business, should contain reference to the company's basic standards of business conduct.

O'Reilly, who was also the leader in spearheading Coopers & Lybrand's award-winning ethics and business conduct program, said the ultimate proof of the success of the ethics program is when ethics becomes a natural and habitual part of the communications fabric of the firm. This means that ethics is talked about throughout the culture, from the water cooler to the regularly scheduled management meetings, to the Board of Partners. This final communications vision was O'Reilly's genius as an ethics leader. How to get there is the trick.

Howard Putnam, the former CEO of Southwest and Braniff Airlines, cautions that managers shouldn't assume that communication is necessarily effective or received the same way it was intended. He tells of leaving Southwest and arriving at Braniff

Airlines as the new CEO, only to learn that the company was in dire financial straits — worse than he had anticipated. He was not sure the company could make the payroll and immediately gathered the company's top executives for a briefing.

Putnam stressed that the airline must conserve as much cash as possible to make it through the critical time ahead. As Putnam hurried to deal with lenders, creditors and suppliers, he assumed his top lieutenants were taking dramatic cost-cutting actions. He was thunderstruck to learn that at the time he was figuratively holding his finger in the dike, one of his executives was lavishly entertaining clients in New York.

Putnam confronted him when he saw the bills totaling $27,000 for food and liquor at Tavern on the Green in New York City. Hadn't he heard Putnam's anguished speech? The former CEO of the now defunct airline remembers his colleague's response. "Yes, but I did it for two reasons. We have always done it and it was in my budget."

Putnam's colleagues interpreted the message about not spending as "not exceeding budget," very different than the concept he had intended to communicate. Putnam uses the incident as a teaching lesson to executive groups, stressing that communication must be constant, varied and tested to make sure that listeners hear the precise message that the speaker meant to convey.

Glenn Coleman, director of communications & training in the office of ethics and business conduct at EDS, also believes that storytelling is an effective way to constantly communicate values and ethics. He often tells a story that he heard at a conference of ethics officers to illustrate the difference between a values-based approach to management and one that emphasizes compliance and rules.

"A man wants to put his dog out in his yard to do doggie kinds of things, so he ties him to a tree on a six foot rope. Now the dog has total freedom to do his things as long as he stays within six feet of the tree.

"Which would you rather trust," asks Coleman, "the rope or the dog? People who work under a rule-based environment are on the six-foot rope. They're free to do as they wish, but never allowed to go beyond the well-defined limit which inhibits their movement and activities. Wouldn't it be better to trust the dog? Give the pooch the freedom, but train him how to use the entire yard. You might build a few fences around the garden and momma's flowerbed — perhaps our equivalent of environmental rules or the Foreign Corrupt Practices Act — and maybe some fuzzier boundaries, called culture and values. But now the dog has much more freedom. And so do we. We can make our decisions in a larger playing field.

"Too many employees," concludes Coleman, "play in a small circle, tied to a tree. That is too limiting. Employees would rather have freedom from control, but also feel responsibility for their own actions. That's what we should be striving to attain. Management should allow and require employees to take risk. In a competitive work environment, we don't want employees to have to run to the rulebook every time they want to do something. So it's better to teach values, which are the boundaries of the playing field. If employees are taking risk within that playing field, then management should stand behind them when they make a mistake or when a course of action doesn't work out."

We like stories, and Coleman's dog story makes a point that is vivid and clear, more so than a booklet that lists business practices, duties, responsibilities or even aspirations.

As many ways as possible

Fortunately, communication in most organizations has evolved from didactic lectures to the sophisticated use of high technology and employee interaction.

BellSouth, the telecommunications company, uses a variety of communication vehicles to enhance its ethics initiative, "A Commitment to Our Personal Responsibility." F. Duane Ackerman, president and chief executive officer, introduced the program by sending a letter to every employee. Each also received an attractive 40-page booklet containing BellSouth's Code of Conduct, information on over twenty different subjects (including the law, BellSouth's policies and sample questions and answers), and a resource guide for further questions. Employees were given a wallet-sized card with the toll-free telephone number of the ethics line. All supervisors held meetings with employees to discuss ethical concerns. Employees viewed dramatizations of ethical dilemmas in a training video, hosted by the ethics officer and several BellSouth supervisors. At the conclusion of the training, every employee signed an affirmative statement indicating they had read and understood the information provided.

But the communication was not a one-time event. BellSouth employees can submit questions anonymously to the ethics office via its website or through their company e-mail address. They are encouraged to call the company's human resources department, the legal department, the security department, the auditing department or the ethics office if they need information and guidance.

A favorite BellSouth communication technique is its refrigerator magnet, a picture of a BellSouth service truck and the message "Ethics is a part of your everyday job . . . just like driving the truck." At the bottom on the magnet is the Helpline number, 1-800-664-4231.

Employees as your audience

The varied and constant communication of company values and ethics can be made even more effective by catching the hearts and minds of employees. Cathleen Sullivan of RedHawk, co-

---

Tenet Health System wallet card

1.800.838.4427
ETHICS ACTION LINE
Ethics and Decision-making • Important Points to Consider

- Have you considered all possible courses of action? Are they legal, ethical and consistent with the Standards of Conduct?
- Has all the information been presented honestly and accurately?
- What are the long-term risks and rewards of each option?
- Will your decision set a precedent?
- How will others view your decision? Can the company live with it? Can you live with it?
- If in doubt, STOP; seek help; use local Tenet resources, if possible. Help is also available from the Ethics Action Line.

author of communications products such as *The Ethics Communication Coach*, recommends that communication elements acknowledge employees' own ethics and values, and then clarify the values of the company by examples from daily work.

Employees know the ethical standards practiced by the company, sometimes better than the management team. So it's important that the stories match reality. To avoid cynicism, one good technique Sullivan recommends is to state the obvious — the company isn't perfect and business constantly challenges us. It's also meaningful to acknowledge the ethics of each employee and stress that individual employees, working together, make up a strong ethical team.

Finally, a good communications program can clarify the values of the company by using examples and stories of different ethical challenges. "In articles, presentations, web pages, posters, pay envelopes and training, use stories of employees who made the right ethical decision," Sullivan suggests. "Employees will feel that they 'got caught' doing something right. This technique helps clarify the meaning of the law, policies and aspirations by positive, as well as the usual negative, example."

What to say

Communicating the content of an ethics training program is self-evident. Communicating and reinforcing the primary values of the organization is also self-evident. But the most challenging communications problems occur when an incident happens and managers are reluctant to share information with employees or outsiders who are watching the incident unfold.

Consider the story of one ethics officer. He was tangentially involved with a political problem involving a senior vice president of the organization. We say "tangentially" because the situation, which he investigated, soon became out of his control. The senior vice president had been accused and was apparently guilty of several ethical breaches for which others in the company had been dismissed. However, this executive was favored and was therefore protected by the chairman of the company, who hoped the matter would go away. The incident was referred to the company's ethics committee. The chairman informed the committee that he needed the executive, who had a three-year contract. If he were fired, it would be an expensive payout. The ethics committee took no action.

The ethics officer knew that many people in the company were aware of the allegation and were watching to see what the ethics committee did. He was perplexed. He had decided that this was not his "hill to die on," the issue over which he would resign rather than compromise his own ethics. He felt that the chairman and the members of the committee needed further education and exposure to ethical principles and the current practices and past experiences of other companies to handle this appropriately. He was willing to stay and continue to work with them.

But what would he say to the rest of the organization or to his own staff?

We advised him to be as truthful as he could be, admitting that he does not control the outcome of all cases and that individuals can hold different points of view about appropriate courses of action in a situation. He may not agree with all of them but his job is to continue to try to influence and educate other executives. Perfection will not be achieved merely by the existence of an ethics committee or values-based program. Perfection may never be achieved at all, as all organizations are made up of individuals with human failings. But his goal — and that of others in the company — was to handle each incident better and to learn from past experiences. If he were to speak words to that effect, sincerely and respectfully, that approach would serve the organization better than his silence or lies or resignation.

We often caution executives to rid themselves of "corporate speak," well illustrated by a Dilbert cartoon strip. A lawyer is cross-examining an employee on the witness stand in court. "Can you explain the meaning of this internal e-mail message?" he asks, brandishing a piece of paper. The employee looks at it and replies, "It says we'll 'use integration tools to leverage the utility of our enterprise-wide processes.'" The employee peers more intently at the piece of paper. "It appears to be something we call communication," he says.

Contrast Dilbert's targeted satire with the e-mail message John F. Welch Jr., CEO of General Electric, sent to several hundred thousand employees after he read that one of GE's units sent out a survey to employees, secretly coded so that allegedly confidential replies could be easily identified. "I don't want to bother you every 72 hours with an e-mail, but something has come up that is just awful, and I want to share what I know about it today and how I feel about it," the message said.[1]

Welch's message couldn't have been more clear, but unfortunately communication within organizations is often circumspect, if not outright lies:

1. "Good speech, boss," in the interest of courtesy;
2. "The customer is always right" in the interest of harmony; or
3. "We have no intention to close that plant" in the interest of internal politics.

More often than not, it is better to tell the truth and to connect the truth telling to the institution's stated values. Whenever the values can be reinforced, even if the message is difficult to deliver, the outcome will be more advantageous and the listeners will receive another message: the institution is true to its ideals.

This takes practice and effort. Glibness usually doesn't work in these situations. Let's assume an organization's stated values are accountability and integrity. Here are alternative approaches:

1. "Boss, would you like some suggestions on how that speech might have been better received?"
2. "Our motto is 'the customer is always right,' but we all know that's not always the case. We may have to accommodate some customers in the short term, but we'll reassess whether we want to do business with them in the long term."
3. "We hope we don't have to close this plant, but there are no guarantees. What we will guarantee is that we'll inform everyone as soon as our decision is clear."

These alternative statements truly communicate and live up to the stated ethical values of the organization. Anything less says the culture is not ready to live up to its values.

Don't forget the 'whys'

Those receiving the communication — employees, customers, investment analysts, and the public — need to know the reason

---

[1] Robert O'Harrow Jr., "Welch Calls Survey 'Clearly Wrong,'" *The Washington Post*, June 11, 1999, p. E3.

for the communication as well as its substance. If there is a new values program being launched, what prompted it? If there has been a problem, what caused it? If the company has stressed one value over another, why was the choice made?

Few companies get consistently high marks for clear and honest communication, so when a story stands out, it deserves to be cited and copied.

No one would suggest that companies copy the actions that led to Sears's $60 million fine and guilty plea to a criminal charge of bankruptcy fraud. When the scandal came to light, no one was more surprised than Sears's chief executive officer, Arthur C. Martinez, to find that Sears had been regularly violating federal bankruptcy laws in collecting an estimated $110 million from 187,000 consumers. It was not a small matter. Sears makes fifty percent of its operating income from its 63 million credit cards, held by half of all American households. Finding out what happened, repaying consumers, and settling with federal prosecutors cost the giant retailer almost $475 million. In dealing with the bankruptcy fraud, Martinez faced perhaps the most challenging communication trial in his career.

But Martinez, who can proudly point to the ethics office, the ethics policy committee with representatives from every business unit and other integrity initiatives he championed after joining Sears, can be applauded for the direct communication to his executives when the scandal broke. First, he summoned his top 200 managers to an urgent meeting at headquarters. He explained what had happened, and then, according to participants, he searched for the reasons. He told every executive to go back and sit quietly at his or her desk, and do nothing but think about their operation, the direction they give, the body language they use, the hidden messages they might be communicating. In spite of the company's emphasis on ethics, does the real communication shout 'make the numbers at any cost?'

Martinez's search for the 'why' continued after that meeting. Sears spent $14 million searching its records to locate past mistakes. At a top executive retreat, he pushed participants to determine whether the company's language about values and ethics was just meaningless rhetoric. The managers huddled and subsequently concluded that the company's aggressive push for performance had resulted in a culture in which making numerical goals took precedence over reporting bad news. Martinez was frank about the outcome and even shared the story with the press.

Martinez's candor right from the beginning, his commitment to restitution and, above all, his quest to understand and communicate the facts of and the reasons for the scandal, earned him the respect of his employees, regulators and the public. As he said, "There's not a dollar's worth of profit worth having if it compromises your integrity."[2]

What about silence?

This section on communication shouldn't end without discussing the opposite of good communication. In contrast to Sears's Martinez and GE's Welch, too many managers exhibit the disability we call ethical muteness in chapter 6. Even if top executives want to communicate, they don't have the vocabulary that will let them tackle the problems at hand. Some even avoid learning any such language, asserting that words like "ethical," "moral" and "values" are meaningless and only serve to confuse. They remain silent because they are ethically illiterate. Our symptom of ethical muteness is a bit different than what Frederick Bird and James Waters called "moral muteness."[3]

In that case, managers may make moral decisions, but defend them in terms of business or economic interests. In our example, ethical muteness means that there is no vocabulary to talk about ethical issues and the organization therefore becomes incapable of addressing the subject. Without the language of ethics and values, it's as if we were exhorting a patient without legs to stand up and run. The effect of ethical muteness is that if the leaders at the top of organizations are silent, it is probable for all sorts of reasons that those at all levels will be silent as well.

Silence is worth a thousand words. It is a form of communication in and of itself, but in this case the message is not one which values-driven managers want to send.

---

[2] Barnaby J. Feder, "The Harder Side of Sears," *The New York Times*, July 20, 1997, p. F8.
[3] Frederick B. Bird and James A. Waters, "The Moral Muteness of Managers," *California Management Review*, Fall 1989, pp. 73-88.

Communication involves dialogue

At a recent conference at the University of Cambridge devoted to the subject of putting values into action, we outlined our suggested ten-point program and spoke about the need for communication.

One participant interjected, "Dialogue!" she said.

It was a good caution, from a knowledgeable source. Her firm, one of the world's largest diversified healthcare companies, was known as a leader in the effort to instill values into a management culture. The history of this initiative started with the vision of two corporate leaders who in 1989 merged their respective companies to form the global giant. They set about to establish a new corporate culture based on several key values, including integrity. According to Professor Ian Jones of Oxford University, who has studied the company, its values and leadership practices were still only words on a piece of paper and therefore a comprehensive training effort was needed to design and implement the new culture.

In conducting these training efforts the manager became convinced that the best communication must be a dialogue. She explained that in spite of the company's best efforts, in 1997 it settled extensive legal claims and government investigations for $325 million, rather than run the risk of possible liability of billions of dollars for alleged illegal medical billing fraud. What had gone wrong?

Despite extensive training in complex regulatory requirements, employees had apparently ignored them. A frank dialogue with employees uncovered the reason. Yes, they had understood the requirements, but since they didn't mirror the company's actual practices, employees concluded they didn't apply to what they were doing. After all, this company was the best. Its employees were ethical and acted with integrity. They must be doing it right.

We could have communicated all day long, she said, but without a dialogue we never would have uncovered what was really going on. You have to encourage a dialogue with employees.

We agree. The best communication is a two-way street. Find ways to make that happen.

Chapter 11

Olin
THE E ZONE e

Olin Corporation, a $1.4 billion chemicals, metals and ammunition company, has integrated communications, training and technology in an expansive way to reinforce its ethics and compliance programs among its 7,500 employees, contractors, suppliers and other key stakeholders.

"You can never do enough communicating," says Robert Gebing, vice president of auditing, business ethics and integrity, explaining why the company has adopted a myriad of communication approaches. "Manufacturing companies like Olin have a history of constantly reinforcing the safety message. You have to keep repeating and varying the safety message, to keep people focused. Ethics and values are no different. They're not flavors of the month — the commitment is real and it's here to stay at Olin."

A method to their madness

Olin's ethics communication strategy is built on several key considerations.

First, the company established a friendly visual identity that symbolizes its commitment to acting ethically in everything it does. Working with an outside design firm, Olin adopted a catchy logo using the small case letter "e" ("reminds some people of PAC-man with a halo," according to Gebing) to represent the E Zone, for ethics. The "e" appears in all its publications, in key words and phrases, such as "**Ethics** . . . It's in **e**verything w**e** do."

"Thankfully 'e' is the most commonly used letter in the English language so the concept was a natural fit as the 'e' repeats itself frequently in all of our business interactions and communications," says Gebing, "and it even appears on telephone stickers that are very visible when the receiver is lifted."

The E Zone, with a population of 7,500, is not on any map, in the phone book or on the Web. According to Olin, it's "that place inside all of us where we make decisions about what's right and what isn't. It's that part of us that knows what to do. It's the little voice that speaks to us, even when we are under pressure or are tempted not to listen."

The E Zone is unusual language to communicate ethics and values but it works. The goal of the Olin program is to empower all of its employees "to visit the E Zone regularly" and to "turn up the volume on that tiny little voice."

One way that Olin turns up the volume on ethics is to vary the communication and tailor it to the audience. While Olin is focused on its employees, it also incorporates its ethics message in its relationships with competitors, customers, communities, suppliers and shareholders. For example, the ethics considerations when thinking about competitors include prices, representations, competitive intelligence, teaming arrangements and trade associations. Shareholders have expectations about the validity of financial numbers as they relate to their capital investment, earnings and dividends. (We're beginning to see what Gebing means when he says that **ethics** is in everything we do!)

Olin believes that one key to its communication success is keeping all communications fun and simple. The "e" symbol is cheery and the materials in which it appears are bright and fresh. The company's ethics communications use simple, vivid language ("Life is fired at us at point blank range") and cartoon characters in some materials.

This design and tone is done with a purpose, to be simple but direct. A few lines from Olin's plain but colorful brochure devoted to the Foreign Corrupt Practices Act (FCPA) shows how clearly Olin communicates its message. The brochure notes that among the "red flags" of a FCPA violation are:

- Unexplained large expenses on a Travel & Entertainment Expense Report
- A sudden, unexplained increase in entertainment or gift expenses by a salesperson

- An agent demanding a higher than normal commission for a transaction
- Any agent or salesperson saying that he or she is working with a government official to give Olin the contract

Those are simple and direct clues about a subject that could be deadly boring.

Gebing stresses three other communication strategies that make Olin's program work: the message is consistent, refreshed regularly and reinforced in as many ways as possible.

Gebing's office produces a family of brochures on specific subjects — from gifts and entertainment to competitive intelligence — and they are available in racks in all facilities for employees to take. "We got the idea from Texas Instruments," says Gebing, "and we find they are very useful. Some are mailed directly to employees at their home, such as the brochures on the ethics helpline and our gift and entertainment policy. That way we can be sure that everyone has one."

Guides are more lengthy documents covering specific legal requirements and are distributed to those who have a need to know a subject in more detail.

Posters are also an effective communication device, because they are inexpensive and can be changed frequently. Post-it notes with Olin's four key values (Integrity, Helping Valued Customers Succeed, Continuous Improvement and Innovation and Olin People — the Winning Difference) are widely used, as are wallet cards and coin-sized telephone stickers with the ethics help-line number.

Gebing recommends occasional promotional items to catch employees' attention. "We created four-way displays for offices and conference room tables — each panel featured an employee and an Olin value. We also gave coolers with the ethics logo and message to nearly all employees — not inexpensive, but it was something of value that wouldn't be thrown away. In all we spent about $200,000 on promotional items, a hard swallow for the budget, but they were unexpected and appreciated."

In addition, Olin communicates through its Web site. "People need access to our policies and procedures," says Gebing. "Many times, people do the wrong thing because they are not

Operators in the computer room "Go-The-Extra-Mile"

Mark Faford recently visited Riverwood International, a key acid customer in Arkansas. Curiously, Riverwood comprises our former Olinkraft pulp and paper mill in Arkansas, which we sold many years ago.

Mark said that while discussing customer service with the key purchasing executive at Riverwood, he happened to mention how proud he was of the customer service function, to which the fellow from Riverwood replied, "I think you're underestimating the value of your people."

The customer explained that sometimes he has to call Olin's Shreveport acid plant after normal business hours to request a just-in-time delivery of acid. After-hours calls to the plant are routed to the operations room, which is manned by hourly employees.

Although the operators are not customer service personnel, the customer said they always take his order and then take the initiative to contact the shipping department and trucking company to make sure delivery of the acid goes through that very evening.

The customer made it clear that he highly values this go-the-extra-mile service. Mark cites this as an example of people going far beyond what is normally required of operators in a computer console room. And clearly, their conscientious commitment is truly helping a valued customer succeed — which is one of our key values.

Success Story
from Olin's ethics web site

aware of the rules." If employees want to send a message or ask a question, the Web site also has a search capability as well as a messaging function that is not readily traceable. It also has an extensive question and answer section, a library of news clippings on ethics issues, Olin "success stories," and a place to showcase comments from employees using video clip technology.

Olin also delivers continuous ethics training, but Gebing believes that training alone will not deliver the message. Frank

Daly of Northrop Grumman has said, "There's supposed to be some magic about marching three hundred people into a room for an hour of training. Then you discover they don't remember it three months later." Gebing agrees: "We believe the answer is to blitz the organization with the message, using a wide range of communication vehicles, all the time."

Communicating communication

Olin is unique among companies because not only did it communicate its core values and ethics resources, but it listened to the feedback and zeroed in on major problems. One of them, perhaps surprisingly, was a lack of effective communication between supervisors and employees and among employees in general.

Gebing explains. "We launched our high energy ethics and values program in May of 1997. The issue of communication really didn't hit us until about six months later. We were pleased that calls to the helpline were increasing, because that meant our employees were hearing the message, bringing concerns forward so the company could address issues before they became problems. But with each successive call we kept asking ourselves, 'Why are people making these calls?'

"In manufacturing, when something goes wrong, we analyze the situation to determine the root cause of the problem. So when we put on our manufacturing hat and did a root cause analysis of the calls, we discovered that most of the calls were about leadership, fairness and respect, and *communication failures* were frequently the root cause. This is what led us to be proactive and add a focus on communications to our program."

Olin developed a primer on communication called "Is anyone listening?" because it believed that being a good listener was the first step toward being a good communicator. The brochure outlined ten ideas about how to be a better listener, as well as suggestions for better communication. But the most effective part of the message on communication was what Olin called "slappers" — verbal and nonverbal "hits" that stop communication.

Have you ever been guilty of these verbal slappers?

Sarcasm	ridiculing, name calling
Lecturing	preaching, ordering

Accusing	blaming, criticizing
Patronizing	placating, humoring, "talking down" to people
Prying	interrogating, asking too many personal questions
Evaluating negatively	judging, "you're wrong, I'm right"
Rejecting	my way or the highway, attacking personal traits
Solving	forcing your solutions or answers on others

Here are some nonverbal slappers, according to Olin. We think they accurately describe many of the techniques we have seen business leaders use, perhaps inadvertently, that sabotage otherwise well-intended messages — whether about company values or daily business matters.

Staring into space

Looking around

Answering the phone

Playing with objects (papers, pens, etc.)

Physically touching or abusing the speaker

Eyeing the clock repeatedly

Rapping or tapping on things

Silent treatment

"We knew communication was important, but we didn't fully realize how important it was," says Gebing. "The feedback on our communications brochure was positive. People understood it, and agreed that concerns were frequently due to misperceptions and misconceptions. Eliminating those by better communication leads to a more constructive atmosphere.

"It's about things that can make a difference," explains Gebing. "Just using the word 'partner' instead of 'supervisor' or 'employee' sends the message that we are committed to each other. If you don't forge that kind of relationship, you end up with absenteeism, 'don't-care' attitudes, inattention and a lack of commitment to always doing what is right. Using the right language to communicate what you intend can truly energize and mobilize a workforce."

The next communication challenge for the E Zone

In subsequent rollouts of its ethics program, Olin is planning to concentrate on the four core company values. Gebing explains.

"When we look at what is happening in the workplace, it is clear that our values and ethical behavior are all interrelated. So it is timely to state our values and emphasize why they are so important.

"For example, let's take a simple training example of a bully in the workplace. When we tolerate that kind of behavior, immediately we have a lack of integrity and respect (value one). We don't foster an environment of helping our customers — internal or external — succeed (value two). We certainly aren't committed to continuous improvement and innovation (value three), and this type of behavior certainly doesn't say much about encouraging Olin people — who are the winning difference (value four). In fact, bullying typically creates only fear and disengaged, resentful employees.

"So our challenge is to focus on our four values, and the behaviors that are associated with these values. Ethics still remains the underpinning in everything we do."

Can an auditor measure communications success?

"It's a challenge and a long term journey," admits Gebing, who spent most of his 25 years at Olin in internal audit and who has just recently returned to run this function in addition to continuing to lead Olin's ethics initiative. "I meet with Olin's audit committee four times a year and have been asked how do we know if our program is working.

"I told them that one way we can measure success is not by the number of frauds or legal problems uncovered, but by the other success stories we can point to. For example, an employee called our helpline to provide information about a coworker who he suspected of using drugs. Because of a fellow employee's concern, we were able to intervene and get the employee into a drug treatment program. Not only did that employee not harm our company or create an unsafe work environment for others, but we were able to help a valued employee with a problem. Preventing accidents or employee turnover has costs savings. Moreover, our employees feel good about our commitment and the fact that we live our values. I count that as a success."

We agree. Olin has identified a key ingredient in establishing a values-based culture: open and honest communication. Without it, the values the company seeks to foster will never be shared or understood. It is a model any organization could well emulate.

Chapter 12

Training

Even the most expansive and effective communication mechanisms are not sufficient to instill values into action. Few employees instinctively know how to make complex ethical decisions or even to think through the process of evaluating potential courses of action and the consequences. Therefore, training sessions that allow employees to exchange views with each other about the importance of ethics and about the issues and values that specifically relate to their daily work are critical.

What is training?

We recently heard an individual argue that "training" was the wrong word; that what we were discussing was "education." He saw training as dealing with specific techniques (such as how to operate a lathe or fix a computer's hard drive, we suppose). He saw education as more broad-based, teaching the nuances of problem solving.

We think such distinctions are not helpful. By whatever term we call it, organizations have found that training — the process of involving employees in a discussion of the organization's values and their role in upholding such values — is necessary for any successful ethics program.

Why train?

Why offer training in values or ethics at all? At one recent seminar of corporate executives, a participant came up to us after the session. He was perturbed. "Does corporate America understand that, in essence, it is taking up the job of teaching values to our citizens?" he asked. We replied in the affirmative, suggesting that many thoughtful executives are doing just that because they have concluded they are filling a void. Too many employees are not receiving any grounding in values from their home, their church, their school or their community experience.

"But that's shocking," he said. "This is a sociological sea change. Has anyone written about it?"

We assured him that there were many good books in the business ethics field that had addressed this, and that we were also writing about it in our latest book. But it was clear to us that he was surprised at the widespread scope of ethics training going on in corporate America, and dismayed by the necessity for it.

We are not so dismayed. While we were once challenged on our assertion that "few" employees instinctively know how to make a complex ethical decision, we suspect we are not far off the mark. It is unrealistic to expect that employees from Maine to southern California would hold the same views about privacy, for example, or that an extroverted employee from a large family in Texas might have the same notions of the formality of social contact as a shy individual from Minnesota. Some employees come from dysfunctional families. Some employees have had no religious training and some have had little formal education. Some have traveled widely and some not at all. Add a mix of generations, ethnic backgrounds, and, for global companies, cultural differences. Why should we expect that every employee would instinctively approach an ethical decision with the same set of values, apply the same criteria, use the same decision-making model and reach the result that the company might hope?

So the good news is that the best organizations have moved beyond training in the "don'ts" and offer training in the "do's," in values. The reason that many have moved beyond publishing a list of prohibitions (the compliance approach) and have engaged employees in a discussion of values is that decision-making has moved down to the lowest possible level in many organizations. Individuals are struggling with issues that emerge in their daily work, but no policy book could possibly cover all situations. Managers need to find a balance between the authority of the corporation and the autonomy of the individuals. Employees need enough freedom to make decisions on their own, but often they need help in developing the habit of sound decision-making, and particularly decision-making based on the company's values. Training is a process that helps individuals develop character, which gives them room for dialogue and self-examination and which encourages sound judgment.

Effective training in values assists employees in two categories of decision-making. First, by raising their level of awareness about ethical issues and reinforcing the company's viewpoint on important values, it is more likely that employees will do the right thing. Helped by the training they have received and the reinforcement that the organization will stand behind them if they pursue the right course, most employees will do so. Without such training, even if their initial instinct is to act ethically, employees may wonder what the company would rather have them do.

Second, training in values helps employees make the right choice when they are confronted with conflicting values, and honestly don't know for sure what their decision should be. Because effective training includes an opportunity for disagreement, dialogue and debate, employees can develop the decision-making skills that require them to consider choices and evaluate the best course of action.

What about the argument that an ethical environment can be obtained if the company just hires decent people with a strong sense of personal values and principles?

The best answer we have heard to that familiar plea comes from Lockheed Martin.[1] Its Ethics and Business Conduct Steering Committee recently reviewed statistics about ethical misconduct across the company, showing that in one fifteen-month period, approximately 70 Lockheed Martin employees were discharged and another 70 suspended for ethical lapses. Additionally, more than 450 employees received some other type of sanction during the same period. As Lockheed Martin itself said, these were good employees who, for a variety of reasons, made bad ethical choices. The reasons, all too familiar to any organization, included pressure to meet a deadline or goal, lack of resources, peer pressure, or a belief that the decision was in the organization's best interest.

---

[1]Lockheed Martin, *Ethics In Our Workplace*, 1998, p. 10.

We call this the NETMA Syndrome: Nobody Ever Tells Me Anything. No organization today can afford to lose one good employee because the employee wasn't aware of the consequences of a wrong decision. Comprehensive training, particularly that encourages employees to ask for assistance when they have concerns, can prevent this from happening.

There is one final reason to encourage training in values, and that rests with senior level managers who may otherwise fall prey to unethical action. These individuals often are well aware of the "shall not's," but without a reinforcement of the importance of the company's values — and in some cases, reinforcement conducted by them — they may conclude that proscriptions on certain conduct do not apply to them or that the company really isn't serious.

For example, many people in business have experienced the boss who liberally uses company employees or resources for his own purposes, yet would immediately fire an underling who did the same thing. Similarly, one study that looked at business felons found that they knew they were breaking the law. Most had a high degree of education and/or a professional background, and the majority was extremely successful. [2] But their arrogance, desire for power and a distorted perception of power that led them to assume they were above the rules contributed to their penchant for financial crime. Perhaps only constant conversation about the importance of company values and their role in upholding such values would have counteracted the immoral behavior.

Some individuals evidence these personal characteristics long before they enter the workplace. For example, fourteen UCLA football players claimed fake injuries, attested to by fake doctors, to apply for handicapped parking permits from the California Department of Motor Vehicles, apparently to avoid a $132 fee per semester for on-campus parking. [3] These otherwise physically fit athletes may have thought that because they were

---

[2] John Dunkelberg, Debra Ragain Jessup and Donald Rubin, "The Anatomy of Fraudulent Behavior," Calloway School of Business and Accountancy, Wake Forest University, 1998.

[3] Associated Press, "Athletes Charged in Handicapped-Parking Scheme," *The New York Times*, July 10, 1999, p. A9.

football players, proper considerations that apply to everyone else didn't apply to them. According to Ali Abdul Azziz, a linebacker, "We did not realize the seriousness of our actions."[4] A representative of the Paralyzed Veterans of America called their behavior a moral outrage. Future employers may call their conduct unethical.

What are we trying to accomplish?

We often use a pyramid diagram to help organizations plan their objectives in conducting values and ethics training. At the bottom level is "ethical awareness." The next level is "ethical reasoning." The third level is "ethical action." Finally the top of the pyramid is "ethical leadership." We suggest managers try to develop training elements for each of these four stages, and move people and the organization through all levels, seeking competence in each one.

To point out the obvious, there is a causal relationship among all four ranks. You need ethical awareness before you can have ethical reasoning. You can't have ethical action without both ethical awareness and ethical reasoning, and you will never achieve ethical leadership without the first three.

Ethical awareness

In developing the first competency, that of *awareness*, we suggest that trainers first explain why business ethics is more important than ever. Many employees are not aware of the reasons why an understanding of business ethics is important to them as individuals as well as to the corporation. Several well-chosen examples can illustrate the point.

When conducting seminars on the subject, we begin by talking about trust. All business relationships, whether they be between an organization and its customers or between employees and their supervisors, are built on trust. We often paraphrase Warren Buffet's remarks after the Salomon Brothers' financial scandal. Trust is like the air we breathe. When trust is

---

[4] Christian Berthelsen, "9 Enter Pleas in UCLA Parking Case," *The New York Times*, July 29, 1999, p. C29.

Stages of ethical development

present, it's never noticed. When it is missing, it's all that's noticed. Trust can't be found in a book of laws or regulations or a compliance manual. Organizations have to trust that their employees will do the right thing.

Here it is often useful to show a short video that dramatizes an ethical hypothetical or dilemma, but one that is not indigenous to the industry or profession in which the individuals work. The reason for this approach is that we want employees to struggle with the ethical situation presented without carrying to the discussion any preconceived ideas or presumed right answers from their own company or industry. We want them to freethink and unearth their ethical juices and bring to the discussion concepts that may have been eclipsed but are there within them. Call it Socratic midwifery if you like, but it works.

In our experience, employees relish the opportunity to be asked their opinion about an ethical situation they have just witnessed on the screen. We're not surprised, because humans have been debating principles of ethics for thousands of years. The ability to do so is innate, but few employees have the chance to reawaken their ethical sensitivity. Here, the discussion and debate heightens their ethical awareness.

If you don't have access to a hypothetical ethical dilemma portrayed in a dramatization, there is still plenty of material for employees to discuss. One of the most effective training tools is the use of contemporary problems. By using real life examples to encourage discussion and debate, managers can delve with candor into the viewpoints held by training participants, without using examples that strike "too close to home."

Here's how it works. Almost everyone knows the circumstances surrounding the impeachment of President William Clinton, yet few would encourage a vociferous debate about the pros and cons of the impeachment issue as it unfolded, if only to keep political harmony in a business environment.

Yet after the fact, the impeachment story becomes a training tool that can focus in on differing values and the tough ethical choices faced by employees who may find themselves in similar situations. The Lewinsky/Clinton scandal, removed of its political implications and immediacy, becomes an intriguing template to test ethical issues in the workplace. For example, if someone in a company suspected a top executive of behaving inappropriately with an intern, what would he do? What if no one had proof, just suspicions? Or another example: every secretary who has ever lied to a caller by saying her boss was in a meeting can identify with White House secretary Betty Currie, who found herself inappropriately facilitating off-hours visits by a certain guest. What might she have done?

Here's another example. If in a crisis a top executive had given certain assurances to managers and these employees defended the boss based on what he had told them, what should they do if they discovered he had lied? Or finally, perhaps here's one for the board of directors: one of the company's directors asked the CEO to provide a job interview for a young lady referred by an elected official. What should the CEO do? What should the other directors do?

Using the well-known facts of a contemporary public problem to unearth the values of employees is a useful technique — it allows managers to probe what their reactions are, without asking them direct questions about their organization. After hypothetical discussions like that, participants are ready for the next stage.

Ethical reasoning

Ethical reasoning is the stage at which we introduce decision-making models and criteria, in order to help employees think through the alternatives and consequences of an ethical dilemma. Much of this "ethical toolbox" actually turns out to be the ideas they have brought to the table in discussing the case in the first stage of values training — the principles of ethics that individuals ought to use in working through a problem. In many cases, they have had these tools all along but may not have used them or been consciously aware of them.

What are some of these tools? Texas Instruments suggests a quick seven-point guide. The first question is whether the action is legal. Presumably if the answer is no, one need not proceed any further. But if it is legal, the next question is whether it complies with the company values. Two more questions, which relate directly to personal, emotional concerns are: if you do it, will you feel bad? And how will it look if it appears in the newspaper? Finally, three guidelines: if you know it's wrong, don't do it; if you're not sure, ask; and keep asking until you get an answer.

Some company "toolboxes" have more devices. Individuals are asked to examine their own values, duties, and alternative courses of action. They are asked to consider if they would feel fairly treated if the situation were reversed; whether the decision would still be right if it set a precedent; and whether the decision would hold up if it became public.

Here are two examples of real life dilemmas that might not be found in any rulebook or legal treatise. In both cases, the individuals are forced to make a decision on their own, with only the values of the organization to fall back on in looking for guidance.

Let's also assume that in both cases, the values of the two organizations are the same: integrity and accountability.

The first organization is a growing, private company whose president is the major owner and is committed to profit sharing with every employee. An employee is asked to attend an educational seminar to receive training in a new product that the company hopes to offer to customers. While the seminar is held at a resort, the weeklong classes are grueling. Wednesday afternoon is the only free time and the employee uses the afternoon to enjoy a round of golf as a break from studying.

At the end of the week, the employee receives his bill at checkout, which includes the round of golf. Is there an ethical issue and what should the employee do?

He could turn to laws, regulations and rules, except that this situation is not covered. Employees are to submit expense reimbursement forms with receipts. That's all. Company rules don't explain whether a round of golf is allowed.

He might conclude that after studying until midnight every night, away from his family for a week, he earned the round of golf. He might conclude that any employee in his situation deserved a round of golf if such an employee had put in a 60-hour week studying and learning for the company.

But having been trained in ethical awareness and ethical reasoning, he might consider the company's values of integrity and accountability. And he might conclude that acting with integrity meant acting as if he owned the company and would have to explain his actions to all the employees. Accountability meant that he was accountable to others and accountable for the financial health of the company and ultimately to its employees and owners. He might therefore conclude that the round of golf was not mandated by a compelling company interest and would ultimately take money from reinvestment in the business or from his peers.

Our second example concerns a board member of a major national charity. This charity provides national services to 1900 other regional and local organizations, which collectively raise billions of dollars for human service needs. The president of the charity is, by all accounts, an inspiring, engaging individual who has a stellar performance record. The board members of this charity reads like a "who's who" of corporate America: the chairmen of IBM, Sears, American Express, and J.C. Penney, to name a few. Prior to one board meeting, the board members each receive an anonymous letter charging that the president had affairs with two sisters and used charity money to cover up his actions. The chairman of the board confronts the president, who denies the charges. Reassured, the chairman informs his fellow board members that he has checked it out and there is nothing to the story. How do we suppose he made his decision?

There were probably no laws or rules to follow in deciding to take the word of the president. The chairman might have concluded that he was justified in ignoring an anonymous letter, particularly in light of an individual whom board members had rewarded over the years for good performance. The harm to a person's reputation might outweigh the necessity to probe further. Finally, he might conclude that if he were in a similar situation, he would not want anonymous letters charging him with such serious actions to be given credibility.

But if the organization's values were those of integrity and accountability, he might have concluded that to sustain integrity and donor confidence, all charges must be investigated thoroughly, because even the smallest hint of impropriety would damage the organization's chief asset — its reputation. Furthermore, ultimate accountability for misuse of donor money resided with the board. To not pursue an investigation would be to ignore one of their primary obligations.

In hindsight, of course, our hypothetical director no doubt wishes the values of the organization had overridden his initial instinct to accept the president's denial. In the real life example, the president of the organization was indicted and convicted of numerous felony counts several years later; even a cursory investigation of the information in the letter by an outside auditor or lawyer would have revealed the information to be accurate.[5]

Ethical reasoning skills and the resolution of ethical problems is a critical part of ethics training. We believe that the most practical approach is the most effective one. All of us have the basic ethical tools and instincts to reason ethically. Solid ethics training, which builds in good ethical decision-making models, will serve to hone these tools and stimulate these instincts.

---

[5] See Dawn-Marie Driscoll, W. Michael Hoffman and Edward S. Petry, *The Ethical Edge: Tales of Organizations That Have Faced Moral Crises*, MasterMedia, Ltd. 1995, pp. 193-206.

Ethical action

The next stage, ethical *action*, is the one in which participants confront the values/action gap and explore the internal company resources that they can use to put ethical decisions into action. In the worst cases, employees feel they have no support systems, don't know how to approach their supervisors or don't know to whom to talk. In the best cases, it is clear what route they can take to resolve and bring to closure any particular problem.

At this stage of the training we recommend that participants talk about company-specific cases and company-specific support systems. Ideally, the ethics task force of company representatives that has been formed to help develop the ethics training will have found and written credible and ethically sensitive stories that have come directly from interviews with company employees. "Real-life" cases at this stage of the ethics training are important if participants are to feel that the training is relevant to their day-to-day activities.

We recommend that the cases be short and uncomplicated, written in a format that is easily understandable. Company representatives, often working in teams (such as a manager and a union representative, or a lawyer and a manager) generally facilitate the case discussions. If the class is large, they might suggest that several small groups work on different problems at the same time, but report back their decision to the entire group.

Here's an example of a short "real life" case. A junior level manager is sitting in a restaurant with his wife. He overhears a senior manager several tables away, talking loudly with his tablemates about a confidential client matter. He looks over to the table and notices that the senior manager has consumed several large alcoholic drinks. What does he do?

This may seem rather simple, but probably not for the junior manager who has a responsibility to protect client confidentiality but who obviously would like not to get fired. Should he go and confront in some way the senior manager? Should he send over a note by way of the waiter? After the participants discuss it, decide on their course of action and report it to the full group for further discussion, the facilitator should then talk about the company's support systems for such a case. If this were to happen in real life, what is the telephone number that the junior manager might want to access at the time? When he got home? When he went back to work? What department would he call and what would he say? Of course this is probably a time when he is going to have to make a decision on his own — again underscoring the importance of a code of ethics and ethics training.

Ethical leadership

This final stage of ethics training is designed to lead participants to the conclusion that developing, strengthening and maintaining an organization based on values is everyone's job. It is not the sole responsibility of the board of directors, the chief executive officer or the ethics officer (although, as stated in an earlier chapter, their commitment is a necessary prerequisite to any successful program). The company's ethical culture is only as strong as its weakest link. Any employee can be a weak link, which is why we recommend that ethics training reach everyone.

The message to the clerk in the mailroom is the same as the message to the senior vice president: fellow employees may very well set their moral compass by watching you and what your actions are. You need to be as much of an ethical leader as everyone else. Everyone needs to recognize his or her own responsibility in upholding the values of the organization.

The primary topic of discussion at this stage of the ethics training, therefore, is a momentous one: what are *my* responsibilities? The use of a company video can be helpful, with a segment from the CEO, along with other vignettes of various individuals from a wide range of divisions and departments, saying in their own words what the company's values mean to them. Niagara Mohawk Power corporation, for example, has prepared an effective video using about twenty employees with short "sound bite" answers to questions like, "What does ethics mean to you?" and "Who is responsible for ethics at the company?" The reaction of fellow employees is positive as they recognize their peers and then identify with what each employee has said.

Finally, to ensure ethical leadership at all levels of the company, the ethical educational program must continue beyond the initial training sessions. Employees must genuinely feel comfortable talking about values and ethics any place and anywhere in the organization, and that talking about ethics is not only okay, but also encouraged.

Objectives and content

Before embarking on values or ethics training, consider the objectives you are trying to reach. Here are some suggested objectives for a training seminar in business ethics:

- To clarify the ethical values and enhance the ethical awareness of employees.
- To uncover and investigate ethical issues and concerns that directly relate to the organization.
- To discuss criteria for ethical decision-making within the organization.
- To examine and enrich the structures, strategies, resources, policies and goals which shape the ethical environment and guide the ethical activities of the organization.

The most effective training seminars must be individually designed according to the business issues of the industry and the organization, as well as its particular culture and mission. While the content of such seminars may depend as well on the length of time and the objectives set for the training session, the most effective programs contain these common elements:

- Supporting remarks by senior executives — in person or on video.
- An introduction to the objectives of the training session by the facilitator.
- A discussion of general ethical principles and business ethics in particular.
- An overview of how companies and organizations are integrating ethical considerations into their operations.
- A discussion of the framework and guidelines for ethical decision-making.
- Comments on various common situations, concerns and myths about business ethics.
- Dramatization and discussion of a general ethical dilemma.
- Discussion of company-specific ethical dilemmas, including identification of the ethical issues, application of company

code of ethics and values and consideration of alternative plans of action.

• Explanation of ethics initiatives at the company or organization, including its guidance system for reporting problems or seeking help.

A successful ethics training program should relate to all levels of the organization, not just upper and middle management. Finally, ethics workshops should occasionally mix different levels of the organization, from hourly workers to executive officers, and even members of the board of directors, in order to promote better understanding and communication among all members of the organization with regard to the company's ethical problems and value commitments. This would help build a stronger and more unified ethical corporate culture.

Leaders in the field

Many companies now have outstanding training programs that reinforce their commitment to values-based management and are generous in sharing information about their successes.

Otis Elevator Company, a United Technologies Company, has incorporated an ethics and values module into its one-year training program called "Otis University." According to Douglas J. Lint, the business practices officer at Otis, the twenty Otis employees who are chosen to participate in the program represent the field/service area, manufacturing/purchasing or sales/marketing. Each group follows a similar course of four, one-week classroom sessions spread throughout the year. Between the classroom sessions the participants return to their normal jobs around the world but continue working on team projects. The objective of the ethics portion of the university is to reinforce the importance of the corporate code of ethics and to generate greater awareness of the role ethics plays in the daily activities of Otis.

Lockheed Martin, the defense industry giant, is guided by six core ethical values: honesty, integrity respect, trust, responsibility and citizenship. But the company does more than just publish the six values. Dilbert, Dogbert and the other characters in Scott Adam's famous Dilbert cartoon series are now integral actors in the company's ethics initiatives.

Steve Cohen, of Cohen/Gebler, the training and communications firm that helped Lockheed Martin develop the program, explains how Dilbert came to play a starring role. "Norm Augustine, the chairman of Lockheed, had the insight to realize that although companies may have several core strategies to pursue, generally you can only reach people with your top priorities. He decided that ethics would be one of them, but he also knew that you had to do more than just write it down and send it out. You need learning across the organization to make it happen. He was willing to do whatever it took to break through the noise and resistance, and to shake people up. He decided humor might do it.

"Our firm helps companies bridge the gap between their goals and vision and the reality of what perceptions and policies really are at work in the company environment. Many training and communications efforts are passive and one-way. Our approach is to create a clear program identity, and then get our audience actively involved in the learning experience. Games are one way to accomplish that.

"Dilbert was the perfect character to use, because Dilbert encounters ethical issues almost daily in the comic strip. The humor provides a gentle but powerful way to get through to people and reveal conflicting values.

"Norm Augustine is a very serious business leader, but he was comfortable with using humor as a tool. He challenged us to develop something that would get people talking, get them to share personal experiences, and facilitate conversation throughout the company about the realities that employees face. He wanted us to be realistic and not theoretical.

"So we set to work with the most amazing client team from Lockheed Martin that I've ever encountered, to develop what became the Dilbert board game, 'The Ethics Challenge.' This team was not an easy crowd. They were always challenging us. We worked for four months to develop a strong program identity, to write the cases and incorporate humor in the game, and to make the entire program 'facilitator-proof.' We wanted it to be easy and fun to administer. Then we surrounded it with a communications program.

"We rolled it out at the company's Leadership Meeting, with the chairman, top executives and division heads. I looked at

The Ethics Challenge • Lockheed Martin

Case No. 7 • Accepting Gifts

You are attending a conference as a representative of your company. A supplier to your industry passes out a small electronic gadget, valued about $40, to everyone attending the meeting. What should you do?

POINTS	POTENTIAL ANSWERS
0	**A.** Accept the thoughtful gesture—since the gift is valued under $50, there is no need to report it.
1	**B.** Accept the gift, but be sure to report it to your manager. If your manager tells you to return it, you are required to comply.
3	**C.** Accept the gift, if declining it puts you or the company in an awkward position. Then immediately consult the Ethics Office for disposition.
5	**D.** Politely refuse to accept the gift.
★	Ask for a few extras for your sick kids.

LEADERS COMMENTS

A. This is a violation of company policy. Employees are not permitted to accept any gift that has a retail or exchange value of $20 or more from individuals, companies, or representatives of companies that have or seek business relationships with us.

B. If the gift is inadvertently accepted in violation of company policy it should be returned.

C. This may be acceptable in limited circumstances. You should, however, try to avoid such situations.

D. Refusing the gift is the best response — see **A.** above.

those who were assembled in the room, taking 'The Ethics Challenge' for the first time, and thought that I had no bigger chance to destroy my career than that meeting. But it was a huge success, and we gained lots of advocates for the program immediately. Lockheed Martin has already trained almost a half a million employees with the game, and it's been adapted for other companies as well.

"But the biggest proof of its success has been the formal and informal measurements that occurred afterward. I recall one participant saying that it was not until he had discussed a case with his fellow participants that he realized he should report suspected wrongdoing. Yet he'd been given that same information for years! That shows that it's not enough just to present information — it's the engagement with the audience participants that makes a training program succeed."

What's next

Cohen is an advocate for live, interactive training, but he predicts that in the next phase of values-based instruction, companies will also take advantage of their existing investment in technology.

"You can do a lot with web-based training," Cohen said. "You can build your program identity, you can introduce new themes, you can sustain knowledge, feature new information or current events, and do tracking and assessments. And the real benefit is, because the technology is there, it costs so little to do so much. Many companies are deploying on-line training in a variety of subjects. We want ethics to be one of them."

Cohen and Gebler are building internet learning portals for many large companies, and have designed an "Innovation Cafè" prototype to deliver web-based communication and community building. Visitors to the cafè can pick up snippets of information, engage in solving real-life instances of sexual harassment or other ethical dilemmas, test themselves, read current news or post messages. Cohen believes that these community-building web forums will supplement in-person training programs, and carry the message forward after the instructional sessions have ended.

Chapter 13

Pension Benefit Guaranty Corporation
HOW TO START AN ETHICS PROGRAM

In many organizations, the impetus to launch a training program in ethics and values often follows a scandal or problem. The resulting crisis and Monday morning quarterbacking invariably leads to the conclusion that employees did not understand the right thing to do and therefore need to be trained in values and decision-making.

But in some organizations that have not experienced a problem there is also a moment of awakening. Someone in top management asks, "Are we missing the boat?" This foresighted individual then tasks an appropriate employee to investigate what other companies or institutions are doing to train employees in ethics and to recommend a process by which they might do the same.

Joan Dubinsky, president of The Rosentreter Group, has developed and conducted ethics training programs for organizations as diverse as The MITRE Corporation and the American Red Cross. She cites The Pension Benefit Guaranty Corporation (PBGC) as one of the best examples of an organization that has most thoughtfully approached the issue of ethics training.

How it starts

"I have seen the stimulus come from a variety of sources," Dubinsky says. "At the Red Cross, for example, the president circulated an article on why business schools were having a hard time teaching ethics. I think the words 'Do it' were part of the president's communication. At defense industry companies, training often revolves around the business needs of each division or unit. Some are more compliance and rules-based in their focus. Some are interested in the challenge of confronting the gray areas of various decisions. Others just want employees to 'call home' for the answer to anything not in the rules book. As more human resource professionals realize that the best companies offer training in ethics and values, we'll see a greater need for creative solutions."

So the boss says to the organizational development specialist, "Let's conduct training in ethics and values." What happens next?

"For a number of trainers, a moment of quiet panic sets in," says Dubinsky. "They may not have a clear picture of what business ethics is all about.

"At that point the best corporate trainers will push back and ask, 'What's the outcome you want to see?' 'What is it related to?' 'Why now?' And at that point they'll bring in outside help."

Hiring an ethics consultant

Many human resource professionals are great trainers, but not expert in the substance of business ethics or values-based decision-making. However, there are experts out there. As human resource managers use their professional organizations and networks to seek out resources, they should also begin to ask important questions.

Dubinsky suggests that those who are looking to hire a consultant to help develop a comprehensive ethics training program should ask such straightforward questions as:

- What have you done and for whom?
- What organizational resources or colleagues can you bring to the project?
- What have the results been? How has the organization changed because of what you or your colleagues did?
- What are your philosophical approaches? Do you have a particular preference for compliance-based programs or values-based programs?

• Are you comfortable developing interactive training programs, using case studies, discussions and exercises?

Perhaps more important than questions to the consultant, however, are the questions that the organization should be prepared to answer. A good consultant will want to learn the institution's standards and values. If there is a mission statement or values code, it should become an integral part of the training and be relevant and understood by everyone in the organization.

A consultant who has been hired to help a company develop ethics training will first identify what the *true* values of the organization are (as opposed to the stated values) and how they are communicated. The tone at the top is critical. For instance, is the culture based on rigid rules and discipline or on open dialogue and debate? Do the senior managers understand the present state of the business ethics movement? What are the values of the industry? What behaviors do senior managers want to promote and how are they doing it now?

Some of the best companies see values-based training as part of management development. Dubinsky uses MITRE to illustrate an organization that has carefully thought through its management objectives. "Senior executives concluded that MITRE couldn't develop a cadre of engineers who were good managers unless they understood business ethics. In its management development program, MITRE included ethical decision-making as a stand alone module and conducted a separate program devoted to compliance issues."

Pension Benefit Guaranty Corporation's tale

The Pension Benefit Guaranty Corporation is a federal agency that insures and protects the pensions of 42 million working men and women in more than 44,000 defined benefit pension plans.[1] PBGC is unusual in that it is not funded by tax revenues, but by insurance premiums, income from investments and pension plans. Its employees are federal government employees, subject to federal compliance rules.

---

[1] See www.pbgc.gov for further information.

Jay Resnick, who is an assistant general counsel at the Pension Benefit Guaranty Corporation as well as the corpora-tion's alternate ethics officer, knew that when James Keightley, the general counsel and ethics officer, raised the issue of an ethics program, he was not talking about compliance. "We had attended conferences devoted to compliance, and once a year we offered what we called 'ethics training,' but that was really more a regulatory approach — how to comply with government-wide standards of conduct regulations and conflict of interest laws. These don't help you with moral choices, they just tell you what the rule is. Jim thought there was something else we should be doing."

"I heard a speech at a conference about a values-based approach to decision-making, and I knew that was what we wanted to pursue. But we wasted some time at first, trying to figure out how to do it."

Phil Hertz, the deputy general counsel, concurs with Resnick. "We wanted to do more than recite rules. It was easy to show employees a rule, but harder when there was no rule. We already had plenty of rules, but they didn't address the day to day issues people were dealing with. There was no procedure to say, 'think about what you're doing and how.'"

Hertz does not find it unusual that the impetus for values-based training, as opposed to a compliance approach, emanated from the legal department. "Lawyers probably give more thought to ethics and values than others, if only because we take courses in jurisprudence. The whole concept of justice forces you to examine what is fair and right. I don't know that other folks within the building naturally get into subjects like this as much as we do."

The office of general counsel, with assistance from the agency's training institute, designed, developed and delivered a corporate ethics course, with attorney Ray Forster serving as subject matter expert.

"Our executive director, David Strauss, agreed with our general counsel that we should pursue the subject," Forster said, "and I was the worker bee who ended up with the assignment. We already trained our employees in compliance rules, but we wanted to set up a course to teach the staff to teach everyone else about how to resolve problems based on ethical principles. So we spent a year doing our own research through conferences and organizations to find out what was happening in the field. We concluded that it would be far better to bring in a professional who had done this before.

"We needed to find someone who had a combination of technical expertise in corporate or business ethics as well as training design skills. We found Joan, who not only understood our language, but also knew ethics and had the vocabulary and background in training on ethical principles to bring to the task. She was just what we needed."

When PBGC contacted Dubinsky she saw that the agency was already headed in the right direction.

"PBGC knew that a good ethics program isn't like installing computer software. You can't buy it off the shelf and plug it in," says Dubinsky. "One of the 'absolutes' in my book is that a consultant and a client must work together in as many ways as possible to design and implement an ethics training program so that the program becomes theirs. This is the key to how long-lived the program will be. The client must support a team-based solution. True, a training program takes longer to develop if the client team is the creative arm, but again, if the program is to be viable, it must be fashioned by the client. A consultant could do the work but then there will be no transfer of knowledge. You want the training group to have new skills. A good consultant will help them get there."

Dubinsky and the PBGC team worked to develop hypothetical case studies for group discussion. They used focus groups, individual interviews and PBGC material. As with other organizations' training efforts, the best cases are developed over time, based on issues or dilemmas that arise from actual workplace experiences. They need to sound authentic and not be perceived as either too simplistic or transparent. Like Dubinsky, we have found that there are few shortcuts when developing this body of casework, but it is well worth the research and time that it takes.

"Case studies based on realistic workplace dilemmas don't just happen," Dubinsky said. "It takes considerable research to pull together, write, and develop effective and teachable case studies."

Dubinsky and the PBGC team finally settled on twelve cases, but Dubinsky urged that the training sessions not begin with a PBGC issue.

"I like to start with what I call a 'case on a right angle,'" Dubinsky says, "one that is not specifically applicable to the client. It allows participants to discuss ethical principles and apply a decision-making model to a situation that is totally hypothetical. They can really argue it out, with no personal stake in the outcome."

Resnick recalls that using a case far removed from the pension guarantee business was an effective technique. "It was a lot easier for people to get involved in the discussion, because it was so different from our own situation," he said.

The Idea Book

Since PBGC had decided to use its own staff to train approximately five hundred of its employees, Dubinksy prepared a comprehensive resource for discussion leaders called the *Business Ethics Idea Book*. It contained everything a trainer needed to know, from a discussion about the difference between compliance and ethics, to the program outline, the case studies and their notes, overhead slides and a bibliography.

In the introduction and primer, the PBGC team set out a very clear goal:

> Our goal is to discern not only what we have the right to do, but the right thing to do. In the complex work facing the PBGC, and every federal government employee, we deal with a myriad of choices in how we conduct ourselves on the job and in how we discharge our duties. The U.S. Office of Government Ethics has created a number of training programs that describe the laws, rules and regulations that govern some aspect of what we do. Our program on organizational ethics builds on that basis and lets us explore the gray area existing between absolute right and wrong.[2]

The PBGC team decided not to provide trainers with a rigid course design, but rather, encouraged trainers to tailor their per-

---

[2] The Rosentreter Group and Joan Elise Dubinsky, *Business Ethics Idea Book*, 1999, p. 8.

Heinz's dilemma

In Europe, a woman was near death from a rare disease. There was one drug that her doctors thought might save her. This rare drug was recently discovered by a pharmacist in the same town. The drug was expensive to prepare; and the druggist charged his customers ten times what the drug cost to make. He paid $200 for the chemicals, and charged $2000 for a single dose. The woman's husband, Heinz, went to everyone he knew to borrow the money, but he could only get together about $1000. He told the pharmacist that his wife was dying and asked him to sell the drug cheaper, or let him pay for it later. But the druggist refused. "I discovered the drug and I am going to recoup my investments."

Heinz was desperate.

DISCUSSION QUESTIONS

- How do you describe Heinz's options?
- What is the impact of each of those options?
- What do you imagine his wife would advise? Her family? Their children?
- What principles are at stake here, from Heinz's perspective?
- How do you describe the druggist's position and concerns?
- What principles are at stake, here, from the druggist's perspective?
- How can these principles be reconciled? Whose concerns are paramount? Are there some principles that deserve greater respect than others?

Business Ethics Idea Book , pp. 134-135

sonal style to meet the interests of their participants. As long as facilitators met the learning objectives (distinguish ethics from compliance rules; think critically about the values of government service; apply a decision-making template; and learn how to identify, appreciate and resolve workplace dilemmas),[3] they could be flexible with their instructional methods.

---

[3] The Rosentreter Group and Joan Elise Dubinsky, p. 14.

Features of ethical dilemmas

Here are some of the most significant features of ethical dilemmas. You may choose to use this list as you summarize the key learning points from either of these two exercises:

- **Ethical dilemmas involve two or more right courses of action, two or more optional courses of action, two or more values that cannot both be equally well served.**
- **Ethical dilemmas are difficult and complex. Generally they are rich in facts and context.**
- **Ethical dilemmas have significant consequences.**
- **Ethical dilemmas involve many stakeholders.**
- **Ethical dilemmas involve human beings emotionally.**
- **Ethical dilemmas may take time to emerge and will take time to resolve. There are very few snap or intuitive resolutions.**

Business Ethics Idea Book , p. 24

The training session

In the first segment of the three-hour course, participants are asked to write down the most difficult personal ethical dilemma they had faced while working at PBGC. According to Forster, this exercise achieved its purpose of encouraging participants to think and to share. "We opened with a promise that no names or notes would be taken," he said. "People were willing to talk and it showed that they really did have a grasp of ethical issues, but not necessarily the framework to solve them. When they shared their examples, the group tried to help the person."

"This exercise worked well," Resnick agreed. "I shared a personnel issue that I was facing. I knew what I had to do as a manager, but it was a wrenching experience for me, because of the other stakeholders involved. It was a tough moral decision. Others had budget issues or other human resource problems — there was a great variety."

Participants were then asked to divide into working teams and to list the top five ethical dilemmas currently facing the

PBGC (or the federal government service in general) in 1999. A representative from each group then volunteered two dilemmas, and the facilitator recorded the issues on a flip chart for the entire group. As participants discussed the various features of the ethical dilemmas and the corresponding fourteen Principles of Ethical Conduct of Government Officers and Employees, [4] resident cynics and skeptics emerged. But a useful discussion about workplace values took place.

By that time, participants were ready to discuss the mini-cases in the *Idea Book*, which were developed with relevance to the work of the corporation. They were concise, but meaningful. For example, "Laura's Story" examines the nature of federal government service and the question of whether PBGC employees should be held to higher standards than ordinary citizens. "When Opportunity Knocks" begs the question of consistency and virtue in management and debates the obligations and duties of a PBGC manager to his or her employees and to the corporation.

The *Idea Book* contained twelve cases, along with end notes and discussion questions, but Forster and Resnick reported that the training classes at best allowed for discussion of two cases and a short wrap-up.

Feedback

"The program got universally good reviews," said Resnick. "This is a very busy agency and three hours for anything is a lot. But most of the evaluations made the comment that the session should have been longer. They wanted more time to talk about more cases, as well as their own experiences and problems."

Dubinsky believes that program evaluation is important, particularly for the design and delivery of future programs. "The questions don't need to be complicated," she said. "Did it meet your expectations? Did you learn valuable skills?"

But the real test of training effectiveness, she states, would be to question employees about six months later and ask for their reflections at that point. Information about how they would

---

[4]Executive Order 12674 of April 12, 1989 (as modified by Executive Order 12731).

change the training session, and which part turned out to be the most valuable, will help future teams redesign the course and construct new cases. Now that Dubinsky has trained the PBGC trainers, the goal is to reach 350 employees initially and to make the sessions available to other employees as well as new hires after that.

Resnick is pleased with what the corporation accomplished. "Hopefully this will make people work better. Our goal was to have people realize it was okay to talk about these difficult issues, and to give them a vocabulary to do so. We know that the tough ethical issues are the ones that trouble your conscience and give you sleepless nights. We want to help people deal with those, and be better managers and employees."

The Pension Benefit Guaranty Corporation may be the advance team for the rest of the federal government. The Office of Government Ethics has commended PBGC for its initiative in this area and is interested in watching the rollout of this ethics training to see how other agencies could benefit. Hertz, Resnick, Forster and the PBGC team are anxious to share their program's content and evaluation with anyone else who seeks to instill values-driven management in a government agency.

Chapter 14

Resources for Assistance

Codes of ethics, communication vehicles, and training programs are significant elements in any effort to implement a values-driven culture throughout an organization. But without effective resources for employees (as well as suppliers, customers and others) to access when a question or problem arises, the endeavor will be only half-complete. Understanding this, some companies have been creative about where and how to provide such resources, taking advantage of technological advances to make as many types of assistance as possible available to employees.

Some of these resources are discussed in earlier chapters. Mission statements, values statements, codes of business conduct, policy manuals and questions and answers are generally the first form of communication that managers produce to help employees. Honda has a Legal Compliance and Business Ethics Policy with an accompanying wallet card that features its investigation policy and information about reporting violations.

BellSouth not only has written materials but also makes extensive use of its web site to provide further information. Visitors to www.ethics.bellsouth.com are immediately connected to a range of resources, as well as clear statements about the company's commitment to ethics.

Our phone lines are open

Visitors to the web site learn about the BellSouth Ethics Line, where they can get advice or report a situation 24-hours-a-day, 7-days-a-week. They can submit a question anonymously directly on the website, or they can submit a question through their intranet e-mail account if they don't mind being identified.

BellSouth resources

THERE ARE PLENTY OF RESOURCES TO HELP YOU

You can TRUST these resources when you need information or guidance.

- **Your supervisor or another manager**
- **Your company's human resources department**
- **The legal department**
- **The security department**
- **The auditing department**
- *A Commitment to Our Personal Responsibility* **booklet**
- **BellSouth's Ethics Website**
- **E-mail at ETHICS**
  (note: electronic mail is self-identifying)
- **BellSouth's Ethics Line 1-800-664-4231**

Ethics: It's part of your everyday job

www.ethics.bellsouth.com

BellSouth's use of an "ethics line" is an example of how and why the business ethics field is moving from compliance-only to a values-based approach. In the early stages of the business ethics movement, companies instituted reporting hotlines. These were toll-free telephone numbers promoted as a way for employees to report wrongdoing. As the calls came in, managers realized that employees would not limit their calls to reporting actual illegalities, since not even lawyers can always discern whether a particular set of facts constitutes a violation of law. Managers also saw value in changing the label of the telephone line to a "helpline" or "guideline", to serve as a source of advice and counsel on ethics and compliance issues. Today, many ethics officers report that over 40% of their calls on helplines concern internal human resource issues and incidents.

How a company designates its ethics telephone lines not only tells us what its values may be, but may influence the effectiveness of this particular resource. The words "help" and "assist" have very different meanings than "hot." The telephone lines that are billed as friendly resources for assistance are used four to five times as often as telephone numbers that are perceived as snitch lines, according to a study done by the Ethical Leadership Group.[1] Its research revealed that it made little difference whether an internal employee or an outside service answered the telephone. But companies that actively invite employees to call with concerns, even if they are not reports of wrongdoing, found the ethics lines to be much more successful.

Some companies resist such telephone lines, saying they prefer employees to contact a manager or supervisor with their questions or concerns. We think they may be missing a valuable resource. Today, employees are just as likely to be out in the field with a customer or supplier than in the office near a supervisor. Furthermore, the Ethical Leadership Group study found that 70% of companies publicize the line to vendors, an important constituency group. Still, the use of such telephone lines can improve. In a random test of one hundred members of the Ethics Officer Association who were in the Fortune 500 and had such lines, a caller to the corporate headquarters was unable to reach the ethics line 41% of the time.

Companies that do not install toll-free telephone lines may think an "open door" policy and a clear code of conduct will suffice. But many employees are skeptical about open door systems that require a subordinate to directly confront a boss or a boss's boss. Rather, they prefer anonymous calls. While some companies staff ethics lines with their own personnel, a significant number have turned to outside professional services, which provide 24-hour coverage, 365-days-a-year coverage, with a person answering rather than a recording.

These helplines have not become vehicles for cynical or revengeful whistle-blowers with false information, as some companies feared. However, companies such as Lockheed-Martin have implemented procedures to minimize the number of false accusations without impairing the usefulness of the ethics line. Callers are asked to state their name, but this information is not included in any further documentation. In most cases, the caller's identity is known only to the ethics officer, as a form of

---

[1] Ethical Leadership Group, "Ethics Phone Lines Best Practices Report," Wilmette, Illinois, December 1998.

corporate "witness protection." At BellSouth, callers are not required to give their name, and ethics managers assign a coded number to the call to track the investigation. If callers choose to give their name, they can ask that it not be released.

To protect the rights of those being investigated, some companies have a requirement that the accused be notified immediately, except when there are extenuating circumstances. This places the burden of proof on the investigators to explain why notification should not occur. In cases where notification would clearly hamper the investigation, however, the option to withhold notification remains open.

Reinforcing values with information

Some of the best resources we have seen are those that also reinforce the company's values and provide further information. Again, BellSouth's web site provides a good example. It clearly spells out the company's five core values: customers first, respect for the individual, pursuit of excellence, positive response to change and community mindedness. The web site also contains a section of "frequently asked questions" on subjects ranging from company assets to personal gain; provides a series of "quick tests;" and includes resource links to other web sites such as the Ethics Officer Association.

BellSouth's website is also being used to simplify administration. For example, employees can now access the annual conflict of interest questionnaire directly on the intranet.

Olin Corporation also provides extensive material on its website, including information about its E-Line, the company's business practice helpline, staffed 24-hours-a-day, 7-days-a-week. One unusual feature of Olin's site is the inclusion of ethics and compliance issues in the news. Chosen for their relevance to Olin's business, the section is divided by topics so that visitors can zero in on the area that is most relevant to their area of work.

We investigated Olin's site after the crash of the ValueJet airliner, thinking that the transport of hazardous "air freight" might be an interesting topic. It was. Olin had chosen to include a condensed version of an article that appeared in *USA Today* on April 27, 1998 about the FAA's stepped-up enforcement of hazardous

"In a chart accompanying the *USA Today* article, Olin
was listed among shippers receiving fines from the FAA.
The chart reference referred to an incident that occurred in
1986 and that resulted in a fine of $90,000 being imposed in
the early 1990s. The incident involved a package containing
a sample of nitric acid that began giving off fumes while
being shipped for analysis from Olin's plant in Lake Charles,
La., to our Chemical Research Center in Cheshire, Conn.
The Federal Express cargo jet carrying the material made
an unscheduled stop in Cincinnati so the package could be
removed. Thankfully, no one was injured in the incident, but
it certainly underscored the need for much greater care
and training in the safe packaging of potentially hazardous
material. Olin employees who need to know more about
proper and legal packaging and shipment of potentially
hazardous materials are urged to call Chris Zavada or Ray
Traggianese in the Chemicals Segment transportation
department in Norwalk."

Ethics and Compliance in the News,
Olin Corporation

material rules, including a proposed fine of $750,000 against Bath
& Body Works for leaking cosmetics. The reason Olin had chosen
that particular article might have been because the company
was also listed as having been fined by the FAA. So the commentary on the website explained that the incident involving Olin's
fine occurred in 1986 and involved a package containing a sample of nitric acid that began giving off fumes while being shipped
by Federal Express. The commentary also gave the name of Olin
employees who are resources for questions concerning the
proper and legal packaging and shipment of potentially hazardous materials.

Alternatives to the web

Not everyone is comfortable using computers or surfing the web,
however, so many companies continue to publish ethics stories,

questions, incidents and information about resources in internal newspapers and bulletins. Digital Equipment Corporation did both; it placed new stories in the newspaper that included a "tease" that referred readers to the website for more information, according to former ethics officer Vic Pompa.

How one develops and distributes information about resources may well depend on the type of company and the skill levels of the employees. At EDS, Glenn Coleman's first "go do" as its ethics officer was to write a code of ethics. In his view, a good program is like a three-legged stool, with a code, policies and values. Using the issue of sexual harassment as an example, Coleman suggests that "respect" might be the overriding value. The code would explain the company's policy on sexual harassment, with the reasons. The policies would outline in greater detail how to complain and what the punishment might be.

Coleman started by developing a code, and at the same time, reviewing all the existing company policies. Not surprisingly, he found that some policies were not needed, some were actually procedures and some could be recrafted as values. Coleman is working first on the code and policies, which he sees as a prerequisite to developing company values.

"Our new ethics initiative will begin with a code," Coleman said, "which we'll hand out with some case studies. We're going to focus everything we can on the web, so that an employee can go straight to a subject, then to a resource page, find out where to get training, who the experts are and what additional resources there are. Even though the company does have some core values, we can't jump right into it. It takes a maturing process, time for everyone to agree on what they are. So we're starting with the basics."

Companies with extensive resources for assistance, from telephone lines to websites to ethics offices and e-mail, make it easier for their employees to make difficult ethical choices according to the company's values.

A little preventive medicine

Let's look at how the issue of resources for assistance plays out in everyday worklife.

The *San Jose Mercury News*, a leading daily newspaper in California's Silicon Valley area, thought it had a clear ethics policy which stated that employees shouldn't make news decisions about companies in which they have a personal interest. The policy was stricter for business reporters, who were apparently told not to invest in local businesses, in order to avoid the appearance of a conflict of interest or damage to the paper's credibility. Yet in one instance, at least, the newspaper found out that not only was its policy not clear, but employees had few resources for clarification.

Chris Nolan, a business columnist for the *Mercury News*, was a longtime friend of Dean DeBiase, whom she knew from their days together working at different jobs. When both Nolan and the DeBiases relocated to the West Coast they remained friends — and for that reason, Nolan says, she never covered him as a business subject. [2]

By 1999 DeBiase was chief executive of an internet company that was about to sell shares to the public. Following a common practice, DiBiase offered to include Nolan on his "friends and family" list, allowing her to buy 500 shares at the opening price.

According to Nolan, she asked the assistant business editor for guidance. Unfortunately, none was forthcoming. Perhaps he forgot the question or thought she'd pursue it with others as well. He admits he said he'd check with another editor, but also assumed Nolan would check. When Nolan didn't hear back, she assumed there was no problem.

Nolan bought the shares and subsequently sold them, making a profit. Later, she spoke with her editors about a free-lance article she was planning to write for *Fortune* magazine about her experience. Again, there were no red flags raised. But when her purchase was reported in *The Wall Street Journal*, the *Mercury News* suspended her, subsequently reassigning her to another beat.

Was the newspaper's reaction too harsh? Both Nolan and some of her colleagues thought so, arguing that the newspaper's 10-page ethics statement was fifteen years old. Some staffers complained they had never seen it. David Yarnold, the executive editor of the *Mercury News*, said that Nolan was disciplined not because she violated a company policy. "This was an issue of vio-

---

[2] Brandon Bailey, "MN columnist suspended over local investment," *San Jose Mercury News*, July 16, 1999.

lating a basic journalistic principle. The issue is that Chris enjoyed benefits that the public at large does not enjoy and as a result places the *Mercury* in a conflict of interest." He admitted, however, that she was not given the advice she sought. "I think there was a lack of follow-through and I'm concerned about that."[3]

Perhaps sensing he was losing the battle of public opinion by claiming Nolan violated an ethics policy that few had seen, Yarnold insisted that journalistic principles don't need to be spelled out in policies. "They're expected to be in our blood: We don't plagiarize the work of others; we don't print unsubstantiated allegations; we don't manufacture quotes; we don't accept questionable favors from sources, even if they are friends."[4]

Nolan went on the offensive, angry that her editors were now accusing her of accepting favors from a source. DeBiase was not a source, she said, "and of all the things that have occurred since this whole episode began, nothing disturbs and distresses me more than to see an editor take it upon himself to name someone he thinks is a reporter's source — in print —without consulting the reporter."[5]

The dispute between Nolan and her editors at *Mercury News* about whose ethical violations were worse continues, but we think the story is more instructive about resources for assistance than lack of clarity in policies.

Newspapers generally have strict policies. At *The New York Times*, for example, top news executives annually report all their personal investments to *The Times'* chief financial officer. That's one approach — keep asking employees to report everything, from their investments to the names of their dinner companions. *The Wall Street Journal* distributes its comprehensive ethics policies to new hires and annually to all staffers, who must certify in writing that they have read it and disclose ownership of any security they have owned for a period of less than six months.

At some point, however, detailed reporting procedures cease to make practical sense, and employees need guidance. For

---

[3] Brandon Bailey, "MN reporter disciplined, will lose column," *San Jose Mercury News*, July 21, 1999.

[4] David Yarnold, "Why we take conflicts of interest seriously," *San Jose Mercury News*, August 1, 1999.

[5] Chris Nolan, "To the Editor," *Wired News*, August 20, 1999.

> **"A**lthough the Merc would have its readers believe
> that I have somehow strayed from the path of ethical,
> professional, and responsible journalistic behavior, that's
> simply not the case. Instead, it's the Mercury's manage-
> ment's failure to have an ethics policy in place, its failure
> to have a mechanism in place to answer and cope with
> ethical concerns raised by reporters, and the paper's
> refusal to take responsibility for its oversights that are
> at fault here."
>
> Chris Nolan
> "To the Editor," *Wired News*, August 20, 1999

example, what is considered a "local" company? If a columnist covers the technology industry, what is a technology company: Disney? AT&T? What are the rules that apply to journalists who work for technology media outlets such as TheStreet.com or CNet? Or, in Nolan's case, does the purchase of "family and friends" shares of an IPO from a friend who is not a source or subject of a column constitute an ethical breach?

In the case of the *Mercury News*, it appears to us that there was a "resource gap" issue. The newspaper had a policy and one of its employees had a question about its application. She didn't get a clear answer and apparently there wasn't a single place she could have found one. Perhaps she failed by not demanding assurances in writing from someone in a position of authority, but most ethical dilemmas don't provide the luxury of time or formality. Employees need answers and they usually need them sooner rather than later.

Nolan's case might be considered as a simple one. What about the tougher cases involving the need for assistance — for example, ones where employees, or even outsiders, suspect wrongdoing?

Resources for outsiders, too

When Dawn-Marie was general counsel of a retailing chain, there were no ethics officers or 1-800-helplines. But she was grateful

that on several occasions outsiders took the time to find someone in her position through the company switchboard, persist in
finally reaching her, and share their tale of woe. In one such case,
the general counsel of a large cosmetics company in New York
called her. "I wasn't sure if I should share this information with
you," he said, "but we've just reassigned one of our most capable
sales representatives out of your territory. She won't call on
your buyer anymore, because of the harassing way he treats
her." Dawn-Marie thanked him for the information and set about
to solve the problem.

Today, widely publicized values initiatives, ethics programs,
mission statements and helpline telephone numbers help outsiders tell companies what is going on within their organization.
For that reason alone they are worth establishing.

Rewarding the whistle-blower

While not all managers have heard the expression *qui tam*, most
know what whistle-blowers are. In the law, *qui tam* refers to
potentially lucrative cases in which whistle-blowers help make a
case of fraud against a company, and recover a percentage of
what the government recovers. The average whistle-blower
award is 18%, which might not seem much for the years of emotional and financial toll that such cases demand. But the stakes
can be high. SmithKline Beecham Clinical Laboratories $325 mil-
lion fraud penalty included a $52 million whistle-blower pay-
ment; United Technologies shared $22.5 million of a $150 million
penalty and lawyers are watching with interest to see what will
be awarded in the Columbia/HCA Healthcare lawsuits.

The bottom line is that no company or organization should
find itself victim of a whistle-blower who decides to call a government anti-fraud unit or to walk into the offices of lawyers who
specialize in representing whistle-blowers. We say "victim" pur-
posely.[6] It is not inconceivable that some whistle-blowers, seeking
to discredit those who may have crossed them in the workplace,
have ulterior motives. Once an employee has contacted an outside source, the investigation may well take on a life of its own.

---

[6] See Dawn-Marie Driscoll, "The hazards of blowing the whistle," *Boston Business Journal*, July 5-11, 1996, p. 8.

But the most important reason for discouraging whistle-blowers is that in a values-driven company, managers should actively seek and encourage information about problems that may raise an ethical question, even if it results in financial harm to the company.

Northrop Grumman tells its employees it wants to hear bad news. The company's "When to Challenge" guidelines are an important part of its values statement. Employees are told that if they are ever asked to do something which they believe is either unethical or not in Northrop Grumman's best interest, or if they become aware of any such activities, it is their right and their responsibility to express their concerns. The advantage of a clear statement and guideline like Northrop Grumman's is that it answers perhaps the most difficult ethical question for an employee: Is whistle-blowing morally obligatory? Must we take action to prevent harm as well as not cause it ourselves? Yes and yes. Ideally, companies support employees to do the right thing by offering resources for assistance.

Chapter 15

Astra USA
IMPLEMENTING RESOURCES
THE ASTRA WAY

If we were fiction writers, we'd put the Astra story off to the side and claim that we couldn't finish the story because of writers' block and an inability to create a believable plot. Is it a tale of how a small company, founded in Sodertalje, Sweden in 1913 and on the verge of bankruptcy after World War I, grew to be an international pharmaceutical giant with a vision of a dynamic future? Is it the story of the contemporary challenge of global management, illustrated by a sleepy corporate office in Sweden ignoring blatant illegalities and unethical conduct fostered by its U.S. president, until the story broke wide open and compelled its attention? Is it the story of a rogue executive, whose actions were aided and abetted by inadequate resources for hearing the concerns of employees?

Because this is nonfiction, we've chosen to tell it here, with the caution that the Astra story is a work in progress. We think the last chapter will be titled "Company Becomes Hero At Last" but the reader may have to stay tuned to see how it actually turns out.

The "Astra Way"

First, the context. Astra, owned by worldwide shareholders, is a successful research and marketing pharmaceutical company based in Sweden.[1] For example, in 1996 its drug Losec, used

---

[1] See www.astra.com for information about the company, speeches and press releases.

totreat peptic ulcer disease, became the best-selling pharmaceutical in the world. Astra's sales in 1995 approximated $5 billion. Astra USA, its American subsidiary, grew from $35 million in 1981 to $330 million in 1995. Its president, Lars Bildman, was credited with much of the success of the 1500-employee company.

But it was also Lars Bildman who made Astra a household name in 1996 — at least in business circles —when he appeared on the cover of *Business Week* magazine with the headline, "Abuse of Power," an investigative story which earned the magazine a coveted journalism award.[2]

The details in the story perhaps would have never come to light if Astra USA had even the most rudimentary resources for employee assistance and feedback. Thanks to Astra USA's experience, however, companies and organizations need not learn the same lesson the hard way. They can just turn to the last chapter of our story about Astra.

According to *BusinessWeek*, the corporate culture at Astra USA was bizarre, to say the least. The overriding theme was a militaristic, isolated environment in which evidence of executive power over employees — including alcohol-induced sexual harassment — was rampant. Bildman insisted on rigid rules about attire, lunch times, personal artifacts and control of all communications. According to many, female employees had to be good looking and men were ignored.

Bildman began his control over new recruits at a nine-week training retreat, requiring attendance not only at substantive sessions but also at late night drinking parties, where the harassment often surfaced. The "Astra Way," recruits were told, meant work eight hours, play eight hours and sleep eight hours.[3] "There was a firewall between family and work," said one observer. "Spouses weren't allowed in the building."

The unique Astra atmosphere continued at its national sales meetings, described as drunken partying and opportunities for more harassment by Bildman and other senior executives. Some lower level male managers followed their bosses' example; others were appalled.

---

[2] Mark Maremont, with Jane A. Sasseen, "Abuse of Power," *BusinessWeek*, May 13, 1996, p. 86.

[3] Kimberly Blanton and Tina Cassidy, "'Astra Way' executive fell on a wayward path; Bildman portrayed as driven by work, pleasure," *The Boston Globe*, June 24, 1996, p. C1.

A few women complained and some obtained out-of-court settlements in return for agreements to remain silent. Others, fearing the loss of lucrative sales positions, suffered through it, deciding the potential for retaliation was not worth it. Those who complained to a supervisor often found the complaint went directly to the president, or was ignored.

In 1991 several women tried to deal with the hostile environment internally by calling a meeting to discuss ways to proceed. Top management found out about the meeting and instead of supporting the women, began to focus on the ringleader. Four months later, Astra had driven her from the company with a settlement and confidentiality clause. The women's group never met again.

Ignorance or disbelief?

Astra's response to the *BusinessWeek* six-month investigation into tawdry tales of mind control, attempted rape, firings and company cover-ups was pathetic. First the company asked female sales representatives to sign a letter denying they had seen or experienced any harassment. Then at the initial interview with *BusinessWeek*, General Counsel Charles E. Yon and several female staffers — in the presence of three legal representatives and two public relations consultants — contradicted information *BusinessWeek* had obtained from others.

Bildman told his Swedish superiors about the pending story well before it was published, yet a senior executive of Astra claimed the company was unaware of the details it received from *BusinessWeek* on April 19. On April 29 the parent company suspended Lars Bildman and on May 13 the devastating *BusinessWeek* cover story appeared.

Despite the gory details in the story, Swedish executives' response seemed pale. At Astra's annual meeting in Sweden in May, CEO Hakan Mogren characterized the allegations as "at best a violation of good style and form. At worst, a number of our employees have been caused inconveniences or suffering."

He added that it was not Astra's rules that were at fault. "It is not until the bubble bursts that you find out what has happened," he said, missing the point that the bubble burst because

Astra had no effective internal resources to channel complaints or problems.

Mogren ended his speech, "Moreover I should like to call attention to the fact that sexual harassment is not viewed in the same way in all cultures. Today it is mainly in the U.S. that this issue has come into the spotlight. As I understand it, this is due, among other things, to the legal environment in the country. Many companies have been drawn into legal proceedings and settlements surrounding this issue."

In other words, blame the victim and the litigious American environment that encourages twenty-five year old trainees to complain about a drunken fifty-year old CEO disrobing in a hotel suite and grabbing them, or about a drunken vice president cornering them late at night in a hotel corridor.

Aftermath

In the face of the *Business Week* revelations and investigations by the Equal Employment Opportunity Commission, Astra had to act. It hired its own investigator to look into allegations of sexual harassment, financial improprieties and other activities, including poor communication from the U.S. subsidiary to the parent company in Sweden. On June 26 Astra fired Lars Bildman and George Roadman, its vice president of marketing and sales. Two other executives, Edward Aarons, director of institutional business and Anders Lonner, regional director and head of Swedish marketing operations, agreed to resign.

On September 10, 1996, Astra appointed Ivan Rowley, a veteran of Astra's Canadian subsidiary, as president and CEO of Astra USA, with a mandate to change the corporate culture.

Seventeen months later, Astra announced it had sued its former president, Lars Bildman, accusing him of using company funds to perform $2.3 million of work on three homes. Astra was also seeking reimbursement of company monies Bildman used for personal vacations and prostitutes, as well as amounts Astra would have to pay as the result of the EEOC investigation.

The next day the reasons for the lawsuit became clear, when Astra announced it had entered into a consent decree with the EEOC to resolve claims of employees who were subjected to sexual harassment and retaliation. The claim fund of nearly $10 million agreed to by Astra was a stiff price to pay for not having established mechanisms to learn of and resolve its internal problems.

Obvious in hindsight

How the problems at Astra emerged is easy to understand in hindsight. The company had a sexual harassment policy, but offered no training on what it meant or who to call if there were problems. The human resources function was minimal, and reported to other functional vice presidents. There were no effective communications channels, either from employees to human resources or from human resources to the parent company.

To be fair, Astra's sales staff was far-flung and not concentrated at headquarters. Most of the egregious conduct took place at off-site sales meetings. "There might have been rumors," said one insider, "but things happened on the margin. Where could you go with hearsay? Nothing was clear cut."

If there was fault to find in an organization without resources for assistance, it lies with the members of senior management who knew of the problems with certain executives but didn't report them to Sweden, or with those executives who

> **"A**stra is sorry for the instances of sexual harassment that took place under previous management. To each person who suffered, I offer our apologies. Astra is committed to eliminating sexual harassment. Every complaint of sexual harassment will be investigated promptly, and individuals who engage in inappropriate behavior will be punished."
>
> Ivan R. Rowley
> president and CEO of Astra USA,
> announcing agreement with U.S. Equal Employment
> Opportunity Commission, February 5, 1998

didn't — or chose not to — notice and who therefore failed by sins of omission.

But such inaction is understandable if the individual whose actions you question is the one who controls your paycheck. In those situations, the best defense is a clear company policy that requires communication of suspected wrongdoing, and one that provides a safe channel to make that happen.

A changed culture

Clearly, Astra USA needed not only to respond to its legal and public relations problems, but also needed to effect immediate and obvious changes in its corporate culture.

Lynn Tetrault, who had been a lawyer at Astra for three years prior to the Bildman crisis, was tapped to step into the role of vice president of human resources, an elevated position. She set about to turn the Asta supership around in mid-channel — no easy challenge for a shell-shocked far flung organization. Tetrault stresses that in a time of crisis, support of top management and new leadership is critical. Astra USA received that sustenance, particularly from the new president, Ivan Rowley. At his insistence, she set to work.

"Our immediate need was to revise our policy on sexual harassment and make it clear that we were talking about a zero-tolerance policy," she said. "But we also had to make clear that we had different avenues of communication for employees who had questions or concerns. We listed the names of the human resource professionals employees could contact but also make it clear they could and should inform their managers.

"The next thing we did," Tetrault explained, "was to design a state-of-the-art training program. Within three months we had trained two thousand people in the organization, starting with the executive committee and then rolling it out to managers and employees. It was important for us to focus on employees out in the field and make sure they felt comfortable communicating with management about their concerns.

"One of the problems we uncovered and immediately addressed was the issue of sexual harassment by customers. We made it clear we wouldn't tolerate it and we'd forgo the business rather than subject our employees to any source of harassment.

"We learned something by listening to our employees in the field. It was amazing how often they found themselves in sensitive situations with customers. We even had male sales representatives who were harassed by female doctors, and initially they were reluctant to let us know. But we made it clear we wanted to help them, and where we had to make adjustments in their physician call list, we did. Now our employees tell us they feel much more comfortable letting us know what's going on.

"We thought this issue was so important that we took our program even further, and when we had complaints about particular physicians in hospitals, we went to the human resource departments in those institutions to let them know what we were doing. They've been very responsive. It's harder to reach sole practitioners or other physicians in private practice, but we're committed to it."

Not just training alone

Tetrault and her team approached their task carefully, realizing that simply throwing a myriad of resources, policies and structures would not work by themselves. Intuitively she and others at Astra knew that to bring about a fundamental change in the values of the company, other factors must also be present, including a self-assessment, commitment from the top and organizational ownership. "We had to evaluate what was going on in the field and what it was we were trying to accomplish," she said.

After the crisis the company had been through, with its free-wheeling, unprofessional and unethical conduct at the top, it would have been easy for the new Astra team to react by imposing a lot of strictures. "We didn't want the pendulum to swing too far the other way," she said, "because it would have been natural to have a knee-jerk reaction and put a zillion controls in place. We chose an alternate course. We wanted to make sure that as we were implementing clear policies and training, we were providing avenues for feedback and participation. We specially tried to change a hierarchical, autocratic structure to one what was based on teamwork."

For that reason Rowley saw the formation of task forces as an important employee resource. "We wanted employees to feel they had an opportunity to provide input and take ownership for the kind of company we were creating."

One of the projects the leadership tackled was to change the corporate culture from one that discouraged mixing family and work to one that was family-friendly.

"We established a task force to look at programs such as flex-time, that would support our new work-family goals and we began to make changes. Even little things, like inviting spouses to management meetings, made a difference.

"We changed our sales training programs. Employees would no longer spend nine weeks isolated in a hotel. We discouraged drinking at sales meetings. We eliminated the hospitality suites and the pressure to socialize. We eliminated regimented policies that made no sense."

Tetrault put a great deal of effort into the company's harassment policies and training programs, but explained that Astra rejected the idea of a 1-800-phone line as an employee resource.

"We wanted to focus on changing the culture so that our employees would feel comfortable sharing information with their managers. We felt that to install an anonymous 1-800 line would run the danger of reinforcing an environment of paranoia and fear which was exactly what we were trying to change. We probably wouldn't have gotten the benefit of the phone line in that kind of environment. It was more important to get employees to let someone around them know what was going on, and to build confidence in the field that they could bring information to their managers.

"We specifically didn't want to alienate our field management. A 1-800 line that would go over their heads or around them would at that point only make them nervous. Over time they might be more comfortable with it, but not then."

Tetrault states that employee surveys became an important resource for employee feedback. "We conducted our first survey in September 1996, which provided our baseline measure. It told us we needed to improve in communication, work-family issues and development opportunities. Ivan Rowley, our new president, took the results and matched it with the objectives he set for the senior team. That process ensured that we would meet our goals.

"A year and a half later we repeated the survey. We got a high response rate and it showed tremendous improvement.

"But the best outcome was the number of women in the field who had left the company and who decided to come back. They would tell us, 'This is such a different place.' That was very gratifying. Astra isn't perfect today, but we've made a lot of strides."

With insight, advice for others

Tetrault is thoughtful about the impact that a sudden ethical crisis can have on a company, particularly on those who are charged with the cleanup. There is a balancing test, she believes, between the desire to make a strong impact quickly, and the danger of moving too fast for the organization.

"I'd caution others not to alienate management in the company, particularly if the new programs are being driven by human resources. You want to make sure that management doesn't feel that human resources is all of a sudden working against them, or putting out a message that employees should come directly to human resources with their concerns, instead of to their supervisors. I think in retrospect we could have done a better job of involving management at all levels in understanding what we were doing, and why. But given the magnitude of the concerns we were dealing with at the time, it was hard to do."

One might question the decision to forgo a 1-800 line and other procedures that ethics programs in benchmark companies have put in place. But it seems clear that Rowley and Tetrault have begun a culture change process at Astra that has started to make things right in a company that was way over the line.

Other companies can learn from the Astra experience, just as other companies have found themselves in similar situations. Mitsubishi Motor Manufacturing of America, for example, agreed to pay a total of $34 million to settle a federal lawsuit over sexual harassment at its Normal, Illinois assembly plant filed in 1996. Among the provisions in its settlement agreement was a requirement that Mitsubishi establish a complaint procedure to make it easier for employees to report problems, and that it follow up on complaints within three weeks.

The Astra story reminds us that changing cultures are always more expensive and harder to implement than establishing the right values and resources for assistance from the beginning. We suspect Mitsubishi would agree.

Chapter 16

Organizational Ownership

Ethics officers don't work in isolation and programs designed to put values into action cannot be totally successful without the full involvement of everyone throughout the organization. Even if other elements are in place — strong commitment from the top, communication vehicles and training — organizations still need to exercise caution before initiating a program that will not have the support and "buy-in" of 100 percent of the people and departments affected. Values can't just be mandated. They probably can't even be suggested or encouraged. First, all employees must believe them as important and true in order to take hold.

This is not as much of a "chicken and the egg" scenario as it may seem. While it may be understandable that some managers would think that the way to achieve endorsement from all parties is to announce a program and roll out its elements, the subject is too subjective and too sensitive. Values aren't like sticky paper to be thrown up in the air in the hope that some will adhere.

Think it through

The key to achieving organizational ownership starts with a thought process that determines who the parties are that will be most affected. As we have urged in earlier chapters, *those* are the parties who should have a say in determining what the values of the organization are and should be. Those are the parties who should work on designing the training and communication programs. Those are the parties who will support it in the field or, alternatively, cynically dismiss it.

Here's a brief example. At a company we know, senior managers who had been stung by an earlier ethical scandal were

intent on developing a new program of values and ethics training. They planned to announce it with fanfare. We asked if union
leaders, who represented the majority of the company's employees, had been involved. The managers were surprised at the
question and adamant about the answer. These managers never
let union officials participate in any activity that they considered
"policy-making" or managerial. They weren't about to start now.
We cautioned them that, for that reason alone, the ethics initiative may fail, but they couldn't see it. At that company, organizational ownership meant command-and-control.

Commitment from the top —
tell the truth

Although we have already explained the necessity for commitment from the top, the notion bears repeating in any discussion
of organizational ownership. No organization — even if every
employee group is well represented in the design and implementation of the program — will fully embrace a values-driven culture
if employees sense that senior managers are not true believers in
the program, or believe in it for others but not for themselves.

Thomas L. Friedman in his book on globalization, *The Lexus
and the Olive Tree*,[1] described what we think is a striking example of both the necessity for sincere leadership at the top and of
convincing one's audience of the sincerity of one's views.
Friedman related a story about business corruption in Russia he
heard from Derek Shearer, who served as United States ambas-
sador to Finland in the 1990s. At the U.S. Embassy it was
Shearer's job to visit Finnish business leaders and encourage
them to invest in Russia, suggesting that this was the best way to
produce stability across the border.

But the Finns replied that they'd do business with the
Russians in Finland but not in Russia where it was too corrupt
and dangerous. They had other choices, so why bother with
Russia? Shearer tried to convince them that the goal of regional
stability was worth the risk. Now Shearer is advising several Wall
Street investment firms. From a business point of view, he advises

---

[1] Thomas L. Friedman, *The Lexus and the Olive Tree*, New York: Farrar, Straus &
Giroux, 1999.

that it is crazy to invest in Russia, where there is so much corruption and unpredictability, until it develops appropriate legal infrastructure.

Friedman used the story to illustrate the necessity for fundamental global legal infrastructure that protects business partners no matter where they do business. Those countries that don't put such systems in place will be left behind, he says.

To us, the story tells another tale. We suspect Shearer was wise enough to know that his Finnish business colleagues were right all along. For whatever reason, he perhaps felt he could not speak the truth to them, but we think he missed a chance to demonstrate ethical leadership by not doing so. Clearly, the audience he was trying to convince did not believe his argument and perhaps even felt that he didn't believe it either, as events subsequently demonstrated.

You can't convince your audience to embrace your point of view if you don't believe it yourself, and your audience won't share ownership of your message if it views the facts of the situation differently than you have described. Match your values message both to your core beliefs and the facts.

A totally aligned and integrated culture

In our view, one of the best thinkers on the subject of developing a mature values-driven environment is Glenn Coleman of EDS. For several years Coleman has described his five levels of an ethical culture — commitment, formulation, action and feedback, re-evaluation and total ethical culture.[2] Many organizations new to the business ethics movement look to Coleman's fifth level as their goal. At that level, communication is open and candid. Trust and integrity are commonplace — unethical behavior is a surprise. Business decisions are made daily with ethics in mind, given as much importance as cost considerations and personnel needs. Discussions of ethics appear on every meeting agenda. Not just employees, but customers and suppliers feel free to ask questions about ethics and raise ethical issues.

---

[2] Glenn Coleman, "The Totally Aligned Ethical Culture — One Step at a Time," presentation at the Ethics Officer Association annual conference, October 23, 1998.

All that sounds very good, except that in Coleman's view, it's not good enough anymore. He suggests that there may be a danger that no one is watching the ethics office and the company management, a particularly critical situation if the two are heading down divergent paths.

Coleman has now added a sixth level to his presentations — "total alignment and integration." At that level, the mission of the ethics and values initiatives must point to and support one or more of the company's goals. If there is not a connection, either the ethics office should alter its goal or raise the issue with company leadership as to why there is a disconnect. From the employee's perspective, the code of ethics and statement of values and principles are one and the same. A few statements of values replace volumes of rules and policies. Legal compliance becomes a value. Work relationships are based on candor and trust. Leadership arises from within and at every appropriate level. The organization becomes the employer of choice. Good employees stay; those who can't work in a highly integrated ethical culture leave.

"I've often stated my job as an ethics officer was to work myself out of a job," Coleman said. Perhaps he is right. In companies that do not have ethics officers, the goal of a totally aligned ethics culture is reached if every employee sees him or herself as an ethics officer, doing the right thing not just because they understand and subscribe to the company's values, but because doing so is one of their own values.

How it's done

Achieving organizational ownership of company values is a continuous process of communication, discussion, and debate throughout all areas of the organization. In some cases, the same is true outside as well. One effective technique is to establish multidepartmental committees as supporting structures to any ethics initiative. At senior levels, with managers drawn from diverse departments across the company (such as human resources, security, legal and auditing being key), an ethics officer has a "kitchen cabinet" to serve as a sounding board and to drive ownership of the program throughout all areas of the business. The committee also helps bring to bear the resources available in participating departments.

In chapter 20 we include the charter of USAA's Ethics Council, a group of four senior level executives who review issues of major significance and take appropriate action. USAA's ethics coordinator works closely with the council. Other companies have found that such a committee plays a useful role, but with a very different membership composition. At Detroit Edison, the Chairman's Ethics Council is comprised of 18 members, ranging from the chairman to union officials, and has both represented and management employees. Such a diverse cross-section of council membership also helps in establishing company-wide ownership.

One risk of a corporate-directed ethics initiative is that outlying areas and locations may not embrace it quite so readily. To prevent this possibility, some companies have deputized specific managers in the field to be responsible for implementing ethics initiatives in their area. These managers then become ethics champions and gadflies, and cascade the process further. Depending on the industry, some companies have assigned responsibility for coverage for discrete risk areas, so that employees have a subject matter expert to turn to when they have questions. These "responsible officers" for each subject area develop an expertise in certain high-risk areas, such as environmental compliance, and may work in teams with a lawyer or manager for responsibility in the area.

We recommend that companies not stop at the employee level in communicating and reinforcing their message about values. Customers, suppliers and strategic business partners are key constituents who should be brought into the ethics tent. Depending on a company's business, nongovernmental organizations (NGOs) might be key opinion leaders in influencing the design of a values and ethics program. Frank Vogl, senior fellow at the Ethics Resource Center, believes that including NGOs in the process of building awareness and support for business values and principles is not just a matter of corporate choice, but an imperative.[3] Too often, he says, multinational corporations approach ethics issues in a disjointed way. They have compliance people doing compliance in one office and environmental

---

[3] Frank Vogl, "More and more, industries must incorporate social issues in management for success," *The Earth Times*, 1998.

officers working on environmental issues elsewhere. They think labor and human rights issues belong to the human resources department. Meanwhile, the company is missing the big picture, which NGOs not only see but also monitor and communicate to advocacy groups.

The necessity for a comprehensive and coordinated approach to ethical practices is particularly acute because of the proliferation of web sites and outsiders exposing every facet of a company's operation. If activists, journalists, investors, citizens, pressure groups, international bodies and government officials are all poking around at every level and in every nook and cranny, all employees must not only act ethically, but feel responsible to report any suspected wrongdoing in the company, before others find it.

The question of ownership of ethical issues in an organization also arises in the context of departmental responsibility. While some companies have made great strides to eliminate the "silo" approach to certain issues (where compensation belongs to human resources, expense reporting belongs to auditing and random drug testing belongs to security, for example), others

> **"What** really drives our business is our people. The people we have out there on the line, making professional judgments, rendering opinions, every single day. The choices they make set precedents for us. They create expectations on the part of our clients. They define the values of our organization.
>
> If you think about our number of people around the world, it's not an organization where legislation works. You really have to have some glue to hold things together. So we created resources to help our people make ethical decisions as they experience them."
>
> Nicholas G. Moore
> chairman, PricewaterhouseCoopers,
> from his *Sears Lecture in Business Ethics*
> at Bentley College, February 9, 1998

are still resisting the idea that challenges to a company's values can and should be answered by everyone.

This question of "who owns ethics" arises most frequently in the arena of shareholder resolutions. If ethics champions see their role narrowly, of driving values-based training programs through the employee population base, whose responsibility is it to decide whether the company should advertise on the Howard Stern Show? Should do business in Burma? Should save costs by eliminating departments and outsourcing? Should reprice under-water stock options for senior executives? Should sell products that don't meet U.S. standards in countries whose standards are lower? The list can go on and on, but these challenging ethical issues, often raised by outsiders, will not go away. In the most ethically mature organizations, operated by values-driven man-agement at all levels, everyone owns these problems and should deliberate the company's position.

Ownership across the globe

There is a new challenge facing many companies today. Not only do they seek to implement values-driven management at home, they must also consider how to achieve it in all their global oper-ations. To do it half-way makes little sense, but even the most naïve managers realize they can't just translate their codes and communications brochures into a foreign language hoping that their oversees employees will embrace the message, as Texas Instruments discovered.

In seeking organizational ownership for company values across cultures, managers must strike a balance between adher-ence to their core values and principles and respect for foreign environments. The two extremes we see are ethical fanaticism and ethical relativism. One says, "My way is absolutely right," and the other says, "There is nothing absolutely right."

Finding the moral ground between these two extremes and achieving organizational ownership of it throughout the world usually require some modification of existing programs. The process is much the same as we have outlined in this book. Here are a few steps to follow:

First, assess what are the risk areas in other areas of the com-pany and locations. Gift-giving, for example, may be a sensitive area in a U.S. purchasing department but not a matter of concern in Asia, where gift-giving is routine and considered hospitable.

Due diligence and business relationships with venture partners may be handled routinely in some countries. However in countries where business partners may not have the same standards or values they may require special risk assessments. The same applies where the venture partner may be a government agency with a questionable reputation for integrity.

Determine what additional or different resources may be necessary in other countries. Reporting and advice mechanisms, for example, might not be easily duplicated in cultures where employees are not accustomed to reporting wrongdoing or where time zone or language differences may impede communication. Local resources will probably be needed.

Finally, be sensitive when developing and crafting communication pieces, including training programs. It is always best if they are prepared by indigenous employees in the country where the material is to be used. If that isn't possible, they should at least be tested thoroughly to surface unanticipated problems or reactions to certain words, concepts or procedures.[4]

Many companies are already aware that operating globally brings with it the challenges of conveying their core values in a way that insures ownership internationally. While a majority of companies who distribute their code of conduct to international employees indicated that it is the same code used in the United States, they also said that they reinforce it with training, in order to fully communicate the importance of global core values.

Diane McDaniel, director of corporate conduct and business ethics at Texaco, says that her company takes the challenge of globalization further. At Texaco, detailed ethics materials are customized for each country, so that the guidelines will be relevant to local laws and customs. In any case, she emphasized the core values and policies of Texaco remain the same wherever company employees work.[5]

---

[4] For additional ideas see Lori Tansey and Kris Day, "Five Common Mistakes in Designing and Implementing a Business Ethics Program," *Business and Society Review*, Vol. 104, No. 2, Summer 1999, pp. 163-170.

[5] "Survey of Global Ethics Practices," *Federal Ethics Report*, February 1999, p. 2.

One last word

Just as many financial advisors advocate the "KISS" strategy to their clients — "Keep It Simple, Stupid" — we advocate the "GBIS" strategy to implement values-driven management — "Get Buy-In, Stupid." To think that an ethics program will succeed without GBIS up-front, everywhere and often, is like thinking your football team will win with only your quarterback knowing the plays. Taking all of our ten steps together, none is more important to values-driven management than organizational ownership. In fact, you will find that it is an essential ingredient to what we say about rolling out many of the other steps.

Chapter 17

Orange and Rockland
THE CHALLENGE
OF INCLUSION

Many companies have done a good job in establishing the basics of a values-based ethics program. Few, however, have given as much thought to including everyone in a leadership capacity as has Orange and Rockland Utilities, Inc., the New York utility serving thousands of electric and gas customers in New York, New Jersey and Pennsylvania,

O&R's focus on organizational ownership of its ethics program was born of necessity, when a scandal scarred its long-service, union employees and exposed some corrupt senior executives. Rank and file employees were not implicated in wrongdoing, but they bore the burden of their company's tarnished reputation. While they had once been proud to wear the O&R uniform, carrying on the tradition of community service and neighborliness begun by generations before them, suddenly they were embarrassed, angry and betrayed by the company they loved.

Power, perks and poor judgment

To understand what O&R has achieved, it is necessary to understand how far the company has come since the days in 1993 when some of its senior corporate officials were accused of embezzlement, abuse of power and election law violations. What were perceived to be arrogant violations of law and of customers' trust outraged community leaders, state regulatory commissions, the district attorney and the community. By August 1993, O&R found itself subject to scrutiny by public service commissions in three states, and a grand jury. The board of directors launched its own internal investigation and heard from employees across the organization. The results were not surprising: a deeply flawed corporate culture that allowed and encouraged the improper use of company funds and an intimidated internal audit system which accommodated the concealment of wrongdoing. Add good financial results, few checks and balances and a lack of trust of senior management, and it was a recipe for disaster.

The cleanup

The atmosphere in the O&R executive suites on the 21st floor in Pearl River, New York was not good, but those who were left with the responsibility to change the corporate culture set about to restoring confidence in the company. It was not an easy job, as employees felt betrayed by what had happened. Understandably, some cynical and suspicious employees felt that an ethics initiative was just a tactic to placate the regulators and investigators and to provide legal cover for the board of directors.

But the company, now under probation for seven years with an inspector general assigned to oversee its activities, took steps to address its problems. Officers established an Ethics Task Force of representatives throughout the organization and began a communication program to share findings from employee surveys and interviews. They also shared information about the company's policies and avenues for reporting wrongdoing.

Within six months, the task force had updated its code of ethics and distributed it to all employees, created an ethics office and helpline system, developed policies to assure that investigations would be conducted fairly, and began an extensive ethics training program.

The Ethics Task Force

Former ethics officer Richard White stated that the turnaround at O&R was helped by the thought given to the makeup of the first Ethics Task Force.[1] One of the original members was a surveyor, a

---

[1] Andrew W. Singer, "O&R's Ethics Council Includes All Levels of the Company," *ethikos*, Vol. 10, No. 3, Nov/Dec1996, p.1.

35-year veteran of the company and a union member. Although as skeptical as some of his other union peers, he offered important suggestions about the rollout of the new code of conduct.

One of the early tasks of the task force was to determine whether a coordinating body should continue to exist after the ethics office was established. It was decided that a reconstituted Ethics Council would continue to meet, comprised of representatives from legal, human resources and audit, as well as union members. The union president was asked to nominate a group of candidates for the council, two of whom would be selected by management to serve. Understanding that the perspective of union representatives was important in a company with 65% union membership, the task force decided to select four union members for the 12-person council. These included the surveyor, a customer service representative, a stock handler and a secretary.

According to White, the union representatives asked important questions. They wanted assurances that the ethics officer's telephone line was secure and that files were safe. In fact, it was the makeup of the ethics council that helped him launch a successful program. Because the company was mandated to include monitoring by an inspector general as part of its plea agreement with the district attorney, some argued that the company didn't need another outsider. The first ethics officer should be someone employees knew and trusted, and so White, who had 29 years experience at O&R, began his new role in February 1995. White, who reported to the CEO and the audit committee of the board of directors, said, "I would never consider not having union people on the ethics council. They bring a practical point of view. They know how things actually work."[2]

Fast-forward a few years — a new ethics officer

When Richard White announced his retirement from Orange and Rockland, the ethics council formed a task force (including the union president) to begin searching for a new ethics officer. The job opening was posted and employees were encouraged to

---

[2] Ibid.

apply. Sixteen did so. Meanwhile, John Ferraro, an architect and eight-year veteran of the company, was on vacation.

When Ferraro returned, his union foreman approached him with the announcement and said, "You should apply for this." Ferraro hesitated. He had no formal training in ethics but decided to participate in the verbal and written interview that the task force had prepared to screen candidates. The top four candidates were invited for a second verbal and written interview and the top three scores were forwarded to the chairman of the audit committee and the CEO. "Every answer I gave, I learned in kindergarten," Ferraro said. "My responses were more instinctive than learned." Ferraro was interviewed and took over as O&R's new ethics officer in July 1998.

Organizational ownership on two fronts

As ethics officer, Ferraro, in cooperation with the council, chooses the twelve members of the Business Ethics Council, which provides guidance and direction in the development and implementation of ethics policies. The council also encourages ethical decision-making and promotes programs that enhance ethical awareness across the company. Ferraro has continued the practice of including four union members on the council, having experienced the value their perspective.

"The wonderful thing about the council is that its members become a liaison for issues to reach me. It's a great advantage for union members, because the represented employees are able to reach them, and they feel comfortable doing so. By having a mix of members, everyone is responsible for our values-based programs. There's no union/management division. Everyone takes off their hats and just discusses ethics. The issue can't be tainted or politicized by any management or labor relations considerations. Ethics in that sense is like safety — it's everyone's responsibility and concern.

"We have a busy council. We consider any issue that relates to our present code of conduct. Right now we're working on a revision. For example, we have a provision that prohibits contact with local politicians. It's very restrictive and therefore it was interpreted by employees to mean that you can't have lunch,

"The mission of the Council is to provide guidance and direction in the development and implementation of policies which shape the ethical environment of the Company. The Council will seek to proactively encourage responsible ethical decision-making and promote programs that enhance ethical awareness among employees. The council will help ensure that ethical considerations remain a top priority of the Company."

Mission
The Business Ethics Council of
Orange and Rockland Utilities, Inc.

can't treat them, and just about can't look at them. It's probably a reaction to our previous scandal. Now if your neighbor was the superintendent of highways, and you work in the gas department, you need to have a good relationship with that person. It's too punitive to suggest you can't even have a cup of coffee with him.

"Our employees said, 'Loosen the reins. Give us some latitude.' The council was our forum to discuss the issue from all points of view and resolve it. Employees were clear in their perspective that the code of conduct was unduly restrictive. 'You can't continue to pound employees with this punitive approach,' they said, and we ended up agreeing that this issue should be addressed."

Ferraro chairs the Business Ethics Council. He also chairs O&R's advisory committee, which reviews ethics cases and applies discipline. The committee is comprised of the director of human resources, the internal legal liaison, the inspector general, and the director of auditing. Once a month the committee reviews cases, without knowing the names of the offenders.

"I'd like union representation on the advisory committee as well," said Ferraro. "I've found it's much easier to apply ethical principles if the union is involved in the investigation, and I think a union member would add value on this committee as well as the council. This is going to be a challenge but I believe it will result in a truly sincere process."

A backward step

Things may sound idyllic now at Orange and Rockland, but Ferraro admits that is not the case. "We still have a young program," he said, "and we took five steps back this year when the union president and then other union representatives pulled their support from our ethics program."

Ferraro tells the sad story. Orange and Rockland was on the verge of a merger with Consolidated Edison Inc. when he heard allegations that some senior managers, just prior to leaving the company, had proposed actions which some employees believed to be unethical — although legal. Since the allegations were highly sensitive, Ferraro bypassed internal resources and went directly to the chairman of the audit committee of the board of directors, backed by the inspector general. The chairman took prompt and appropriate action and the matter was over. At least Ferraro thought it was over.

Not unexpectedly, the facts of the case were distorted and rumors reached members of the council, who confronted Ferraro. "You voted not to know the details of cases," he reminded them. "Do you want to revote and change your operating procedures and become involved with investigations?"

The council decided that resolution of cases was still within the purview of the advisory committee.

As a result of distorted facts and rumors the union president withdrew his support of the ethics process. In a letter, he wrote that the IBEW had always been "a strong supporter of the Ethics Program at Orange and Rockland. In the beginning all of the employees, my members included, were skeptical as to whether the ethics program would work but assurances were given at all levels. The fears of everyone were, temporarily, put to rest."

But, he went on, the positive feelings did not last. "I am left with no other choice than to withdraw any support from Local Union 503 IBEW until such time as ALL employees are treated equally."

Ferraro is hopeful that when the merger is completed, the union representatives will return to the council. He believes that no values-driven program can reach its full potential without their involvement, and he hopes to establish separate ethics councils in individual company locations that will also include union members.

"I honestly feel that working with many of them came close to a spiritual experience for all of us," Ferraro said. "It was that important and meaningful. I'm not going to give up. I have a 'carpenter bee' philosophy. I work slowly and persistently, chipping away at a surface. I'm just going to keep working my way in to try to gain back their confidence and participation."

Ferraro's comment bears emphasis. Underlying all religions is the concept of morality, but in many workplace arenas, "God talk," as Catholic Worker Movement founder Dorothy Day once described it, is deemed inappropriate. But one evidence of the shift in our secular culture towards that of the sacred, or spiritual, may well be the pursuit of values and moral conduct in everyday life, including in the workplace. It is surely more acceptable to talk about "values" than religion. And for many, the two concepts are connected. It is not surprising, therefore, to hear that inclusive efforts to develop an ethical program are a "spiritual experience."

Employees — whether managers or represented workers — don't check their values or aspirations at the workplace door. The work of building an ethical culture meets the need of many individuals to pursue something other than just secular, materialistic activities. It may be what Professor Robert Coles of Harvard calls the intersection of secular thinking with the constant search for moral, if not spiritual, sanction.[3] Perhaps the pursuit of values in every facet of our life is what being human is all about. What a tribute to an organization like Orange and Rockland for an employee to discover — and express the fact — that his higher aspirations can be fulfilled in part at work. But Ferraro is not alone in his quest.

Commitment from the top

One of the tunes on our broken record called *implementing values-driven management* is "commitment from the top," discussed in chapter 6. No values-driven program can succeed without it. With its scandal behind it and its ethics infrastructure in place,

---

[3] Robert Coles, *The secular mind*, Princeton University Press, 1999.

Orange and Rockland is fortunate to have a new president, as a result of its merger with Con Ed. Kevin Burke, who was tapped to lead O&R in mid-1999, believes in not only the benefit of a values-driven approach to management, but in including all employees in its development and implementation.

"I have observed and concluded that bad management gives rise to unethical cultures," said Ferraro. "The opposite is also true. Good management style helps produce an ethical culture. In a short time, Kevin Burke has made an impact on O&R. He's very approachable, wants to learn about what we've been trying to do, and has made an immediate impact on employees, who perceive him to be fair and honest. As a result, our ethics process has benefited."

Burke shares Ferraro's sentiments about organizational ownership. "Ethical values evolve from within each employee," said Burke. "They are not defined by a union contract nor are they reserved for management. We are all equally empowered to proudly emulate our ethical convictions and dedicate ourselves towards achieving a positive, values-based program that includes all employees."

The only way to make music

Ferraro is a firm believer that every segment of an organization — directors, executives, departments, remote locations, hourly employees and others — must feel a proprietary interest in an ethics program if it is to succeed. His role is perhaps the least important. "I *serve* the council. Its members are the ethics advocates and program directors, not me. It is better for them to function together, on their own, away from me, because if in the future there is no ethics officer, they an still emanate ethics throughout the council and the company.

"I look at it this way. A values-driven initiative is like making music. If you were to gather the best musicians to form an orchestra and provide them with a score, one that outlines the rules and regulations to execute the piece, if they do not play in unison the result is noise, not music. If a whole section, union musicians, decides not to play, the piece becomes fragmented and loses its spirit. Most tragic is if they all choose not to play. The result is a silent piece of paper never discovering its potential to become beautiful music.

"It's the same with ethics and values. You can have the best-written code of conduct with all the required legal ingredients, but if it doesn't result in an ethical, employee-empowered culture, all you have is a two dimensional silent compliance manual. You need everyone involved in bringing the culture to life, making ethical music together."

Chapter 18

Consistent Standards and Enforcement

When we first described our ten-point program for implementing values-driven management, we were sure that consistent standards and enforcement had to be an integral part of any program's effectiveness. After all, we reasoned, the most effective way to undercut an ethics program is to establish a uniform standard of conduct or values and then to discipline a low level employee while ignoring a similar wrongdoing by a senior executive or star performer. Another way to ruin a well-intentioned program is to carefully craft company values and standards but then, by direction or negligence, end up with several standards depending on the individuals, departments, locations, or countries involved. This should be avoided at all costs, we said.

Then we changed our minds.

The issue of inconsistency

We became persuaded that the goal we sought was *consistent core values across an organization.* Inconsistent application was permitted if it could be explained convincingly to our mothers —never a bad test for any ethical dilemma. For example, individuals at senior levels of an organization can, and perhaps should, be held to higher standards of conduct than others. Similarly, there may be divisions, departments or areas of a company or organization that should be held to higher standards of conduct than the rest of the company. There are some industries, companies, or organizations that should be managed and run with a more stringent set of values than others, such as government agencies or regulated industries. Not all individuals, companies or institutions are created equal. To paraphrase a familiar saying, much is expected from those to whom much has been given.

Here is a more detailed look at some of these differences.

Application of values

Not all ethical dilemmas about uneven application of standards or values involve misconduct. Consider the following scenario and stated organizational values of "care" and "respect" and "responsibility" in a hypothetical company called Bliss Manufacturing. Bliss has a general policy of prohibiting employee solicitations in the workplace, except for the company-endorsed annual United Way drive. The intent of this policy is to

> **"W**ell, you know, there's a difference between a parking ticket and a speeding ticket. So, what we do, is we have a disciplinary council. It's made up of colleagues. And you know what's interesting about America — we find that your colleagues will be tougher on you than I probably would be. We have a system where we take violations, and if they're egregious violations you get fired. If they're violations of judgment, whatever they might be, there may be a different sort of punishment.
>
> If I had to make a point on this, it's the visibility of our process and actually showing our people that we do hold people accountable— that is most important. You can have all the rules you want, but you need a couple of examples. And people are pretty smart. People know if you make a small violation, you deserve a small penalty. But if you make a bigger violation, you deserve a bigger penalty. And I think that's the example. And I guess we're in a world today where accountability is more the theme than permissiveness."
>
> Ivan Seidenberg
> CEO and chairman, Bell Atlantic Corporation,
> from his *Sears Lecture in Business Ethics*
> at Bentley College, April 13, 1998

guarantee that workers do not feel pressured to contribute money or join organizations and to respect their privacy.

The son of a well-liked manager was involved in a serious automobile accident and his supervisor and co-workers wanted to plan an event to raise money for the boy's continuing care and to use company resources to inform all employees. The supervisor approached the ethics committee to ask if this would be permitted. The committee generally encouraged employees to take responsibility for their own decisions at the local level. But in pointing out relevant factors, the committee stressed considerations such as the pressure on co-workers to participate and contribute money, the precedent such an event might set, the use of company resources for this cause but not another, and obligations to other needy employees. Ultimately, however, the committee left the decision to the supervisor. The supervisor went ahead with plans for the event, much to the consternation of the ethics committee, which in hindsight thought it should simply have denied the request. Now it was left with the problem of uneven enforcement of company policies.

We won't try to solve this dilemma, except to point out that it is typical of situations occurring in the workplace —which we'd call a weighing of two "rights." In truth, it doesn't present the same ethical considerations such as a more pressing decision about whether to continue manufacturing a product that has great usefulness but might cause harm.

In thinking through the ramifications of a values-driven management culture, however, it is necessary to understand and consider the instances in which the same values or standards of conduct might not apply to everyone equally.

Are there double standards? yes and no

Dave Walsh, vice president, ethics, at Niagara Mohawk, the large upstate New York utility company, cites one example of what he calls "different," not "double" standards.

"Our represented employees are paid for overtime according to our collective bargaining agreement. So if one of our line mechanics were working from 7 a.m. until 9 p.m., he'd be paid

"Our code of conduct requires that each employee must observe the highest principles of business ethics while performing their assigned duties. The adherence to these principles is a constant ... but because assigned duties can vary greatly, the way people act out these principles can also vary. It's a subject of much discussion and, sometimes, disagreement."

David J. Walsh
vice president, ethics, Niagara Mohawk

overtime for the extra hours. If one of our executives were working from 7 am until 6 p.m. in the office and then attending a United Way dinner until 9 p.m., obviously we wouldn't pay him extra. That's part of his job. Similarly, the line mechanic can't drink while he's at work. The executive at the dinner might have a drink, because we feel that you can conduct yourself the same as any other attendee at those events after normal business hours. He's not being paid those hours to be there. At some point your life is your own even when you're representing the company, as long as you conduct yourself appropriately."

The challenge of creating realistic standards is one that takes thought and discussion, Walsh says. "We're in a conservative mode right now, after some problems. But we have to be careful when we are crafting policies not to make them so conservative as to be unrealistic. If we do, we'll end up with a double standard, as some people will follow them and others won't."

Walsh gives the example of the company limit on extending or accepting invitations. "The previous limit prohibited invitations that went beyond a 'minimal' amount. But our employees were looking for more certainty. They wanted to be sure they were following what the company had in mind.

"It turned out that it wasn't that simple to decide what was 'minimal.' At first, we thought $25 per quarter would be about right. You couldn't accept or extend an invitation beyond that limit. But then someone noticed we had company tickets that we use to bring customers to the Buffalo Sabres games. Each ticket was valued at higher than $25. So essentially we were saying that we thought it was unethical to bring a guest a ticket to a Sabres game. Obviously that wasn't right. So after much discussion, we raised the limit to $75 per quarter. In the present business climate and given today's prices, that is much more realistic and achieves our goal."

Organizational standards and individual standards

Companies that resist articulating and imposing specific corporate values on all their employees sometimes use the excuse that doing so would be too patronizing or paternalistic. If they hire principled, ethical employees, they perhaps assume that all of them would hold essentially the same values. But in practice that does not turn out to be the case.

Bobby (Barbara) Kipp, a partner at the global accounting firm PricewaterhouseCoopers (PwC), is director of the firm's ethics and business conduct office. She believes that the ideal goal should be an alignment of individual work behaviors with corporate values. "We don't necessarily suggest that people leave their personal values at home and just subscribe to ours," she explains. "But we do expect people to live by our code of conduct, and the values that we have said are paramount to our business. If you do it right over time, if you are upfront with people when you recruit them, and make it clear that this is what is expected of them at work, and that the organization's culture supports and rewards those behaviors, then you will get the right people joining, and they'll be happy staying. What we might say to our people is 'if any of your individual values are not in line with ours, you do need to leave them at home.' Chances are, people with serious values mismatches won't stay with the firm very long.

"For example, people who thrive on being individual 'stars' might feel that an organization where teaming work and sharing are highly valued is not the right place for them. It's also important, if a company is serious about its values, that they also look to the organizational process and policies also. If you expect your people to live your values, then the organization has to be serious about living the values as well."

What works for a large organization such as PricewaterhouseCoopers, with 150,000 partners and staff based in over 500 offices in 150 countries, may not be applicable to smaller companies. In organizations with fewer people, or in workplaces where people primarily interact with each other rather than with customers in the field, it is easier to tell if an employee does not exhibit the same values and standards of conduct that the company espouses.

"Those companies have the benefit of transparency," Kipp says. "They are more apt to be able to rely on company folklore and storytelling to communicate what is expected. A large company can't just rely on that.

"This isn't simply a mater of having a lot of people, it's also the sheer volume of throughput. For an organization such as PricewaterhouseCoopers, with say, 25% growth and 15% staff turnover, this means that up to 60,000 people need to be assimilated each year. Folklore and story telling takes time and personal attention, something that simply isn't available for organizations operating on this scale."

Dave Walsh is careful about the language he uses when discussing what individuals do and what companies can require. "I don't like the words 'moral' or 'morality.' Let's take the issue of gambling. It's not inherently unethical or immoral to gamble; in many instances it is legal. But I prefer to use the word 'fair.' Is it fair to our customers to allow gambling at work? It's also a productivity issue. We just don't want our employees spending time on it at work."

Organizational standards and industry standards

How does a company integrate its standards and values with those of the rest of the industry? This is a challenging issue, particularly for those operating in highly competitive fields.

On the one hand, trade association or industry codes of ethics and models for behavior are often limited. Kipp cites the American Institute of Certified Public Accountants' code as an example. "While helpful, the AICPA standards only relate to a limited segment of our professional activities and our concerns. It is beneficial in that in the subject areas it covers, it sets shared guidelines for the industry with regard to such issues as independence, conflicts of interest and contingent fees. On the other hand, we can't rely on the AICPA to be the standard-bearer for all of PwC because our services extend beyond accounting and auditing. Our code covers other subjects, such as the respect we show to fellow employees and clients."

Industry codes of ethics can, however, be particularly helpful if they set an elevated standard that all competitors agree to abide by. One ethics officer explained the process that his organization was struggling with. "We are trying to craft a segment of our values statement and code of conduct that would impose high standards on our marketing professionals. We think it is the right thing to do, but we also understand that none of our competitors have done so. Our marketing professionals are resisting, because they feel we are hamstringing them and they will lose out on business opportunities.

"This is one instance in which it would certainly be easier if our national trade association took on this issue and developed a code that all the major industry leaders would agree to abide by. At that point, we would be competing solely on the basis of price and quality of service — not on the basis of who has the best scoop on the other. Until that happens, we will have different standards than the rest of our peers. On the other hand, values do define the culture and that includes but goes beyond standards and ethics. For example, one organization can believe its success depends on careful, cautious, sustained action, and that can be valid, given their strategy. In our organization, we value agility and courage, because those values support our strategy."

Enforcement of the same rules — equal or not?

Harry Britt, global manager of ethics and business conduct at PwC, says that the firm works hard to ensure consistent standards of discipline. "We do our dead level best to treat everyone equally," he says.

Interestingly enough, Kipp has a somewhat different opinion. "In the big picture, Harry may be right. But *de facto*, the application of discipline differs."

What's going on here? Dissension in the ranks of the same ethics office?

No, we hear this debate and discussion all the time. Britt and Kipp are both right.

Harry: "The code of conduct is policy. So it should apply to everyone in the firm, across the board, whether you are a senior manager or work in the mailroom. If I misuse my office computer, I'll get the same discipline as anyone else. There are no exceptions."

Bobby: "We should and do make allowances for mitigating circumstances. In many areas, we hold higher level people to a higher standard. For example, if there were allegations of sexual harassment in an office, we would expect the person in the mailroom, who overheard or suspected it, to know that he had an obligation to report it. But we would expect the office manager to do more. He should know that any suspicion of sexual harassment is serious and should be reported immediately. And in addition, we would expect him to take action.

"Similarly, we have a rule about giving and accepting gifts. It's generally a $100 limit. But if the chairman of the largest company in the United Kingdom, for example, gave our chairman a gift that we thought was valued at $150, we would not expect our chairman to refuse it. He should probably accept it graciously as long as he was convinced it was not given with the intent of influencing a specific decision. But if our mailroom supervisor were given a gift of something worth $150 from an overnight shipping company that wanted more of our business, we would expect him to refuse it. We think that, in some areas, the standards need to be adapted to specific dynamics, while fitting into the overall principles and their foundation."

The answer, Britt and Kipp agree, is a process insuring that individual incidents are handled consistently and discipline is reviewed by the same people in the organization. "I don't know of any large, dispersed organization that has cracked this nut," Kipp says. "But I know many, like PwC, that have taken steps to put as much consistency in the process as is possible. Here the ethics office reviews cases that come to us and we have confidence that there is consistency at each level."

Britt cautions that companies cannot rely on helpline data or even the ethics office as the sole source of information about whether standards are being enforced uniformly. "We support the idea of ethics liaisons across all areas of an organization. In PwC, for example, we have 35 individuals acting as liaisons for our 6 service lines. When we meet and talk together, we discuss problems and information, and the liaisons and our office share their concerns and experiences with each other. It's a good link to the field to help us find out where the worries are coming from."

Dave Walsh has 8000 employees working at Niagara Mohawk to service an area of 24,000 square miles, but his system of enforcing uniform discipline is helped by two factors. First, union officials represent the majority of his organization. Therefore the company has a long line of arbitration decisions that provide guidelines for consistency.

"We usually agree with the union on two issues," says Walsh. "First, should the employee have done what he or she did? Probably not. Second, should something be done as a consequence? Definitely yes. It is the answer to the third question, the 'what,' that sometimes causes arbitrations. But we arrive at an answer."

For the nonrepresented employee, Walsh insures consistency by overseeing the human resource function and by the use of the Ethics Oversight Committee, which handles allegations against officers of the company. Walsh also reports to the committee concerning general ethics matters and how they were handled.

At some companies, disciplinary action procedures and sanctions are thorough. At New York Life Insurance Company, supervisors are given a detailed guide to the disciplinary action process, modeled on the sanction guidelines published by the National Association of Securities Dealers. The guide does not prescribe fixed actions for particular offenses, but helps managers through the decision-making process. According to John H. O'Byrne, vice president of New York Life, these are only guidelines. Actual circumstances on a case by case basis will determine the disciplinary action. Disciplinary actions are reviewed by third parties to ensure consistency and fairness.

As You Formulate Your Recommendation for Discipline:

Determine the seriousness of the offense by considering the:

- **Extent of harm or injury to customers and/or the company and/or other agents/managers**
- **Absence or presence of a reasonable explanation for the conduct**
- **Evidence to determine whether the conduct was intentional or reckless, negligent or inadvertent**
- **Evidence of misrepresentation, forgery and/or misappropriation**

In general, the misconduct can be viewed in a progression:

Less serious	*Serious*	*Most serious*
Inadvertent	Negligent	Reckless; willful
No harm to customer or company	Some harm to one or a few customers	Serious harm to a customer/customers
Reasonable explanation for conduct exists	Explanation for conduct exists but does not excuse	No explanation exists

Managing Partner's Guide to the Disciplinary Action Process,
New York Life Insurance Company

What if it's not an ethical issue?

Deciding what is fair to one set of individuals versus other individuals may depend on the subject matter. In some companies, the first evaluation that must be made is whether the issue concerns a core value of the organization or a serious violation of the code of conduct. In some cases, managers conclude that the issue doesn't rise to that level of concern, even though it engenders a great deal of discussion.

For example, PricewaterhouseCoopers, like many companies, recently changed its policy on office space. In a move to reduce costs for real estate and accommodate professionals who rarely use a company office, the firm utilizes "hoteling," the practice of assigning office space to employees only when they need it. According to Kipp and Britt, the move caused considerable discussion among those who were affected, but not a single call was made to the ethics office about it. Individuals didn't think the process was unethical.

Similarly, PwC instituted a new policy on independence. Independence is the ability to act with integrity and objectivity in fact and appearance with respect to work performed for clients. Personal obligations must be sufficiently separate from client interests to allow services to be truly objective. The independence rules are often complex, and previously there had been different standards depending on the level of the employee. For example, Kipp, a partner, could not invest in any PwC audit client. Managers had been less restricted, so Britt, who is based in Boston, was prohibited from investing in an audit client of the Boston office, but could invest in non-Boston clients. The independence policy was changed to be more restrictive for managers. "Everyone has been talking about this new policy for managers and we got a lot of questions on how to apply it," says Kipp, "but again, we didn't receive any complaints that the policy change itself was unfair."

Dave Walsh spends considerable time with his human resource, audit, legal and environmental allies to discuss and resolve the line between ethical violations and other issues. "I get involved primarily if it rises to the level of a potential termination, but our staff in the field spend a lot of time hashing out other issues. When does a case of an abusive supervisor rise to the level of an ethics case? Issues involving safety violations or poor job performance are clearly not ethical matters, but sometimes the line isn't clear. It helps to keep discussing these cases and arriving at consensus on what we should do."

On the job, off the job

Many organizations are struggling with the issue of whether an individual's character and behavior off the job should fall within an employer's purview. Years ago, the answer was clearly "no." If the actions were not job related, not on company time or company property, it was impractical, if not impossible, to discipline an individual.

In the late 1970's, Dawn-Marie received an anonymous newspaper clipping in the mail about an employee who had been listed in his town's police reports. He had been apprehended and charged with unlawful conduct over the prior weekend. The conduct alleged had nothing to do with the individual's job in the company. The chairman was appalled and wanted him fired. "You can't," she said. "For one thing, he's only been charged, not convicted."

The chairman insisted on being kept apprised of the development in the case. "It doesn't matter," Dawn-Marie insisted. "It's not job-related."

Several weeks later, she learned the case had been "continued without a finding" and the employee had been put on probation for six months. If he behaved himself, the case would be dismissed. It was a rather inconclusive verdict, but enough to help her make her point. The employee could not be fired.

Today, her answer would probably be different, depending on the employee and his position. Employers are struggling with such issues as alleged spouse abuse, driving while intoxicated, nonpayment of taxes, personal bankruptcy, public drunkenness, or simply outrageous behavior in public —all of which reflect on the company.

Bobby Kipp and Harry Britt, who deal with these issues at PricewaterhouseCoopers, say that while there is no hard and fast rule, they are helped by a process of review that takes these instances into account. "If we learn of it, we inform the general counsel or others in our organization to see if such behavior has also manifested itself at work or whether it fits in a larger pattern," Kipp says. "When someone is out in the public, particularly if they hold a senior level position at the firm and are identified as being with PwC, we definitely believe it reflects not only on them but on all of us. And if there is a problem, such as substance abuse, we work with them to get help."

Dave Walsh agrees and says that Niagara Mohawk has high expectations of its managers and executives, all the time, on and off the job. He cites one example. "We had a case of a manager who was involved in a car accident, off work time. He had indicated to his senior officer that he was at a particular place, when in fact he was someplace else. We discharged him because his officer lost confidence in him. We probably wouldn't have discharged a mechanic in the same set of circumstances. This is not unusual. If we were faced with a case of someone not paying child support, in financial difficulty, or with substance abuse problems, for example, we'd probably talk to the individual and his boss and that person might not stay with us. We have an expectation of how people at a senior level conduct themselves in their personal lives and in the community, as well as at work."

Different standards for different departments?

There is widespread agreement that life and work aren't fair, and what applies to one may not apply to another. Sometimes the application depends on the department involved. For example, in most companies, those working in a purchasing department have much stricter regulations and reporting requirements than those working in other parts of the same organization.

Dave Walsh explains how it works at Niagara Mohawk. "The code of conduct spells out the expectations for all employees, but it notes that standards are more stringent for the purchasing department, for example. Our code allows very modest entertainment and gifts. But in purchasing, the standard is 'none.' This issue of different standards for different individuals is one that occupies a lot of my time!"

Similarly, some companies or organizations may have stricter requirements than others because they may be government contractors, deal with sensitive matters or material, or are regulated by public agencies or hold a monopoly. This is one reason that we feel strongly about the need for clear communication and regular training for all employees. Individuals who may have joined an enterprise from another industry or working environment may not immediately appreciate the reason why the standards of their new employer are necessarily higher than those of their previous employer.

Dave Walsh again refers to the example about Niagara Mohawk and the general issue of gambling. "Our standard of comparison should not be between us and the company that allows betting pools at work. The fact that they are doing something doesn't make it right for us. Our test should be, 'Can we look at our customers and say to them we are taking their money and using our time to place bets on NCAA pools?' The answer is no."

Merging two cultures

PricewaterhouseCoopers was the product of the merger of Price Waterhouse and Coopers & Lybrand, two of the top six accounting firms in the world. While the nuts and bolts of any large merger are challenging, it is even more difficult if the values and standards of the two organizations are different. Luckily that was not the case.

"We had the good fortune of two organizations that were very aligned," says Kipp. "We conducted a policy-gathering comparison. Where there were differences, people got together and worked it out.

"If there were any differences, I would say in matters of enforcement and discipline, Price Waterhouse had a culture of dealing with matters immediately, including affecting compensation. The Coopers process was to note the incident and reflect its compensation impact at the end of the year."

Does geography matter?

Small companies have the luxury of a limited geographical area and can determine the values that are paramount in their employee or customer base. Their biggest challenge may be integrating employees who join from another part of the country and may bring a different set of values or style of work ethic.

For large companies such as PricewaterhouseCoopers, however, geography poses a challenge. "New York City is a separate world away from many parts of the midwest or south," Kipp says. "What might be tolerated or not even noticed in a big eastern city might be considered rude or unacceptable in other places of the country. We have to be sensitive to that, yet try to uphold the same standards across the firm. We don't have a different set of values depending on where you live or work."

Working in other countries, however, presents a significant challenge to firms that are trying to roll out a single set of values and code of conduct. Kipp and Britt find that integrating their initiatives across the globe will take patience and understanding.

"We have to be very sensitive not to push American standards on the rest of the company or the rest of the globe," says Kipp. "We're in an information-gathering stage right now. We want to understand what others have been doing. We know that PwC in the United Kingdom, the Netherlands and other countries already have some programs that are ongoing. We need to respect what they have done and share our information with them. We can be most helpful as a resource, but it won't work if we come in and try to tell them to do it our —the American — way. We won't get anywhere if we try that."

PwC's business is divided along both industry lines (e.g. energy, financial services) and service lines (e.g. tax, audit, consulting). But as it relates to business conduct standards, Kipp and Britt state that the first consideration is geography and the others fall in line afterward. This does not mean that their excellent program (an American Business Ethics Award winner in 1998) will be operative just in United States offices.

"We are identifying business conduct champions outside the U.S. Together we will define and communicate our global standards of business conduct. We first need to identify common standards, communicate them, offer training programs, suggest mechanisms to raise concerns, and then do some level of compliance checking. Those are the major elements we are striving to implement world-wide.

"We know our present United States code of conduct won't work well outside of this country. So we're in the process of drafting a shorter one, with general principles in it. We'll offer it to other PwC firms with the idea that whatever they'd like to do should fit within its parameters. We understand that in other countries, many of our peers view themselves as professionals who already operate to a strict ethical code of conduct. They may feel they don't need anything else, and until they believe that having higher standards of ethics gives them a competitive advantage, they may be slower to adopt more extensive programs. But we are fortunate that our PricewaterhouseCoopers Global Board believes we should have a global business conduct standard, so that is what we are trying to achieve."

Chapter 19

The Boston Globe
MUDDIED STANDARDS, MUDDLED MANAGEMENT

This is a classic ethics story, one in which a profitable and well-respected company lost its way. It is the story of an ethical crisis that top executives mishandled at every possible point — not because they were bad people, but because in an effort to be overly fair, they forgot that the fairest approach is one of consistency.

The story is about a daily newspaper and a popular columnist, but that's almost irrelevant. Substitute "technology company" and "top salesman," "law firm" and "rainmaker," "hospital" and "prominent surgeon" — or any other combination of an organization and its superstar — and you could have the same tale of woe.

The following is what happens when a company lacks consistent response to, and enforcement of, its core values and standards.

A summer of discontent

The summer of 1998 was not a good one for the Globe Newspaper Company, publisher of New England's most dominant newspaper, *The Boston Globe*. Looking back, critics could say that in three short months the paper needlessly self-destructed.

For the past thirty years, the *Globe* had built a stellar reputation and a circulation to match. Under one editor alone, it won 12 Pulitzer Prizes. The paper attracted the best reporters, took an aggressive stance on civic issues and in all categories outshone its cross-town rival, the *Boston Herald*.

In 1973 the *Globe* hired a brash young writer named Mike Barnicle, who soon began writing columns that championed Boston's working class. Cops, single mothers, gas station owners, elderly immigrants and young veterans found themselves reflected in his prose. As Barnicle's voice grew more powerful, so did his clout within the paper. As one writer described him, "He was not even 30, yet he fashioned himself as a self-made newspaper hero unafraid of his bosses."[1]

Even as the paper promoted him as Boston's Jimmy Breslin, Barnicle's critics said he pushed the envelope of journalistic standards. The *Globe* settled at least two lawsuits alleging that Barnicle fabricated quotes attributed to real people. Chicago's famed columnist Mike Royko complained Barnicle was copying his work. Staffers complained he was arrogant and aloof, all while earning an estimated $200,000 salary at the *Globe* and a near equal amount for television commentary. He hobnobbed with actor Robert Redford, the Kennedys and O'Neills, and media stars Tim Russert and Don Imus.

If Mike Barnicle filled a void at the *Globe* by speaking for the common man, the paper's editors were acutely aware that its ranks were thin when it came to minority staff. In 1990, the paper welcomed a young black writer and poet, Patricia Smith, who in 1994 was given a coveted columnist position. Unfortunately, Smith's past record was not free from blemishes, and after questions arose about the veracity of her column material, the *Globe*'s editors decided that a reminder was in order. To avoid the appearance of favoritism, in January 1996 editor Matthew V. Storin reminded Smith and Barnicle about the *Globe*'s "rules of the road." They had to write truthful columns and provide backup to verify their contents. Everyone was now on equal footing.

If that sounds like basic "journalistic standard 101," it should. The problem was that the standard had never been uniformly applied or enforced. To have fired Smith in 1996, Storin would have had to confront Barnicle, something he was unwilling to do. Storin admitted to his own media critic that people said that Mike Barnicle made things up. But Storin also acknowledged that he never had reason to doubt the authenticity of Barnicle's columns.

---

[1] Sean Flynn, "Scandal Rocks Hub Daily," *Boston Magazine*, October 1998, p. 55.

"Life is full of gray areas, but the intellectual contract that makes mainstream newspapering possible is stark and clear. Editors have to be able to trust what reporters and columnists write and say. Journalists do not make things up or present others' writing and thought as their own."

Howell Raines
"The High Price of Reprieving Mike Barnicle,"
The New York Times, August 13, 1998

So the loose standards continued, the *Globe* pretending its columnists were writing the truth and some of its columnists pretending to write the truth. In fact, in the midst of staff complaints to editors about Smith's work, Storin nominated her for a Pulitzer.

But in June 1998 the façade cracked. One doubting and diligent editor amassed persuasive evidence that Smith had been writing fiction instead of newspaper columns. When confronted, Smith admitted to the fabrications and resigned on June 18.

So a company took a little longer than it should to dismiss an untruthful employee. Is that so bad?

No, that's only the misdemeanor. The ethical felony followed, shortly after the predictable community outrage over the firing of a black female writer and the double standard the paper permitted for its white male "recidivist fabricator and serial plagiarist" (a description that one of Barnicle's column subjects offered).[2]

By July, when it seemed the *Globe* would ride out the Patricia Smith storm, Storin left for vacation in Italy. Enter the classic ethics case, with all its elements.

Surprise   The worst ethical crises happen without warning. On August 2, Barnicle's column consisted of a series of funny one-liners prefaced by, "I was just thinking . . ." An alert reader tipped

---

[2] Alan Dershowitz, "Why I've Not Yet Been Vindicated," *Boston Magazine*, October 1998, p. 51.

the *Boston Herald* that several of Barnicle's quips came from George Carlin's book, *Brain Droppings*.

A Public Free-for-All Ethical scandals are wrenching even if they are played out in the privacy of the corner office. Perhaps the board is informed, but after the fact, perhaps the final press release gives a clue announcing the resignation of an individual "for personal reasons." If the individual is unimportant, the resignation may go unnoticed.

The ethics case of the *Boston Globe* and Mike Barnicle involved the worst-case scenario. Not only was the scandal fresh material for the media and every opinion leader, the competition broke the story. Its front page headlines screamed the news, while *Herald* columnists and reporters embellished the burgeoning scandal with more fodder to feed the media frenzy, predicting an editorial shakeup and chastising Barnicle for past sins. Soon the weekly *Boston Phoenix*, the leading alternative newspaper, chimed in with its own in-depth reporting on Barnicle, while the influential *Boston Magazine* revived its 1991 "Barnicle Watch."

The media excitement continued as Barnicle argued jokes are impossible to source and denied ever reading the Carlin book. Storin, from his vacation retreat, immediately decided to suspend Barnicle for a month, playing into the public attention and feeding the debate about whether the *Globe*'s journalistic standards were uniformly applied, since they had forced Smith's resignation a few months earlier.

The punishment turned out to be too little, too soon. Just a few hours later, a Boston television station ran a clip of Barnicle holding up the Carlin book and recommending it to viewers as a good summer read.

Now the *Globe*'s editors felt they had been lied to. Storin, again calling from Italy, demanded Barnicle's resignation.

One has to wonder what Storin was thinking, knowing the personality of his star columnist. Perhaps Storin thought if he asked nicely, Barnicle would say yes. Barnicle refused to resign and instead mounted a public defense that he might have argued privately to Storin, if given the chance.

A superstar offender A superstar in or causing trouble is bad enough, but if the superstar engenders strong feelings, not all positive, the case is tougher to deal with. In the *Globe*'s case, its high profile sinner was described as aloof, contemptuous, and lazy. Barnicle had "played by his own set of rules and gotten away with it,"[3] according to one observer. Barnicle, who by this time was a regular on such popular shows as Imus in the Morning and The Newshour with Jim Lehrer, was a well-known public figure. Opinions were rarely neutral about the columnist; fans loved his brash, contemptuous view of the world but others thought his ego had overtaken his renowned writing skill. His own words in a 1983 interview captured his personality: "I got license, freedom, nobody breathing down my back. Hey, I'm a lucky bastard. It's a fuckin' pisser, isn't it?"[4]

Prior warnings to the offender   Barnicle's career was described by the *Boston Phoenix* as "marked by numerous instances of borderline plagiarism, legal problems sparked by apparently egregious misquotes and . . . credible accusations that he faked some of his columns."[5] Reporters digging into Barnicle's misdeeds uncovered a $40,000 payment for a 1973 column, and a $75,000 settlement paid to Harvard Law School professor Alan Dershowitz for another column. A 1993 column about two rogue policemen appeared too strange to be true but apparently Barnicle's editors never double-checked the account.

In the aftermath of longstanding questions about Barnicle's writing habits, the "rules of the road" discussion and fact-checking system Storin instituted in 1996 perhaps should have been the last sermon to the sinner. But are plagiarized jokes the same as fictionalized news? No one had a clear answer.

A popular referendum on ethics   Tough ethical decisions should be made in the privacy of the office, after thorough investigation and careful reflection. In the case of the *Boston Globe*, by asking for Barnicle's resignation rather than firing him, or by refusing to suspend him for a longer period while they investigated, the paper lit a fire with gasoline. Barnicle took to the airwaves, pleading his case on talk radio and national television. Don Imus's lis-

---

[3] Dan Kennedy, "Twenty-five years of trouble," *The Boston Phoenix*, August 13, 1998.
[4] Dan Kennedy, "Barnicle's Game," *The Boston Phoenix*, August 13, 1998.
[5] Ibid.

teners were urged to contact the *Globe* with support for the columnist. Soon the voicemails and e-mails at the *Globe* were full. Everyone in Boston, it seemed, had an opinion on the Barnicle affair and was not hesitant to express it. Barnicle urged a public vote on his column and the *Globe* was powerless to stop its columnist's campaign.

Outside pressure on the decisionmakers Should an ethical decision rest upon the prestige of those arguing various points of view? Should a law or accounting firm bend to its biggest client? Should a company bend to its biggest customer or its sole supplier? Consistent standards and enforcement are good insurance against this happening. The *Globe*, lacking clearly articulated values, was ripe for advertiser pressure that soon materialized. Thomas G. Stemberg, CEO of the office-supply chain Staples, subtly threatened to pull his advertising, proclaiming that Barnicle's column was a "key element of the *Globe*'s attractiveness as an advertising vehicle."[6]

The pressure apparently worked. Barnicle halted his media tour in time to meet with publisher Benjamin B. Taylor on August 7th. The following week Storin returned from vacation to meet with Barnicle and Taylor. On August 11, Storin announced that the *Globe* had changed its mind. Its executives would not seek Barnicle's resignation, but would suspend him for two months.

The rationale? "Though there were clear offenses and violations of professional standards, I did not feel . . that the punishment fit the crime,"[7] Storin said.

Say that one more time? Clear violations of standards but we changed our mind? No wonder the *Globe* staff and the community were confused. Storin and Taylor had only muddied the ethical waters.

Allegations of double standards, complicated by bias Having consistent standards and enforcement makes it easier to deal with an individual who has transgressed. Having no clear standards makes the judgment call that much harder. Having no

---

[6] Flynn, p. 120.

[7] Sinead O'Brien, "For Barnicle, One Controversy Too Many," *American Journalism Review,* September 1998.

clear standards, and having applied what few standards there were unevenly, only compounds the chaos. The *Globe* created chaos, complicated by racial and gender bias, when it forced Patricia Smith to resign and then only suspended Mike Barnicle. Black community leaders were vocal, not because Smith was sent packing, but because Barnicle was not. African-American staffers at the *Globe* were particularly upset.

No company support   One test of the integrity of an ethical decision is whether the brass can explain it to the troops. The *Globe* troops, by and large, were not happy with its management's flip-flop on ethics and the decision to retain Barnicle. The *Globe*'s ombudsman, Jack Thomas, wrote an editorial denouncing the double standard, arguing that both columnists compromised the ethics of the newspaper and damaged its credibility. As *Globe* writer Howard Manley said, "That they are willing to risk the work of an entire newsroom to save one person is unbelievable."[8]

Allegations of protection   The following is a recipe for disaster: mix serious ethical lapses, one superstar and an alleged double standard, and stir up community opinion. Bake for two weeks and you get allegations of protection. The Barnicle fiasco seemed to demonstrate that the *Globe* had a culture of protection and corruption. Storin covered up Smith's lapses as early as 1995, yet recommended her for the Pulitzer in 1998. His critics claimed Barnicle had been protected for years by a series of editors and publishers. Perhaps *Boston Magazine* stated it best: The newspaper allowed its columnists to be "shielded by institutional hubris that crippled the moral authority of the *Globe*, which eventually found it impossible to reveal the truth without also admitting complicity."[9]

Divided we fall   When a full-scale ethical scandal erupts, threatening the integrity and core of an institution, its managers must be united in their view of the situation and the core values they wish to enforce. It appeared to outsiders that Barnicle was able to divide his bosses with alternating anger (against the predators who decided to ruin 25 years of his work) and humility. While

---

[8] Kennedy, "Barnicle's Game."

[9] Flynn, p. 51.

> **"A**nd, perhaps once or twice a year, I used my memory to tell true tales of the city, things that happened to real people who shared their own lives with me. They represented the music and flavor of the time. There were stories that sat on the shelf of my institutional memory and spoke to a larger point. The use of parables was not a technique I invented. It was established ages ago by other newspaper columnists, many more gifted than I, some long since dead."
>
> Mike Barnicle
> "My Way," *The Boston Globe*, October 29, 1998

Storin was still in Italy on vacation, Barnicle met with publisher Taylor, apparently pleading his case and promising to be quiet. So, by the time Storin came back, the perception was that Taylor won when Storin bravely announced Barnicle's reinstatement with only a suspension, insisting to readers that the columnist was now on a "high wire without a net." [10] There would be no room for future ethical lapses.

But the *Globe* was silent about past ethical lapses and the investigators weren't yet finished.

Rush to judgment   Complicated situations deserve the luxury of time and attention. Granted, making and articulating clear decisions is hard when the competing press is breathing down your neck, but one of the great mysteries in the *Globe* case is why the editors didn't just suspend Barnicle for several months in the beginning, demand his silence, and investigate him fully.

The public outcry over the *Globe*'s apparent cave-in to Barnicle only served to bring out his critics. A *Readers Digest* executive notified the *Globe* that it had researched a 1995 Barnicle column in the hopes of reprinting it and could not verify

---

[10] Matthew V. Storin, "A Letter from the Editor," *The Boston Globe*, August 16, 1998.

it. The *Globe* knew about the accusations but waited until Barnicle was at his summer home, without his notebooks, before demanding the backup for the column. The next day the *Globe* decided it couldn't wait and demanded his resignation again.

Barnicle quit. "It became a feeding frenzy,"[11] he said, explaining that he no longer wanted to be the issue distracting a great metropolitan paper from its daily work.

Further criticisms followed: Barnicle had plagiarized from a book about Louisiana Governor Earl Long; Barnicle had lied about his resume. Like a fighter reeling from the punches, Barnicle still tried to fight back, asking the *Globe* to run a final column arguing his case, as Patricia Smith had done. When it refused, he offered to pay $36,000 for a full-page ad. It still refused, relenting only two months later, running his op-ed piece, in which he distinguished between news stories and "true" stories, "flawed in the retelling."[12]

Above all, unclear standards, unenforced   By now Storin might have figured out that the *Globe*'s summer of hell began long before, when the paper developed a reputation as a haven for underworked brats. He had a golden opportunity to raise professional standards when he took over in 1996, but seemed to fear confronting powerful and popular favorites. He ducked the issue of whether rules for columnists could be clear, saying, "columnists of that nature have been a kind of gray area."[13] Admitting that questioning Smith about her columns would also raise many of the past suspicions about Barnicle, Storin seems to have missed the point that it was his own lack of clear standards or enforcement that caused the subsequent problem with Barnicle. But Storin did understand that his own muddiness may have confused Smith and led to her relaxed attitude about truthfulness: "It may have been the noise about Mike, unfair though it may be, that gave her the wrong impression,"[14] he said.

---

[11] Mark Jurkowitz, "Barnicle resigns after new questions on reporting," *The Boston Globe*, August 20, 1998.

[12] Mike Barnicle, "My Way," *The Boston Globe*, October 29, 1998.

[13] Sinead O'Brien,"Secrets and Lies," *American Journalism Review*, September 1998.

[14] Ibid.

So Storin preferred to take the nonconfrontational way out, keeping standards loose, challenging no one until the suspicions were so grave, or the public voices so loud, that he could not ignore them. Perhaps he was only following the prevailing culture, as most Americans give journalists low marks for integrity. In a study released after the *Globe*'s imbroglio and other television and newspaper scandals, nearly 90 percent of those surveyed said they believe reporters use illegal or unethical methods, and over 65 percent said they believe stories are fabricated and published as real.[15]

Some institutions are blessed to have individuals with high standards of their own, and the *Globe* was no exception. Eileen McNamara, a 1997 Pulitzer winner, approached Executive Editor Helen Donovan with her concerns about Smith when she heard Storin was submitting the young columnist's work for a Pulitzer. When Smith resigned, McNamara tackled the issue of standards again in an unequivocal column. Rejecting the notion that Smith was forced out because of bias, McNamara stated, on the contrary, "It was the worst sort of racism that kept us from confronting the fraud we long suspected. If we did ask, and she did tell, we might lose her, and where would we be then? Where would we find an honest black woman columnist who wrote with such power and grace?"[16]

Howell Raines, in an editorial for the *Globe*'s parent company, *The New York Times*, also understood basic journalism values and criticized what he called the double standard at the *Globe* prior to Barnicle's resignation. "If you have to choose between a worthy but erring colleague and the newspaper itself, you choose for the paper. After all, all the members of this profession know the rules when we sign up."[17]

Well, maybe. Mike Barnicle either forgot the rules, if they were ever explained to him, or convinced himself that what he was writing was parable. But everyone is human. It is up to man-

---

[15] Michael White, "Survey: People Deem Media Unethical," *AP Online*, October 17, 1998.

[16] Eileen McNamara, "A Matter of Integrity," *The Boston Globe*, June 27, 1998.

[17] Howell Raines, "The High Price of Reprieving Mike Barnicle," *The New York Times*, August 13, 1998.

agement to remind employees of the rules and the values for which the company stands. By failing to state or enforce clear standards, *Globe*'s management failed Mike Barnicle, its readers and itself.

Mike Barnicle himself said so, long after he was fired. "Reconstruction dialogue in a 1995 column is a clear failure to abide by today's standards. It was not always so but is now." [18]

And the cost of not being clearly told what the standard was and the punishment for not abiding by it? "Banishment from the place where I've spent most of my adult life. My penalty was to have my work, my life — private and professional — savaged." [19]

It could happen to anyone. It is a lesson for all.

---

[18] Barnicle.
[19] Ibid.

Chapter 20

Audits and Evaluations

Managers should not establish values initiatives, training programs and other infrastructure without constantly measuring how effective they are. Substantive audits should include detailed investigations into potential violations of law or regulation and whether individuals are making decisions based on the values of the organization. On the process side, audits should reveal whether communication vehicles such as helplines or websites are working, whether employees have acknowledged receiving training and whether employees are even aware of resources available to them.

Many companies already perform compliance audits and evaluations, for example, by listening to the way telephone representatives impart information or by reviewing advertisements, offering documents or bid processes. Auditing how employees adhere to an organization's values is a bit more difficult, but many companies are finding effective ways to judge whether the program is working.

A necessary step

In an all-perfect world in an all-perfect organization, the right people do the right thing all the time. They don't need anyone to check up on them.

But that's not the world we live in. Too often we are influenced by factors that compel us to act differently than we otherwise might — from compensation systems to peer pressure to examples set by others.

Remember the story of the Emperor's new clothes? The emperor paraded around town naked and yet everyone told him how distinguished he looked, until a child shouted out, "The emperor has no clothes!" The moral of the story is that it took the innocence of a child to verbalize what everyone else was thinking.

This type of social behavior happens in companies and organizations all too frequently. An individual's private thoughts may be different than those of others, even if he or she behaves like the rest of the crowd, applauding a dull speech or promising revenue numbers that can't be delivered. It takes courage to admit the truth.

In the previous chapters we explained the necessity for resources and institutional support to encourage employees to follow their right instincts. Without those resources, individuals will act as expected, often looking to see what others do. But even with resources available, individuals sometimes are more persuaded by social pressure, and don't use the resources at hand. For example, Wall Street stock and bond traders have a reputation (at least until recently) of behaving boorishly towards women, minorities or others who do not fit their aggressive, macho image. Even those who did not like the behavior joined in or ignored it, because it was more important to be part of the crowd than to raise a fuss. In such an environment, it takes a clear and strong values message on the part of management at all levels to counteract the prevailing culture of the industry.

We can point to more serious examples of crowd following, but the point is the same. The behavior of individuals can be influenced by others around them, despite clear values messages from the company and despite resources for assistance. Therefore, audits and assessments are a necessary ingredient in any values initiative to see if values are being followed. If they are not, audits can help determine what has gone wrong.

Let's take two simple examples. A manager is at a conference at a resort with the boss and another senior executive. At a break in the conference schedule, they play golf. The boss and the other executive add the greens fees to their expense account. The manager isn't sure that is the right thing to do, but he wants to conform and doesn't want to embarrass the boss by asking. So he perceives the action as the standard. Over time, it does become the standard for managers attending conferences. "Everyone does it."

"Auditors can set a moral tone by basing their inter-actions with co-workers on honesty, integrity, respect, and compassion. They can also ask tough questions, which increase awareness of the organization's ethical clime.

Is the ethics program designed to help workers become better individuals? Does management walk the talk? Are wrongdoers punished and ethical giants rewarded? Or does management throw out the wheat with the chaff?

When ethical behavior is inspired, demanded, and rewarded, the organization profits — in more ways than one. That's why it is so important for internal auditors to take a strong stand in favor of the straight and narrow. After all, no internal auditor was ever accused of being asleep at the wheel because the organization erred on the side of goodness."

Christy Chapman
executive editor, *Internal Auditor*
February 1999, p. 6

Or take the example of Joseph Jett, the disgraced bond trader at Kidder Peabody, who was accused of causing $350 million in losses from a "phantom trading" scheme.[1] According to Jett, he pointed out to his superiors that the computer program was booking profits that might not be real. The superiors were not concerned, and, in fact, told him to segregate his assets off the accounting balance sheet, so General Electric, Kidder Peabody's parent company, wouldn't know the amount of capital Kidder was using to trade. So Jett kept two sets of books, even past the quarterly financial disclosure deadlines to General Electric shareholders.

---

[1] There was extensive press coverage of the scandal when it occurred in 1994. For Jett's version, see Joseph Jett and Sabra Chartrand, *Black and White on Wall Street: The Untold Story of the Man Wrongly Accused of Bringing Down Kidder Peabody*, William Morrow & Co., 1999. For another perspective of Jett's book, see Steven Brill, "Rewind," *Brill's Content*, July/August 1999, p. 35.

If he had thought about it, Jett, educated at MIT and Harvard Business School, might have gone to General Electric auditors, outside counsel or regulators to ask, "Is this okay?" But Jett, who received a $9 million bonus one year, seems to have taken the attitude, "You want numbers, I'll give you numbers." After Jett was summarily fired, auditors crawled all over Kidder Peabody to try to understand what had been going on. Jett could have enlightened them earlier, had they inquired.

Now married — internal control and values auditing

Companies regularly audit financial operations and compliance with specific laws and regulations. But can organizations check whether they are adhering to a values-based management culture? Yes.

A wide range of commentators has stressed that the function of internal control includes a consideration of the ethical environment in which employees operate. For example, the 1998 Best Practices Council of the National Association of Corporate Directors, in its report dealing with fraud and illegal activity, called for increased "fraud awareness" by directors, who must focus on the company's business activities and the culture in which it operates. [2] In the NACD's view, one of the most effective deterrents to fraud is the "tone at the top." Furthermore, the report recommended that management report to the board on its efforts to deter fraud and to maintain a culture of high ethics.

In 1999 the Blue Ribbon Committee on Improving the Effectiveness of Audit Committees suggested that a diligent audit committee question not only such areas as accounting principles, reserves and accruals, but also risk assessments and external environmental factors that affect financial reporting. [3] The 1992 Committee of Sponsoring Organizations of the

---

[2] *National Association of Corporate Directors Best Practice Council on Coping with Fraud and Other Illegal Activity*, National Association of Corporate Directors, Washington DC, 1998.

[3] *Report and Recommendations of the Blue Ribbon Committee on Improving the Effectiveness of Corporate Audit Committees*, New York Stock Exchange and National Association of Securities Dealers, 1999.

Treadway Commission focused on the components of internal control, including the integrity, ethical values and competence of personnel.[4]

Public accounting firms such as KPMG and Pricewaterhouse Coopers have responded by publishing comprehensive guides for audit committees and corporate executives, reminding them of their responsibilities to oversee risk management. We applaud such clear warnings as the following from KPMG:

> Dominant or autocratic management can also be a cause for concern in an established company. Such leadership can put a strain on the enterprise's controls and corporate governance processes and set the wrong "tone at the top." Ensuring that management fosters an atmosphere that supports a strong control environment is a core audit committee responsibility.[5]

Among the items on PricewaterhouseCooper's audit committee self-assessment checklist is:

> The audit committee reviews company policies and procedures for the regular review of officers' expenses and perquisites, including the use of corporate assets, inquires as to the results of that review and, if appropriate, reviews a summarization of the expenses and perquisites for the period.[6]

An auditing structure

As noted in chapter 6, commitment from the top is necessary if any values-based program is to be effective. Prominent corporate governance experts agree, emphasizing that the board and senior managers should get their arms around the corporate culture as

---

[4] Coopers & Lybrand LLP, *Internal Control-Integrated Framework*, The Committee of Sponsoring Organizations of the Treadway Commission (COSO), 1991. COSO is an alliance of five professional organizations: The American Accounting Association (AAA), the American Institute of Certified Public Accountants (AICPA), the Financial Executives Institute (FEI), the Institute of Internal Auditors (IIA) and the Institute of Management Accountants (IMA).

[5] KPMG, *Shaping the Audit Committee*, 1999, p. 13.

[6] PricewaterhouseCoopers LLP, *Audit Committees: Best Practices for Protecting Shareholder Interests*, 1999, p. 54.

well as its numbers.[7] Ethics and values are important elements of the internal control function.

Some companies have ethics committees, ethics councils or other company-wide task forces that oversee their programs to incorporate values into operations. Others have this kind of committee as well as an ethics committee at the board of directors' level. Others use the audit committee of the board of directors, which is generally charged with the oversight of the company's internal controls and comprised solely of independent directors.

For example, after scandals and government investigations rocked Columbia/HCA, the giant hospital chain, the company hired Alan Yuspeh as senior vice president for ethics, compliance and corporate responsibility. The board of directors of Columbia/HCA appointed a specific committee charged with the oversight of ethics and the company has a similar internal committee comprised of senior officers. Yuspeh and his department report directly to the CEO and the ethics, compliance and corporate responsibility committee of the board. In addition, each Columbia/HCA hospital has a senior executive who acts as ethics and compliance officer at that institution.

Whatever structure an organization chooses, we recommend that the values auditing oversight function be performed by individuals at a high level who have demonstrated integrity and independence. Such individuals should be educated about business ethics and be champions of the organization's stated values. A formal charter or mission such as USAA's can be helpful in memorializing the function and structure of the committee, and it should be reviewed and adopted annually. A company committee most often reports to the board of directors or the audit committee of the board. Committee members follow a practice of meeting privately with the ethics officer, if there is one, or with internal auditors, security or other individuals charged with performing the auditing function. The most effective committee members keep current with the best practices in the industry. One technique we recommend is the practice of developing and discussing hypothetical

---

[7] Curtis C. Verschoor, "Internal Control: A Weapon in the War Against Fraud," *Director's Monthly*, February 1999, pp. 7-9.

USAA Ethics Council Charter

Scope and Purpose

The USAA Ethics Council (the Council) is responsible for functioning as the most senior-level focal point for consideration and resolution of ethical issues and the establishment of ethics policy on behalf of the CEO and USAA's Board of Directors.

Functions

The council performs the following functions:

Acts as the focal point for ethical issues by providing liaison to the CEO, Board of Directors, and company Presidents/Staff Agency Heads with regard to ethical issues, and by being accessible to all employees.

Monitors and approves training programs to educate employees and management on the purpose and maintenance of the Ethics Program.

Conducts periodic reviews of the USAA Code of Business Ethics and Conduct handbook and recommends changes to the CEO as appropriate to meet the needs of USAA.

Assures consistency and quality of the ethics program across all operating locations and report status to the CEO.

Formulates advisory opinions and resolves problems involving ethical issues or management actions necessary to ensure compliance with the USAA Code of Ethics. Informs and advises the CEO on all matters that the Council expects may require corrective or preventive action by the CEO or the Board of Directors.

Provides assistance to the CEO to carry out his overall role of policy and program guidance and direction on the standards, development, implementation, monitoring and enforcement of USAA's Ethics Program.

Reports annually to the Chair of the Board Governance Committee of the USAA Board of Directors regarding the status and effectiveness of USAA's Ethics Program.

Duration

The Council shall continue in existence at the CEO's discretion.

Chair

The Chair of the Council shall be appointed by the CEO.

If the Chair will not be present at a meeting, the Chair shall designate another member to act as Chair.

Membership

Council membership shall include at least three members of the Executive Council selected by the CEO.

General Counsel shall be an ex officio member of the Ethics Council.

Council members shall not appoint substitutes to represent them in any Council meeting.

USAA Ethics Council Charter (continued)

Council members may invite selected individuals to attend meetings as is appropriate to the meeting agenda and anticipated actions to be taken by the Council.

Meetings

The Council shall meet on an as-needed basis, as deemed appropriate by the Chair.

The Council shall meet under the CEO's personal guidance and direction at least three times a year.

Two Council members shall constitute a quorum for conducting Council meetings.

The Ethics Program Coordinator shall prepare and distribute to all participants an agenda for each meeting.

The Ethics Program Coordinator shall provide administrative support to the Council to include scheduling of meetings.

Minutes and Reports

The Ethics Program Coordinator shall prepare and distribute minutes of each meeting and, after coordination with the Chair and General Counsel, shall distribute them to members of the Council and such other persons approved by the Chair.

The Ethics Program Coordinator shall be responsible to coordinate the collection, preparation, and distribution of reports and other materials deemed necessary by the Council.

Subcommittees

The Chair may establish such subcommittees as deemed appropriate to accomplish the functions of the Council within its scope and purpose. The Chair shall remain responsible for the actions or decisions of any such subcommittee.

In 1999, the Council's membership included:
President, USAA Alliance Service Company
President, USAA Life Insurance Company
Senior Vice President, General Counsel and Corporate Secretary (Ex officio)
Senior Vice President, Business Integration

cases drawn from the experiences of other similar companies or organizations, so that committee members will develop a familiarity and comfort level dealing with issues of conflicting values or ethical concerns.

All members on the committee should recognize the committee's unique role and responsibility and should be prepared to dedicate their personal time and attention to the task at hand (no proxies allowed). Committee members should be knowledgeable about the company's risks and controls and should work to develop a high degree of candor, inquisitiveness and objectivity with respect to the issues that come before it. While the number of members varies by company, the committee should be large enough to represent a balance of views and perspectives, yet small enough for frank discussion and action.

We suggest that committee members rotate on and off the committee, so that as many senior level managers will have an opportunity to serve. At most organizations, regular committee meetings are generally scheduled well in advance. The agenda should reflect the organization's current concerns and meet the committee's goals and objectives. And as is the practice with many audit committees, new members should receive extensive orientation.

Auditing values at BellSouth

BellSouth's approach is a good model for other organizations. The ethics, compliance & business conduct organization, along with internal auditing and security, reports to the senior vice president, corporate compliance and corporate secretary, who reports to the chairman and CEO. Jerry Guthrie, BellSouth's corporate director, ethics, compliance & business conduct, says that this is as close to an ideal organizational structure as you can get. Referring to it as the governance organization, he emphasizes the objectivity of having a reporting chain outside any normal operating or staff functional area and the synergies gained from having his function in the same organization with internal auditing and security. He adds that as corporate social responsibility becomes an increasingly important topic in industry ethics discussions, being in the same organization with the corporate secretary function adds to the synergies and value of

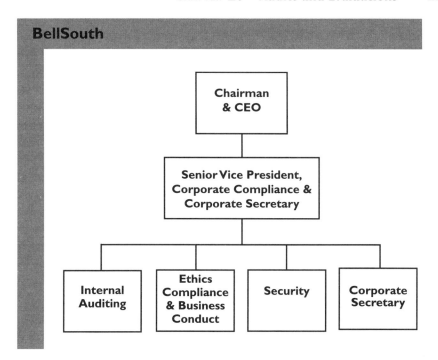

this organizational structure. In addition to this structure, he believes a strong partnership with the legal organization and human resources is essential.

At BellSouth, the CEO chairs the corporate ethics and compliance committee. There is also a designated executive in each major subsidiary group who has ethics and compliance oversight responsibilities for that entity. The ethics and compliance committee is the champion of the company's ethics and compliance initiative because, as Guthrie says, "the tone is set at the top." The committee provides guidance, direction, and acts as a final authority on clarification or interpretation on policy issues. But it is the audit committee of BellSouth's board of directors that has the ultimate oversight role. Guthrie meets with them twice a year to keep them informed on trends, issues and activities going on in ethics, compliance and business conduct.

The audit committee often asks Guthrie how he measures the success of the ethics and compliance program. He attributes what he believes is the best measurement of a program to Bill Giffin, Sears' ethics vice president, who said that Sears measures the success of its program by the number of people they help, not the number of people they catch. Guthrie said that he monitors the number and nature of inquiries they receive through the toll-free contact line and other resources; he looks at such indicators as the percent of callers who ask for advice vs. the percent of callers who have complaints. He also notes the percent of calls that are anonymous. He cautioned that there are ambiguities in using such indicators with total calls as an example: Is it good or bad to have an increase in calls? In BellSouth's experience, almost half of the calls are for advice, which Guthrie sees as a positive indicator. Many of the questions concern polices about practices in the workplace: "Can I use e-mail at work?" "Can I work for a vendor after I retire?" The fact that employees are asking these questions and understand that there may be a conflict of interest in a particular contemplated activity shows that the ethics message is coming through.

The effectiveness of the ethics message is not left to chance. As Guthrie speaks to employee groups throughout BellSouth, one of his key points is that ethics and compliance are part of the everyday job and the immediate supervisor is the best place to start when an employee has a concern. He believes that one of his organization's primary roles is to raise awareness throughout the corporation and to help employees know that there are many resources available to help them when they have a question pertaining to their job. To accomplish this, Guthrie and his staff don't wait to be invited to speak to internal groups. They make known their desire to participate in organizational meetings to all levels of leadership and get themselves invited to speak to raise awareness of the role of the ethics office. After their presentation, they mingle with the organization's managers and are available to anyone who might want to discuss an issue with them. Call it "assessment by walking around" — it works.

While Guthrie believes that face-to-face communications is the best vehicle, he also states that he uses every available technique to get out the message. On field trips, he brings pens and magnets advertising the BellSouth EthicsLine, the employee toll-free contact line. He provides quotes and "sound bytes" for executives to use when talking about ethics and compliance subjects.

One of BellSouth's most comprehensive communications vehicles is its website, which is available both to internal audiences through the intranet and external audiences through the internet (www.ethics.BellSouth.com). Here a viewer can find a variety of things: BellSouth's code of ethics, called *A Commitment to our Personal Responsibility*; questions and answers on a number of subjects; PowerPoint presentations; streaming videos of the "Ethics at BellSouth" series; and an interactive game of case studies based on inquiries.

Audit the program, too

We've suggested that audits and evaluations of ethics and compliance programs not be limited to instances of wrongdoing or problems. If executives are serious about implementing values-based management, they should be equally serious about evaluating how well their program is succeeding.

Guthrie was not hesitant to have such an audit performed of his program at BellSouth and to share the results with the company's ethics and compliance committee and the audit committee of the board of directors. Guthrie asked an outside firm, the Ethics Resource Center, to perform the audit after his organization had been operating for two years. The team of auditors conducted interviews and focus groups at corporate offices and in the field, with all levels of employees. The results were positive while containing some suggestions for improvements. He has also used internal auditing to audit specific aspects of his operations, like the security of his computer systems. Guthrie said he plans to regularly evaluate his program, using either internal or external audits. He concluded that he believes this to be the most effective way of measuring the success of an ethics and compliance program.

Guthrie is not alone in struggling with how to audit the success of BellSouth's initiatives. Carrie Penman, former ethics officer at Westinghouse, said, "Everyone's struggling with audits and measurements. There hasn't yet been a good tool out there to measure the effectiveness of programs. Most ethics officers track helpline calls, but that usually doesn't cut it when the board asks them how to measure adherence to company values. I'd like something that is detailed yet practical, but it may be difficult to design something that will be applicable to a wide range of organizations and industries. I'm not sure one size fits all."

Penman's experience at Westinghouse has given her an appreciation for nonquantifiable measurements as well. Her views about the most useful assessments may sound unusual, but many managers — whether or not they are ethics officers — would agree with her. "I trust my gut instinct. At Westinghouse, I answered the phone myself. I could tell you which locations called most often and which ones I never heard from. I could tell you which locations and managers had problems, and which were the most responsive to what we were trying to do. I could hear tones of frustration or anger from callers from certain areas of the company, and I could tell the difference in the attitude of various managers when I took an issue to them to resolve.

"As I developed more confidence in my gut instinct, just by doing my job day to day, I could say to our auditor, 'Here's where you ought to go and check.' I would pay as much attention to what I was not hearing as to where the calls were coming from. A lot of my auditing came down to assessing management style. If I suspected managers were telling their employees, 'Don't tell me your problems, just get the job done,' invariably I knew it would be indicative of bigger problems."

Not by audits alone — a hot car race

In some companies, auditors know how to audit financial statements, but individuals who are trying to audit adherence to a company's values may understandably find it a bit more difficult until a crisis occurs that reveals the obvious.

One incident in the automotive industry raises the question of whether an audit or evaluation might have prevented a major breach of integrity. Would the red flags have pointed an ethics sleuth in the right direction? We're not sure.

As is so often the case, the story begins with an aggressive battle to achieve sales goals. Cadillac, manufactured by General Motors, had been the nation's best-selling luxury car for 57 years. But in 1998, knowledgeable industry journalists were predicting that Ford Motor's Lincoln would dethrone Cadillac, as Lincoln had out-sold Cadillac through November of that year.[8]

---

[8] See Robyn Meredith, "Oops, Cadillac Says, Lincoln Won After All," *The New York Times*, May 6, 1999, p. C1.

Losing the "we're number one" bragging rights to a competitor was serious business in the Motor City, where the rivalry between Cadillac and Lincoln was as traditional as Harvard and Yale's on the football field. Despite the fact that Cadillac sales had been decreasing for years, by the end of 1998 Cadillac had out-sold Lincoln in a stunning come-from-behind victory by a mere 222 cars out of over 187,000 sold.

Or had it? When Cadillac's sales fell 38 percent in January of 1999, internal auditors quickly uncovered the obvious. By May 1999, Cadillac was forced to admit it had sold 4773 fewer cars in December than it had reported.

General Motors not only lost its place as the number one luxury car seller, but it momentarily lost the ability to present itself as a company of integrity — no small matter, when the product they sell carries around precious cargo.

The lesson here is two-fold. First, individuals often act according to the goals and incentives superiors set for them. No one should be surprised when they do. If "how" employees make financial objectives is as important as actually making them, then employees must know that operating with integrity is their first obligation. Otherwise, they may end up as just the latest name in a list of discredited companies such as Prudential Securities, Columbia/HCA, Archer Daniels Midland and Cendant.

Second, audits and assessment must be geared to the "how" of achieving results as well as the results. Perhaps there were some employees in Cadillac's marketing or sales division who could have accurately described the corporate culture and behavior that was taking place in the month of December 1998 and could have predicted the outcome.

An attorney at GM with direct involvement in their ethics initiatives, Michael Robinson, is not so sure that audits before the end of December 1998 would have made a difference in this case, as sales data don't exist until they are submitted. A review of information on December 1, December 10 or December 17 likely wouldn't have revealed anything unusual, he said.

"Auditing plays an important role in properly checking for abnormal, out-of-line conditions," Robinson said. "But while certain auditing refinements can improve detection of potential problems, the failing in this case was one of basic judgment.

Companies do not audit themselves into operating with integrity in all they do — they achieve that status when every employee knows that's their first obligation."

The General Motors story, however embarrassing, had a positive outcome. When the issue was first reported to General Motors by an outside source, its ethics team leaped into action. According to Robinson, legal, audit and security personnel worked quickly to pursue the allegations and bring all the facts to light. The leadership of the company was forthright about what had happened, apologized to Lincoln, and then used the story as a teaching tool for its management ranks.

"This incident came up at about the same time we were beginning to roll out our new values-based program to the entire company," Robinson explained. "It was a challenge, because we wanted our 4000 executives around the world to be the champions of our 'Winning with Integrity' program, and we needed to enlist their wholehearted support. To do that, we had to confront this story publicly to kill any skepticism or cynicism. People needed to understand that there had been repercussions, and that the company didn't operate that way. When we convened everyone for a global conference, we hit the issue head on."

Roy Roberts, GM's vice president of internal vehicles sales, service and marketing, was explicit in an employee newsletter. "Now is not the time for finger pointing," he said. "Our reputation for integrity remains a key to our success. It is our moral imperative. And just as important, our customers expect and demand it."[9]

In reflecting on the incident, Robinson agrees that there might have been employees who could have alerted company officials about the fraudulent sales numbers, but he understands why, even in the best of companies, they might not have done so. "No matter how much you tell people that there are resources for them, and tell them there are people to ask or give information to, we know that employees can be between a rock and a hard place when they are involved in a difficult situation. It's especially true if they are part of a team culture, are longstanding employees, or don't want to go against their peers or their supervisors.

---

[9] Roy Roberts, interview in *GM Edge*, July 1999.

"That's why a values program has to be a continuous effort, supported by the top. We have to tell employees that we understand what is difficult and that we are there for them when they do the right thing.

"I'm gratified the company chose the course it did," said Robinson, relating the General Motor's quick and frank admission as the facts unfolded, as well as its candid discussion of the problem in employee meetings. "Maybe this will set a tone for the whole industry. We sometimes hear that 'everyone does it,' or similar excuses. Well, General Motors is not going to operate according to the lowest common denominator. We just have to keep getting that message out and reinforcing it wherever we can."

Chapter 21

Olympic Games
TARNISHED GOLD?

Executives and managers sometimes ask, "How can you tell if a values initiative or ethics program is worth the time and effort? Can you measure the bottom line results?"

We tell the truth and say that auditing and assessing the benefits of an ethics program is sometimes difficult. But we have any number of illuminating stories about organizations that make no effort to instill values or a code of behavior into their operations, that ignore warning signs of potential problems, and that conduct no audits or assessments of their operations.

On a global scale there's perhaps no better contemporary example than the International Olympic Committee.

No comprehensive code, no audits

If any organization should have exemplified values, it was the world famous biennial summer and winter international athletic competition. Think of the word "Olympics" and what comes to mind? Until recently, it might have been pure ideals and the best and most talented young people from hundreds of nations, competing in sports and games — scenes of living together in a global village, waving flags, going for the gold, shedding tears of disappointment and of joy.

But after December 1998, the image of the Olympics may have changed forever, to that of a self-appointed body of 114 relatively unknown, allegedly corrupt individuals, accountable to no one, who control a big business by owning the copyright of

The Olympic Oath

"In the name of all competitors, I promise that we shall take part in these Olympic Games, respecting and abiding by the rules which govern them, in the true spirit of sportsmanship, for the glory of sport and the honor of our teams."

the word "Olympics" and the universally recognized symbol of five multi-colored rings.[1]

A code of conduct backed by regular audits for all members of the International Olympic Committee (IOC) could have prevented the golden image of the Games from becoming tarnished. But in the rarified world of private nonprofits, with no mandate to allow open access to its proceedings, there is a need for strong leaders who have a clear sense of values to insist on accountability for ethical behavior that will apply to everyone.

A fast breaking scandal

The Olympic Games scandal had its roots in the 1991 secret vote of IOC members who awarded the 1998 winter games to Nagano, Japan. Nagano led in each of the five rounds of voting, beating Salt Lake City, Utah, by a vote of 46 to 42, in the final ballot. When the competition for the 2002 winter games came up, Salt Lake City was again ready with a strong bid — so strong, in fact, that several commentators said the city would have beaten the other nine competing cities on the merits alone.

But apparently winning the bid for rights to host the Olympic Games is not done on the merits and Salt Lake City, which had tried four times over twenty-five years to be selected, was not leaving anything to chance. It watched how other successful cities pursued the Olympic gold and followed suit. Salt Lake City was indeed selected to be host city in 2002, but its competitive

---

[1] *The Salt Lake Tribune* provided extensive global coverage of the unfolding scandal of the International Olympic Committee, including background information about the IOC and past Olympics. *The Tribune*'s archives are accessible at www.sltrib.com.

practices for securing the rights were called into question at the end of 1998.

In a surprise announcement, KTVX Channel 4 in Salt Lake City disclosed that in 1991 the organizing committee had developed a "scholarship program" which supplied $393,871 worth of tuition, living expenses and athletic training for 13 individuals, including six relatives of IOC members who were voting on Salt Lake City's bid. When the allegations came to light, the committee's rebuttal that the monies were humanitarian assistance looked ridiculous.

As is so often the case in a fast-breaking ethics scandal, more revelations emerged. More than one million dollars in shotguns, rifles and skis, luggage, clothes and athletic equipment were given to visiting IOC members, despite a rule that barred members from receiving gifts worth more than $150.

Loose structure, no common code of values

When the scandal broke, the IOC's members ranged from 86-year old Hadj Mohammed Benjelloun of Morocco who joined in 1961, to 40-year old Prince Albert of Monaco who joined in 1985. Of the 114 members, 48 were from Europe, 21 from the Americas, 20 from Africa, 20 from Asia and 5 from Oceania. Juan Antonio Samaranch of Spain had been president since 1980, presiding over an executive board of eleven IOC members serving four-year terms.

There was no clear nominating or election process that allowed one to become an IOC member. The executive board proposed new members, who were generally approved by acclamation. Members could serve until age 80, unless grandfathered. The average age in 1998 of the IOC's 102 male and 12 female members was 61 and a half. Voting on cities to host the Olympics was the most important function for most of the IOC members. According to one member who retired in 1994, the IOC "lives among itself. The members are like cardinals in the Vatican. Governments come and go — it doesn't matter to us." [2]

---

[2] Christopher Clarey, "Perquisites and Total Autonomy," *The New York Times*, December 21, 1998, p. D8.

Unlike the cardinals at the Vatican, however, who appear to be a cohesive unit, the IOC members, all volunteers, appeared to have no common organizational ties — and their informal approach to their duties started with the informal way they were chosen.

With such a variety of nationalities, cultures, ages and experience, it would seem desirable for IOC members, all volunteers, to be bound by a comprehensive and well-audited code of conduct to insure against diverse business and cultural practices that, if revealed, might be considered unethical. Unfortunately, that was not the case.

Not salt water taffy

Was Salt Lake City guilty or merely an innocent victim? Longtime IOC executive board member Marc Hodler of Switzerland suggested that the city was just the most recent victim, boldly stating that the Olympics were for sale, with blocks of votes delivered to bid cities by agents for payments of millions of dollars.

Whether consultants, lobbyists or agents received payments and whether the treatment of visiting IOC members was lavish hospitality or bribery, the damage had been done. A pall was now cast over the games and the financial stakes were high. Included in the estimated $2 billion worth of construction projects for infrastructure in Utah to support the Olympics was $60 million of public money. Six years before they won the bid, citizens were so anxious to win the Olympics that they voted to impose new taxes on themselves. Now they were appalled. Salt Lake City's bid committee spent almost $15 million in private money to pursue the winter games. Organizing officials needed to raise $859 million through sponsorships and ticket sales to balance the budget for the event.

While to young athletes the Olympic Gold may still represent an ideal worth striving for, the reality is that the winter and summer games are billion-dollar businesses. Just how big the business is can be found in the fact that NBC agreed to pay $3.55 billion to broadcast all the games for the years 2000 through 2008. Ever since Los Angeles reported earnings of $227.7 million from the 1984 Summer Games, cities, countries and local Olympic Committees have aggressively pursued the right to host the

> **"T**he Olympics are no longer a corner clambake.
> Two hundred countries are invited with half the planet
> watching. The host city is on global display for 16 days
> and on the international map forever. Salt Lake City's
> budget for the Winter Games is $1.4 billion. That ain't
> salt water taffy."
>
> John Powers
> *The Boston Globe*
> December 24, 1998, page C1

games. Not surprisingly, the price has gone up. Now the IOC tariff is $55 million for major sponsors, more than 10 times as much as the amount it charged during the 1984 Olympics.

With revenues of approximately $10 billion every four years, the IOC is in the catbird seat. The IOC decides which sports will be included and negotiates the television and sponsorship contracts that fund the games and its operation. The Salt Lake City event, with an operating budget of $1.45 billion, is expected to have an economic impact of $2.8 billion.

According to *Inside Big-Time Sports: Television, Money & the Fans*, vast commercialization of the Olympics helps the networks recoup their rights fees and generates millions of dollars in revenue for the IOC. International marketers and the local organizing committee parse the Olympic commercial pie into sponsors, "official" suppliers of goods and services and exclusive advertisers in various categories, some of whom spend upwards of $100 million to associate with the five rings.[3]

The United States Olympic Committee (USOC) was seeking to raise $1 billion to support the Salt Lake City games and to outfit the United States teams before and after 2002 and hoped to earn $250 million as its share of the event. But when the scandal broke, U.S. sponsors were not rushing to cut checks. U.S. West,

---

[3] David Klatell and Norman Marcus, *Inside Big Time Sports: Television, Money & the Fans*, New York: MasterMedia, Ltd., 1996.

one potential sponsor, lost little time in making its views known, stating in a letter that "the ideals and spirit of the Olympic Games and the values and high standards of the athletes draw companies like ours to sponsor the process and to use these powerful symbols of commitment, determination and fair play in our marketing, management and community affairs efforts.The very core of these ideals and the spirit of the games are now under scrutiny and perhaps tainted.This is an extremely serious issue for all of us."[4]

David F. D'Alessandro, president of John Hancock Financial Services, was clear about the status of the $40 million Hancock pays every four years to sponsor the games. "Perhaps the IOC will only do the right thing when it understands that its revenues as well as its reputation are in peril."[5]

The warning signs were there

At least one Utah industrialist was not surprised at the turn of events. Jon M. Huntsman Sr. had been an enthusiastic supporter of Utah's unsuccessful bid for the 1998 winter games, even contributing $100,000 to the cause. But in 1994 he pulled his support from any further efforts because of his concerns about how the bid procedure was being carried out and a lack of fiscal accountability. "The activities that surrounded the Olympic bid committee never passed what I would call a smell test," he said. "It was out of control almost from the very beginning."[6]

In Lausanne, Switzerland, the IOC launched an investigation into the allegations; in Utah the organizing committee's ethics panel began its own investigation; the United States Olympic Committee named former Senator George Mitchell, facilitator for the Ireland peace process, to lead its inquiry into the bribery charges; and the FBI began investigating possible criminal violations. The IOC imposed an immediate ban on members visiting

---

[4] Mike Gorrell, "Mitchell May Be Chosen To Head Olympic Probe," *The Salt Lake Tribune*, December 22, 1998.

[5] David F. D'Alessandro, "How to Save the Olympics," *The New York Times*, February 14, 1999, p. 40.

[6] Bob Mims, "Huntsman Says Bid Process By S.L. Was 'Out of Control,'" *The Salt Lake Tribune*, December 18, 1998.

> **"Well**, one has to play by the rules of life. If one does not play by the rules of life, then everyone loses. That's why it's so important that we selected our leaders carefully and from those who have proven track records of integrity and honor. But for anyone to suggest or infer that in dealing with the international arena that bribery and payoffs are essential is absolutely false. It's nonessential and not done by those who have respect in the international business arena."
>
> Jon M. Huntsman
> Salt Lake City industrialist, *Salt Lake City Tribune,*
> December 18, 1998

cities bidding for the 2006 winter games: Sion, Switzerland; Turin, Italy; Zakopane, Poland; Klagenfurt, Austria and Helsinki, Finland.

Not surprisingly, once the scandal in Salt Lake City broke wide open, other allegations surfaced. Apparently Salt Lake City bid organizers were just the most recent players in a long process of bribery.[7] The night before Nagano, Japan was selected to host the 1998 Winter Games, Japanese officials gave IOC members luggage, laptop computers and promised to fund a $25 million Olympic museum in Lausanne, Switzerland, home of President Samaranch. The German magazine *Der Spiegel* alleged that Atlanta used bribes to win the 1996 Summer Games and Toronto, a loser in that sweepstakes, outlined apparent abuses of the bid process by IOC members in a report to the IOC. Sydney's practices were questioned, as was an allegation that the press in Australia knew of extravagant payments to IOC members but in the interest of civic solidarity, declined to report them. Investigators in Sweden, Japan, Russia and Britain followed trails of money laundering and other illegitimate activities through Olympic committees.

---

[7] While out of print by 1999, *The Lords of the Rings: Power, Money and Drugs in the Modern Olympics,* by Vyv Simson, alleged widespread corruption within the IOC long before the Salt Lake City scandal arose.

Conflicts of interest emerged all over the map, and not just between gift-givers and gift-takers. Jean-Claude Ganga of the Congo, accused of accepting over $250,000 worth of valuables, was a close ally of Samaranch, and led the drive to allow him to raise the retirement age and continue in office until age 80. Several members of the Salt Lake City Olympic Committee who were also doing business with the IOC woke up to the dangers of conflicts of interest and resigned. A USOC member who "consulted" to bid cities on the side also resigned. Salt Lake City's Mayor, Deedee Corradini, a member of the SLCOC, announced she would not run for re-election, forgoing a chance to welcome international visitors to the Games as the city's mayor. James Easton, one of only two American members of the IOC, acknowledged his Salt Lake City company provided a job to the son of an IOC member, while at the same time urging the expulsion of fellow IOC members who accepted improper favors.

Even Olympic history was fair game for critics. Researchers revealed that former IOC President Avery Brundage's construction company was promised the job of building the German Embassy in Washington if Berlin was selected as the site of the infamous 1936 Games. Others asserted that Olympic officials stood by as demonstrating students were machine-gunned in Mexico in 1968 so the world would see a sanitized view of Mexico City and its Summer Games.

The Special Bid Oversight Commission, headed by George Mitchell, was not subtle in its sweeping indictment of the scandal. It placed the blame on the lack of audits and checks and balances at every level: the bidding city, the USOC and the IOC. In an organizational culture that was potentially illegal and inevitably corrupt, the report noted, "It strains credulity to believe that so many responsible citizens could participate in such a long and highly public campaign to influence IOC members and spend so much money in the process, but that only Messrs. Welch or Johnson were aware of the improprieties surrounding these activities."[8]

It was not only Salt Lake City board members who dozed through the process, although all the books and records were

---

[8] Linda Fantin, "USOC Report: S.L. Organizers Must Have Known," *The Salt Lake Tribune*, March 2, 1999.

apparently available to them. The USOC made no attempt to audit bid committee books and records. In fact, USOC members also accepted lodging, entertainment and gifts from Salt Lake City. Even the board's independent auditors came under criticism, as board members explained that Ernst & Young assured them all four annual audits were clean.[9] "Clean" perhaps meant that no one was stealing, but the auditors apparently accepted without comment the committee's procedures that allowed checks to IOC members to be paid without documentation.

But the seeds of scandal were there, if anyone with a green eyeshade wanted to look closely. In 1988 auditors for the Utah Legislature documented many questionable practices at the three organizations that later became the Salt Lake City Bid Committee. It was headed by the two individuals who later found themselves at the center of the IOC scandal. Allegations of abuse of public funds, accepting improper gifts, expense irregularities, high lobster, steak and liquor bills, and payment of bills without receipts or documentation were cited. Apparently no one paid attention then, or later.

The aftermath

The stories of scandal had their effect. Stockholders and directors of companies that were anteing up millions of dollars for the Olympics questioned whether the company's fragile institutional image would be sullied by the association. Some predicted the IOC would wake up from the controversy and discover that its brand is worth much less than it thinks, allowing competitors like the Goodwill Games and individual sport competitions like World Cup soccer to lure away sponsors and fans.

Until this scandal, the IOC had not expelled one of its own members in four decades. After the investigations, four resigned, the IOC expelled six and reprimanded nine. But critics complained members from small, poorer countries were singled out, while favorites, such as executive board member Un Yong Kim of South Korea, only received a warning. Samaranch himself, who received thousands of dollars in gifts from Salt Lake City, received an IOC pat on the back — a vote of 86 to 2 to keep him

---

[9] Mike Gorrel, "Bid Committee: Who Knew What, When?" *The Salt Lake Tribune*, January 17, 1999.

in power. But United States government officials continued to investigate possible illegal actions by the IOC chief, while Swiss officials considered revoking the tax-exempt status of the IOC. In August 1999 Justice department prosecutors obtained their first guilty plea in a criminal case arising from the Salt Lake City effort. David E. Simmons, the former chairman of Keystone Communications, pleaded guilty to a tax violation in connection with the hiring of IOC Vice President Un Yong Kim's son, for which he was reimbursed by the bid committee. Simmons also agreed to cooperate with the Department of Justice in its investigations and prosecutions of committee leaders.

Finally, even the award of the next Olympics site engendered outrage. In June 1999, by a secret 53-36 vote, Turin, Italy beat out Sion, Switzerland for the 2006 Winter Games, even though Sion had the best rating from a technical evaluation committee. Jean-Loup Chappelet of Sion was blunt, accusing IOC members of voting out of revenge against an early IOC whistleblower, Marc Hodler of Switzerland. "We were robbed,"[10] he said.

Message from Salt Lake

The lessons of the scandal are simple. A code of conduct without audits or assessments is meaningless. If the IOC is to keep its nonprofit status and its volunteer members unpaid, its leaders need to think about whether the intent to do good works is sufficient to counteract the lure of perks and the temptations of outright personal gain available to IOC members.

An ethical framework that includes audits and assessment is even more critical in the case of an organization like the IOC because of the difficulties of policing the body that controls the Olympics and billions of dollars. As a "private" international organization, the IOC was exempt from laws that govern corruption in international transactions. But as nine-time Olympic gold medal winner Carl Lewis said, "I don't know of any organization that has more power or makes more money that is less regulated in the entire world than the IOC."[11]

---

[10] Indira A.R. Lakshmanan, "Irate Swiss claim IOC was amiss in selecting Turin," *The Boston Globe*, June 20, 1999.

[11] Associated Press, "IOC Ready to Expel Some Members," *The Salt Lake Tribune*, January 13, 1999.

Chapter 22

Revision and Reform

The last of our ten points is that a program to instill values into an organization must be more than a precise model that sits on a shelf gathering dust. It must be a living instrument. Circumstances and situations often change from month to month, year to year, requiring managers to reevaluate the goals and contents of even the most carefully thought out values program. Some companies go as far as to use specific words in their materials that anticipate constant change, rather than resting comfortably on a static program.

At Motorola, for example, the ethics initiative is called "Motorola Ethics Renewal Process." In an attempt to be flexible and meaningful for the company's 150,000 employees, 60 percent of whom work outside the United States, the emphasis is on the word "process." Rather than relying on a formal program or a detailed audit, Motorola managers have determined that to meet their goal of being the most trusted company in the world, its employees needed a flexible process by which to discuss tough issues.

Motorola and companies like it are unusual, however, in the depth of their proactive commitment to change. More often than not, the revision and reform that we advocate are reactive, caused by external circumstances.

Events precipitate change

There is nothing that spurs change faster than a scandal. Roger Tetrault, chairman of the board and chief executive officer of McDermott International, Inc., tells the story of taking over leadership of the company in March 1997. Three weeks later, he learned that one of McDermott's joint venture companies had been involved in an on-going conspiracy to rig bids. Two years later, the price tag of the Justice Department investigation and the company's legal bills was over $5 million. In Tetrault's view, what was even worse than the exorbitant cost of the scandal was the management time and attention that was diverted from building the company during the two years it spent in defending itself.

McDermott had a compliance program before the scandal broke, but Tetrault set about to improve it. Two changes he made immediately included declining to bid on any contract in which the company suspected overseas business partners were not complying with United States standards, and a commitment to help prosecute employees who break the law.

Tetrault is resolute about the changes that were needed in his company and he challenges those in other companies: "Is your compliance program a mishmash of legalese or does it speak to the gut issue of right and wrong and crime and punishment? Does it have teeth?" he asks. "If it doesn't, you'll never touch those very smart people who are going to someday hurt your company."

Tetrault suggests that companies take a survey to find out whether employees think the existing compliance programs are sincere. "You may be surprised at the results. You may find that what your management says and what your employees believe are two different things as we found out two years ago."[1]

Only where there's a will

Roger Tetrault is obviously committed to implementing a values-driven management culture at McDermott. In the aftermath of a scandal and with his personal pledge to institute change, he will no doubt be successful. The more difficult circumstances arise when reform is needed but the will is lacking. Royal Caribbean Cruises is a case in point. Described as having a "culture of crime," the cruise line pleaded guilty to routinely dumping haz-

---

[1] Roger E. Tetrault, "The Development of an Ethical Culture," presentation at the 1999 Conference Board Business Ethics Conference, May 17, 1999.

ardous chemicals in coastal waters, violating federal water pol-
lution laws.[2] That doesn't sound too bad, until you learn that this
dumping continued after the cruise line had been convicted
earlier of illegal dumping charges and had promised to stop. It
didn't stop, continuing to lie to the Coast Guard.

The cruise line had paid a $9 million fine for illegal dumping,
obstruction of justice and engaging in a fleet-wide conspiracy.
But nothing changed. Two years later it was forced to pay an $18
million fine again, despite the fact that an outside auditor
warned the company that it was continuing to violate the law.

One wonders whether there will be any reform of the culture
at Royal Caribbean any time soon. When the latest fine was
announced, the company said it had made a mistake. A Justice
Department lawyer retorted that they were not in the business
of prosecuting mistakes. Perhaps Royal Caribbean was gambling
that after the first fine, federal authorities would leave them
alone. By continuing the illegal dumping, the cruise line report-
edly saved tens of thousands of dollars per ship.

It's easy to see that the management culture at Royal
Caribbean needs serious reform and revision. In fact, it needs to
embrace all ten steps in our suggested program to implement
values-driven management, but from their past behavior it
seems hard to imagine that any of the ten will soon be adopted.

Change due to learning

The companies and organizations with the best values programs
are always in tune with feedback received from employees, customers and others. But listening is not enough. When managers
begin to hear the same tune over and over, they must challenge
themselves to react, revise and refresh what they are doing to
address it.

Olin Corporation, which we discussed in chapter 11, is such
an organization. Olin has a variety of resources for employees,
including its ethics help-line. According to Bob Gebing, vice president, business ethics and integrity, a large number of employee

---

[2] Matthew L. Wald, "Cruise Line Pleads Guilty to Dumping of Chemicals, " *The New York Times*, July 22, 1999, p. A10.

Respect

We All Need To Feel Valued

Knowing how to show respect for other people is not an inborn skill. In fact, all of our instincts tell us to look out for Number One. We want to protect our turf. Run off the intruders. Defend ourselves.

It's only as we learn how to live and work together that we come to understand the importance of respect. When it's missing, we feel unimportant. Left out. Resentful. When it's part of our environment, we feel valued. We feel like a part of things.

That's why this brochure was created. To get people thinking about respect. Respect for our families, our friends, our coworkers, or selves. Respect for our customers and suppliers. When we act and speak with respect, we protect the dignity of the individual. We also minimize negativity and conflict. We defend our values and ethics.

Respect is one of the keys to an effective, constructive business environment. An environment that makes everything we do easier, better — and more productive.

Respect —It's a two-way street
Olin Corporation

callers described a tone of insensitivity or discourtesy, which in totality added up to a feeling of lack of respect. The same issue surfaced in surveys Olin conducted after holding its training programs. "The message from our employees was loud and clear," said Gebing. So Olin produced a new brochure on precisely addressing the issue of interpersonal relations.

In Olin's characteristic bold colors and graphics, the cover stated, "Respect. It's a two-way street." The inside of the brochure gave ten tips for promoting respect, and suggested other problems that might be going on when employees feel a lack of respect. Is disrespectful language symptomatic of personal problems? Insecurity? The need for control? Employees can read the brochure and get some ideas and suggestions for an effective response. On the back of the brochure, as usual, Olin lays out all the resources that employees have available to get additional help or clarification.

Respect is a simple issue, and Olin's response was thoughtful and effective. The reason to praise Olin, however, is not for the content of the brochure, which is admirable, but for its sophisticated response to an issue that was bubbling up to the surface. By listening and reacting, Olin keeps its program values-centered and refreshed.

Change due to altered environment

Everything may be progressing swimmingly in your shop, but you pick up the newspaper one day and read about a competitor's woes. The lurid details of a scandal or settlement agreement with regulators should cause alert managers to revisit their own operations, including the content of ethics and values programs. If, for example, Bear Stearns Securities has just settled charges with the Securities and Exchange Commission for $38.5 million relating to its securities processing operations, its Wall Street peers should immediately perform a self-assessment to see if they might also be at risk for similar violations or relaxed standards. At the very least, communications and training programs should use the Bear Stearns example as a teaching tool, so that employees will feel free to ask questions and raise concerns.

Companies are always in danger of being caught by shifting sands, unless they carefully monitor new developments in their industry and in their regulatory world. This naturally calls for them to revise their own operations to reflect these changes. There are numerous examples of behavior and practices that were tolerated, or even encouraged, one month which may be considered crossing the line the next. Consider the issue of managing earnings. When SEC Chairman Arthur Leavitt gave a speech in September 1998 attacking what he considered bad financial reporting, alert CPAs, finance officers and others took notice. Now, what some might have considered accounting irregularities could well be regarded as financial fraud. The difference is not minor. *Fortune* magazine listed a sampler of CEOs named for accounting fraud, including Donald Ferraini of Underwriters Financial Group (reported nonexistent revenues, 12-year sentence), Richard Rubin of Donnekenny (concocted false invoices, faces 5-year sentence), and Steven Hoffenberg of Towers Financial (defrauded investors of $450 million, 20-year sentence).[3]

These executives may well have deserved their criminal penalty. The more important question is whether the next team to take the field will stumble as well, due to negligence, arrogance, lack of information, peer or supervisor pressure, or the simple desire to go along to get along.

Change because it's right

Sometimes managers feel that if a procedure or practice has been initiated in the name of ethics or compliance, it is untouchable. Not so. Sometimes a fresh look is needed, as well as a courageous hand to stop the continuation of an idea whose time has passed.

The Chairman's Ethics Council at Detroit Edison took just such an action at one of its first meetings. Joseph Saunders, an audit manager, reported to the council on an employee conduct survey his office was prepared to send out. Saunders launched into his 25-page presentation, explaining that the survey, originally designed to report and uncover conflict of interest, was an annual undertaking. From its original design to reflect conflict of interest issues, it had been expanded to encompass other company policies such as environmental standards and business expenses.

Saunders had barely started his presentation when questions flew at him from council members, whose members included a broad representation of employees, from union representatives and corporate staff and line managers. The questions were blunt and direct.

"I've been here 34 years. Are you asking me if I've ever observed wrongdoing during that time?"

"If we have to sign our own names to these, why would we answer 'yes' to questions that ask if we've ever accepted travel from an outside supplier, given outsiders access to confidential

---

[3] Carol J. Loomis, "The CEO as Felon," in "Lies, Damned Lies, and Managed Earnings," *Fortune*, August 2, 1999, p. 82.

"Like all companies, Detroit Edison always had values that guided our behaviors. Some of those values were articulated though most were not. They just grew up over the years. Through the years, we held values that were typical of the electric utility industry. Rules and process oriented. Top-down management — a parent-child relationship. And the CEO was the parent who had all of the answers. (What a rude awakening employees had when I took over.)

"Employees counted on their 'Detroit Edison family' to take care of them through retirement. But today's labor market no longer supports the concept of 'lifetime employment.' Does that make Detroit Edison or any of the thousands of firms that are wrestling with changing the employment model unethical? I hope not. Our challenge is to find a model that is true to our obligation to run a successful business and one that is responsive to the needs of our community and employees. We believe that preparing our employees for the changing world and equipping them with the skills they need to ensure 'lifetime employability' is the best and most ethical thing we can do. We must prepare employees that not only have technical skills for the 21st Century, but also leadership and human skills that never go out of style."

Anthony F. Earley, Jr.
Detroit Edison chairman and chief executive officer,
"Responsibility: The Price of Greatness,"
University of Detroit-Mercy, March 23, 1999

company information or are aware of unreported environmental violations?"

"If the purpose of the survey is to increase employee awareness of the policies, why don't we just train them instead of sending out a survey?"

"If we're doing this to collect data, how useful is it really going to be?"

"What do other companies do?"

"Have we thought through the entire process? After we raise awareness we'll have questions from employees. Do we have the training and resources ready to handle them?"

"Why is the survey being distributed just to managers? It's often the clerical and administrative staff who really know what's going on."

Council members offered suggestions and continued to challenge Saunders as well as each other. Finally, one member expressed what quickly became the group's consensus. "You're bringing this survey to us to partner it with the council, but you can't do that. We have real concerns with it."

The council — which some had said had no real authority, given its 'advisory' role — had stopped the survey dead in its tracks. Saunders promised to redesign the survey instrument to test procedural awareness and to present it at the council's next meeting.

John Howell, Detroit Edison's ethics officer, was surprised but gratified at the outcome. "I had no idea the council would do that," he said. "I thought maybe they'd change a couple of questions. This shows the council does have real power to affect change, to prevent us from doing the wrong thing, and to direct us in doing the right thing."

Some change is difficult

Sometimes revision and reform is necessitated by the organization discovering that an ethical principle or value it had held as sacrosanct has become the subject of debate and divisiveness. We are not about to suggest that in the face of any opposition, managers cave to those who can shout the loudest. However, raised voices sometimes give a clue that organizational ownership is lacking and either revision or further explanation is needed.

Earlier in the book we cited the example of the use of technology and respect for company property and privacy as a complex issue many managers are facing. It is appropriate to revisit that issue again. Professor David W. Gill, the Carl I. Lindberg Professor of Applied Ethics at North Park University, has warned that if technology is transforming the way business is organized and carried out, it must necessarily transform the way we approach business ethics. [4] Gill critiqued the current crop of

---

[4] David W. Gill, "The Technological Blindspot in Business Ethics," paper at the Fifth Annual DePaul University Conference Promoting Business Ethics, October 30, 1998.

business ethics textbooks and found them lacking, having little awareness of the impact of technology on business and few using cases to address contemporary technology issues. He's undoubtedly right, because we see that the intersection of technology and business is confounding organizations as well. If they can't keep current with its challenges, it is no wonder that business ethics textbook writers can't either.

No less an august institution than Harvard University found itself embroiled in a difficult ethical case concerning technology. Ronald Thiemann, respected dean of the Harvard Divinity School, was forced to resign after university computer technicians discovered thousands of pornographic images on Thiemann's computer. What makes the case difficult is that although the computer was university-owned, it was located in the dean's office in his university-owned home. Evidently the cyberporn was legal, but the staff was "unavoidably and involuntarily exposed to inappropriate materials which they found to be not only offensive, but severely distressing," according to Harvard's president. [5]

Others thought differently. Harvard Law School Professor Alan Dershowitz questioned why the technicians weren't disciplined for revealing the content of someone's computer in his office, a gross violation of one's right to privacy. "The notion that a person is entitled to less freedom because that computer and that home are part of his compensation package is abhorrent," said Dan Kennedy in *The Boston Phoenix*. [6] The debate continues beyond Harvard's ivied walls. Even a poll aimed at human resource professionals arrived at a split verdict. By a slight margin, 48 percent thought that Thiemann, a minister who had founded the Center for the Study of Values in Public Life, had exhibited conduct unbecoming for a person in his position. But 43 percent thought what he did was legal, harmed no one and was done on his own time. [7]

While this ethical dilemma may illustrate to some the tension between "big brother and constitutionally protected free

---

[5] James Bandler and Ross Kerber, "Harvard defends role in dean's resignation amid porn claims," *The Boston Globe*, July 3, 1999.

[6] Dan Kennedy, "The second annual Muzzle Awards," *The Boston Phoenix*, July 1, 1999.

[7] "News Poll," *Workforce*, July 1999, p. 20.

speech" on the one hand, and "standards about the use of company property and hostile environments" on the other, to us it suggests that Harvard might need to revisit its policies on technology. If the institution decides the policies shouldn't be changed, at the very least they should be re-explained to those who are expected to live by them.

Rules are often changed, but programs based on values are no less in need of constant scrutiny and revision. How that revision is done should be developed according to the framework and culture of the institution. There is no single right way — it is the process that is important.

Chapter 23

Guardsmark and Ira Lipman
LIVING VALUES, CONSTANTLY RENEWED

The story of the development of values-based management at some companies is usually a story of an ethical crisis followed by a thoughtful response. Occasionally the story is one of ethical awakening, when a senior manager is inspired by current events and the example of the best practices set by his corporate peers.

The story of Guardsmark, the fifth largest security firm in the country, and its founder, Ira A. Lipman, offers a kaleidoscope of images. With every turn of the lens, these images coalesce into a unified story of clear moral values — developed by family, nurtured and honed across a lifetime of work dedicated to protecting human life and physical assets, exemplified in public service. "Truth, courage and judgment are the hallmarks of our service," is Guardsmark's description. Those three values apply equally to Ira Lipman. As he renewed these values by actions in his own life, so too, his company renews its values in a unique process.

On the front lines of civil rights

Ira Lipman demonstrated his instinctive moral character at a young age. As a sixteen-year-old high school student in Little

Rock, Arkansas, he was on the front lines of the segregation battles that raged in the late 1950's. In that tense atmosphere he could have kept his head low, but instead he befriended one of the nine black students who integrated Little Rock Central High. He also realized that thanks to the emerging world of television news and the presence of NBC's John Chancellor in Little Rock, the moral crisis confronting Little Rock was fast becoming a national story. Lipman dared to help, calling Chancellor anonymously from a pay phone outside the school to provide him with important details on the story. In an atmosphere that had made the name Emmett Till a household word signifying martyrdom, Lipman was putting his life in danger.[1] But his inherent sense of justice and morality propelled him forward, as it would in his adult years, when he built a national security company based on the same core values.

Lipman's father, Mark, was a private investigator in Little Rock, so Lipman grew up with the investigation business and understood the importance of security. Lipman began to work with his father, but in 1963 started his own company specializing in uniformed security services. He named the company Guardsmark, after his father. Guardsmark grew quickly, ultimately acquiring Mark Lipman's company, which became the Mark Lipman Division of Guardsmark — its investigative arm. By 1999 Guardsmark had 115 branch offices and operated in more than 400 cities, employing 14,000 people. The annual revenues of this privately held company exceeded $300 million.

Ahead of his time

Guardsmark adopted its first code of ethics in 1980, a time when the business ethics movement was still young.

"We felt the right thing to do was to have a code of ethics," recalled Lipman. "We wanted a sheet of music that all people in the company would understand, something that says, 'This is what we stand for.' That first code was developed by our managers and corporate staff, at our monthly management meetings. We did it together and agreed upon it. Today, however, we've learned that the best way is a bottom up process."

---

[1] David Halberstam, *The Fifties*, Villard Books, 1993, pp. 680-681.

In its first ten years the code was revised three times, but in 1991 Lipman decided that it should be revised every year, and asked his managers and corporate staff for suggestions. To make sure that employees knew the code was changing every year, Lipman decided to institute a sunset provision in 1992, making the code invalid after a certain date.

"We'd sit in meetings year after year and look at the code," said Lipman, recalling the earlier revision process. "But we wanted to make sure we changed it and that people *knew* we changed it. The sunset provision really got people involved and participating, because we asked for their suggestions. A sunset provision means that you are forced to revise it. Too many people write something up and never return to it to see what else is needed, due to societal changes, new developments in the company or changes in the industry. We do this every year.

"The sunset provision and revision process also make people reread the code, because they knew we'd be asking them for ideas for the new code. Then, when the new code is published, everyone reads it again, to see how it has changed."

In 1995, when Lipman decided to expand the company's ethics office, he also decided that he wanted to "blaze new trails," according to Stephen I. Kasloff, the company's corporate ethics officer. "Mr. Lipman wanted the whole company to have the opportunity to be involved in the annual revision and renewal process, so he asked us to solicit comments from all members of the Guardsmark family," said Kasloff.

"We wanted the input of all 14,000 men and women of Guardsmark," Lipman explained, "so that people can really feel that they make a difference. We're very proud of that. It's not a dictated code used for marketing purposes — it's a living document."

The continuous improvement process

"We live and breathe the code of ethics at Guardsmark because it's a year-round process," said Kasloff. "First we send it out every January in the pay envelopes to every employee. We include a letter asking for suggestions about how to make it better. Then in February or March, a letter is sent to each field employee from his or her manager asking for comments or suggestions about the code. Again, the letter is included in the pay envelopes.

"We include 'ethics code revision' as part of our learning curriculum. This, too, produces recommendations for revising the code.

"I also call managers asking for suggestions. By July I have all the suggestions compiled for review by our corporate ethics committee. In 1999 we received suggestions from 304 employees. Some were duplications but in all we received 168 different recommendations for changes. The ethics committee, which is comprised of four members, considered each one and recommended that approximately thirteen be adopted.

"When the ethics committee's report is finished, it then goes to the President's Meeting, consisting of executive management, regional managers and corporate staff. The President's Meeting participants debate each one and the final revisions are then prepared for inclusion in the new code."

Ira Lipman does not pull rank at the President's Meeting. "I have just a single vote," he said. "I'm a consensus person, and we all have to agree on the changes or else if opinion is divided, we refer it for further study. We don't adopt every recommendation of the ethics committee, but we agree with probably 85 percent of them."

Attention to detail

There is no doubt that Guardsmark's employees pay careful attention to the code of ethics. Its eight sections are clear and straightforward, as is the introduction:

> The **Guardsmark Code of Ethics** is our Company's statement of values. Our first **Code of Ethics** was created in 1980. The **Code** expresses the unity of **Guardsmark's** business purpose and ethical vision — and it empowers us in carrying out our mission, in earning the trust upon which it rests, and in being true to the best in each of us. That trust is built from every action of each individual. It is not won, but earned through living each day those values and principles which nurture it. Our mission is to be the best security service company in the world, to do the right thing, and always to exceed our customers' expectations. [2]

---

[2] Guardsmark, Inc., *Code of Ethics*, 1998, p. 1.

The code also contains resources for assistance. The sunset clause and the company's toll-free number are printed in bold at the end of the code, together with the names of the ethics committee members and the company's address, for ease of contact.

In 1998 and 1999, as in past years, employees suggested important changes in the language of the existing code. Among the additions they requested in 1998 was the idea that a supervisor's responsibility includes the duty to "exercise supervisory authority fairly."

Under "commitment to excellence," in 1998 employees decided that the responsibility to reduce waste and maximize efficiency should be done "without compromising our standards." Although the "commitment to excellence" section already contained a provision for reporting potential code violations, in 1999 an additional paragraph was added specifically addressing "requests which conflict with this code of ethics." This resulted from the separate suggestions of a corporate staff member and a field supervisor.

In 1998 the company added "internet access" to the code's prohibition on the use of company or customer equipment or software for personal use, and in 1999, at the suggestion of a security officer, this prohibition was extended to specifically include electronic mail.

Two days of celebration and renewal

Soon after Ira Lipman founded Guardsmark, he realized that he would need to recognize excellence if he were to succeed in promoting it across the company, and the first company award was created and given in 1967. Today "Winning Wednesday®" and "Terrific Thursday®," the Wednesday and Thursday prior to Labor Day, are designated a company-wide celebration of achievement and numerous awards are given at this event.

In 1991, the year before the code of ethics sunset provision was added, Lipman decided to incorporate recognition of the new code into the company's traditional celebration of excellence. "Winning Wednesday® and Terrific Thursday® are our Academy Awards," explains Kasloff. "The final ceremony of the two-day event is the official signing of the new code by everyone at the event. It's the perfect conclusion to the celebration because it dramatizes that our ethical commitment is indivisible from our business commitment. If we are going to continue to be successful, who we are and what we do must be the same."

The back page of the code of ethics, called "personal commitment," is the signature page of the code. One hundred signatures were reproduced in 1998 under a declaration that states ". . . by our signing we encourage everyone to join our pledge to adopt personal standards of integrity, responsibility, honesty, self-control, self-respect and self-confidence, and our pledge to strengthen our weaknesses and build on our strengths. We further accept the responsibility of incorporating the values of this code into our thoughts and actions each and every day. We will honor the spirit as well as the letter of this code. We will lead by example." [3]

The formal signing ceremony does not end the revision and renewal process, however. "We ask everyone who is in the Memphis headquarters that day to sign the code," says Kasloff, "even if there is not room for all their signatures on the back page. We videotape the ceremony so that each of our offices can see it, and then we ask each office to have a signing ceremony as well.

"Thereafter I send out a letter to each person who sent in a suggestion for revising the code, and we publish their names in *Update*, the company's biweekly newsletter."

Update contains a major feature story each September about the code of ethics and the signing ceremony to further communicate the company's renewal process. "We highlight the photograph of the signing of the code year after year," explains Lipman. "We want to make a strong point that this is important."

A living document

After the code of ethics is revised, the company sends it out to the far corners of Guardsmark's operations. It is posted in easel form in every office and published as a stand-alone booklet for distribution. The code has been included in orientation booklets and in security officers' manuals. But Guardsmark does not wait

---

[3] Guardsmark, Inc., *Code of Ethics*, 1998, p. 7.

until an employee is hired to expose him or her to the code. Every person who applies for a job at Guardsmark has to sign the code as a part of the application process, so they are aware right from the beginning of the standards the company expects.

"Our code is an integral part of our business because the very business we are conducting is one of integrity," Kasloff explained. "We are safeguarding our clients' assets, and our employees don't work at our facilities — they are out on other people's sites. We have to conduct ourselves with the highest standards.

"Because we are so spread out, we use the code as a learning tool," said Kasloff. "It's an ideal vehicle to use as a learning device, to explain to managers and employees — and even our customers — what we are all about."

Indeed, the code of ethics is of such importance to the company that a six-foot high framed edition of the code stands prominently in the ten-foot high lobby of Guardsmark's corporate headquarters, alongside a like version of the company's diversity policy. Thus prospective candidates and other visitors entering the company's headquarters see the code of ethics and the diversity policy even before reaching the elevators.

Kasloff and his colleagues also use the code when responding to complaints from the field. "We take complaints and questions seriously because when someone takes the time to write or call and express a concern, it usually means that something has genuinely moved them. We've learned that at times the real issue is something other than that which is being expressed. For example, sometimes it's a case where a person feels a supervisor isn't listening. If you don't feel you are being listened to, you may feel you don't count. And in these cases the code is not being followed because our code requires supervisors to establish an atmosphere of participation and communication, and to show respect and empathy for all employees. It all comes back to the code."

Not just ethics, but diversity

With Ira Lipman's personal commitment to civil rights developed as a young man, it is not surprising that one of Guardsmark's most important and longstanding values is that of diversity. The company's first policy articulating its adherence to equal opportunity was promulgated in 1965, two years after Guardsmark was founded and just a year after the historic Civil Rights Act. The company established its first code of ethics in 1980, a sexual harassment policy in 1982 and a "no slur" policy in 1988. The present diversity policy and statement, including ideas from all the past documents, was drafted in 1997. Like the code of ethics, it was signed that year by all regional managers, branch employees and corporate staff members who signed the code of ethics revision at the annual signing ceremony in Memphis. The company also introduced a new diversity management award in 1997 to recognize the branch offices with the best overall diversity achievement and management programs. Whenever the company hosts a conference for a group of employees they tour the National Civil Rights Museum in Memphis and have the opportunity to hear first-hand from Ira Lipman about the importance of diversity and equal opportunity.

"No country can become great without diversity. No company can become great without diversity. And no person can become great without understanding and practicing diversity," said Lipman.

Kasloff, who oversees the company's diversity efforts, sees the diversity policy and statement as an important companion to the company's code of ethics, and reflective of the founder's own moral values. "Mr. Lipman battled segregated schools in Little Rock as a teenager in the 1950s and worked for integrated facilities in Memphis as an adult in the 1960s. He's been involved in human rights and social justice issues his entire life, so the attention he places on these values is a beacon for all 14,000 employees. It is a key to what makes this company great."

Not just at Guardsmark

Ira Lipman and Guardsmark have long been recognized as leaders in their commitment to values-driven management. This has been expressed in part through involvement with many ethics organizations and centers, including the University of Pennsylvania's Zicklin Center for Business Ethics Research at The Wharton School, the Ethics Officer Association, the Society for Business Ethics, the Ethics Resource Center and the Center for Business Ethics. Moreover, in 1996 Guardsmark was awarded one of the American Business Ethics Awards sponsored by the American Society of Chartered Life Underwriters and Chartered Financial Consultants, in recognition of its strong ethics program.

But the real test of excellence is not whether business peers honor you when things are going well, but whether they turn to you in a time of crisis. Luckily for human service organizations across the country, Ira Lipman's reputation as a values-centered business leader was well known when the United Way of America was rocked by scandal. When its former president and chief executive officer William Aramony was ousted in 1992, the United Way of America's board of governors elected Lipman to the board and promptly asked him to serve as the first chairman of the ethics committee of the board of governors.

Lipman knew where to start, drawing on his own initiatives at Guardsmark and the extensive ethics program he had developed there. The UWA committee worked to draft a code of ethics for both the board and the staff, and not surprisingly, it contained two important features. First, staff and board members are asked to sign the code annually. Second, staff and board members are given the opportunity to review the code annually and recommend new language as needed.

The revision process is important with any code or program. Charles Kolb, former general counsel of the United Way of America, gives an example of how Lipman's idea worked at that charity.[4] The first version of the code of ethics included a section on nepotism, but two board members disagreed on what the provision should include. One felt it was inappropriate to hire family members; another thought that any appearances of favoritism could be worked out. The board decided to allow it, but the following year the code was amended to address the real issue of concern: favoritism by anyone, for any reason.

According to Kolb, Lipman's influence did not stop at leading the United Way of America to the forefront of best practices in ethics and values. Lipman generously underwrote the cost of conducting the first ethics training workshops, not only for the staff of United Way of America, but for local United Way volun-

---

[4] Charles E.M. Kolb, *Developing an Ethics Program*, The National Center for Nonprofit Boards, 1999, p. 10.

teers and staff from around the country, thereby further promoting his high standards of excellence.

In diversity as in ethics, whether outside his company or within it, for Ira Lipman it is all one vision and one set of values — values of excellence and integrity — consistently pursued and applied year after year, over a lifetime.

Chapter 24

Are You Finished?

The task of putting values into action is never finished, which is how it should be. Like the three most important words in selecting real estate (location, location, location), the most important words to remember in maintaining a values-based culture are diligence, diligence, diligence.

But there are clues to indicate whether or not the program is working.

Employees are motivated

Loyal, capable employees are so critical to most enterprises today that we've come to call them human assets, intellectual capital or even investors who are as entitled to tangible rewards as shareholders (who, after all, only invest their money, not their time and effort).

The focus on the behavior and satisfaction level of individual employees may seem misplaced in a discussion of an organization's values culture, but an essential dynamic occurs between individuals and organizations. Individuals do not operate in a vacuum. They gain meaning, direction and purpose by belonging to and acting out of organizations, social cultures that are formed around common goals, shared beliefs and collective duties. Corporations, like other social entities, can and do influence individual decisions and actions. A values-driven program can have a positive influence on employee motivation and performance.

The importance to individual workers of such a program is not to be minimized. A range of recent surveys demonstrates the significance of ethics initiatives in helping employees sort out conflicting priorities and deal with pressure. An April 1997 study by the Ethics Officer Association and the American Society of Chartered Life Underwriters & Chartered Financial Consultants found that 56% of workers feel pressure to act unethically or illegally on the job. Forty-eight percent admitted they had engaged in such actions. These transgressions ranged from deceiving customers to cutting corners on quality.[1]

Even human resource managers, who should know better, aren't immune from pressure. A recent study of human resource professionals found that more than half had observed workplace conduct that violated the law or the organization's standards of ethical business conduct. Nearly half felt pressured to compromise such standards to achieve business objectives.[2]

While such surveys may only report the bad news, ethics officers and other professionals share information about the good news. In their view, employees are significantly aided by clear values statements that give them a ready defense against pressure to act unethically. In addition, resource mechanisms help them answer their questions quickly, no matter how insignificant. For example, one in six employees recently surveyed agreed with the statement that the traditional standards of right and wrong are no longer relevant and one-third either agreed or were ambivalent. But the survey also found that employees are receptive to corporate solutions which outline policies proscribing conduct and which encourage employees to police themselves.[3]

Frank D. Walker, chairman of Walker Information, Inc., has conducted numerous studies that have indicated that a worker's perception of the values and ethical practices of an organization will affect his or her commitment to the organization and their

---

[1] American Society of Chartered Life Underwriters and Chartered Financial Consultants and Ethics Officer Association, *Sources and Consequences of Workplace Pressure*, 1997.

[2] The Society for Human Resource Management, *The Society for Human Resource Management/Ethics Resource Center Business Ethics Survey*, 1997.

[3] American Society of Chartered Life Underwriters and Chartered Financial Consultants and Ethics Officer Association, *Technology and Ethics in the Workplace: The Ethical Impact of New Technologies on Workers*, 1988. See also Dawn-Marie Driscoll and W. Michael Hoffman, "Allow Employees to Speak Out on Company Practices," *Workforce*, November 1997, pp. 73-76.

> **"S**ome people would characterize ethics as a relatively soft concept. This is 1998. Competition is fierce. The winnings go to those who are the quickest. But we view ethics as a hard-core value. Because the values that are the product of consistent ethical behavior are what hold widely distributed organizations together. And that's one of the most compelling reasons for a firm like ours to have an ethics program in place. We are widely distributed. We're all over the world. And having resources that people can use every day is very important. You can't legislate moral behavior; you've got to have principles, values, and standards by which people can make decisions."
>
> Nicholas G. Moore
> chairman, PricewaterhouseCoopers,
> from his *Sears Lecture in Business Ethics*
> at Bentley College, February 9, 1998

intention to remain with the company. In his 1999 Society for Business Ethics presentation of some of these studies Walker said, "We do believe that by developing and offering a formal position and policy related to ethics and compliance that organizations will be ultimately rewarded." We agree. A company that cares enough about its employees to pay attention to their real concerns will ultimately be compensated by a loyal and satisfied workforce.

Ethical behavior pays

Managers oriented to the bottom-line may find "ethics pays" a difficult fact to prove. The corollary may be a better test: unethical behavior can be costly. One needs only to read the headlines in the business section of a newspaper to understand that the price of misconduct is rising:

Texaco $176 million racial discrimination settlement after tape recordings of improper conversations among its top executives were released.

Archer Daniels Midland $100 million antitrust fine for price-fixing.

Louisiana-Pacific Corporation $37 million fine for customer and environmental fraud, including lying to inspectors.

Laboratory Corporation of America $187 million in fines and penalties for health care billing fraud.

Mitsubishi Motor Corporation $34 million to settle a government investigation of pervasive sexual harassment.

Caremark $250 million to settle a government investigation of illegal health care billing practices.

LaRoche Holding AG $500 million in a vitamin price-fixing case, and *BASF AG*, $225 million for its role in the same conspiracy.

Royal Caribbean Cruises, Ltd. Two fines — $9 million and $18 million, two years later — for deliberately dumping oil and hazardous materials in coastal waters.

These are examples of real costs, but can you measure savings? One ethics officer confidentially shared his frustration in reporting to his board of directors about the company's ethics and business conduct program. One director asked him how he could statistically measure the program's success. He had to explain that one can't always measure preventive medicine, but that increased employee use of the confidential helpline, employee satisfaction surveys and the prompt resolution of festering problems were distinct benefits that may help the company avoid becoming a newspaper headline in the future.

You're ahead of the curve

Some managers prefer a checklist approach to implementing a program. They think through the vision and can then measure the roll-out by seeing if all the "action items" or programmatic steps have been achieved. If all ten (or twenty or thirty) have been finished, they are satisfied.

Unfortunately, even if you compare your efforts today to the best practices models available, you can't be confident that your work is completed. You don't achieve "ethics" or "values." It's a continuing process, a total way of behaving, not a one-time effort.

"It's the core values."

Lewis E. Platt, chairman, Hewlett-Packard,
announcing Carly Fiorina as CEO, and explaining
H-P's reputation for a gender-blind environment
The New York Times, August 22, 1999, pg. 1

The best you can strive for is to be ahead of the curve, always striving to be one of the most ethical organizations while understanding that, like sainthood, perfection will never be attained.

We like to use the analogy of affirmative action. An organization can have an impassioned mission statement about diversity as well as a myriad of procedures, efforts and measurements to recruit and retain and promote minorities in the workforce. In truth, with all these endeavors, the climate for integrating minorities into the employee pool may be no better than before. But if affirmation action — or putting values into action — is an important goal, you will never stop asking, "How can we do this better than we are now?"

Also many corporations are recognized as having excellent ethics programs even though they may have been motivated by an ethical crisis or had an ethical problem after they were up and running. To name a few such benchmark programs:

- **Sears** (despite problems in its automotive repair shops and credit collection departments)
- **Northrop**, now **Northrop Grumman** (despite problems in its Pomona testing labs)
- **Nynex**, now **Bell Atlantic** (despite problems with employee and vendor improprieties)
- **Coopers & Lybrand**, now **PricewaterhouseCoopers** (despite problems with some partner actions in Arizona and Los Angeles)

The goal is to not be discouraged by missteps or problems along the way. Rather, it is to continue to match or surpass today's professional leaders in business ethics.

In addition, we have mentioned scores of companies and organizations throughout this book, many of which are developing exciting new initiatives to put values into action. They are joined by new peers in the business ethics movement every day. As the work of ethics practitioners is never finished, neither is ours, as chroniclers. The second edition or sequel to *Ethics Matters* will include their stories and ideas. We think we'll call it *Ethics Works*, because it does.

One more thought

When Peter Drucker, the legendary management guru, was thirteen, a teacher asked him what he wanted to be remembered for. Drucker, still prolific in his 80's, continues to ask himself that question, "because it pushes you to see yourself as a different person — the person you can become."[4]

So too with our quest for the ethical edge. Managers should not want to be lauded for the good procedures they set in motion, but rather for the values these procedures deliver, ones that create a management culture that is always striving for excellence. These enlightened managers know that ethics matters.

---

[4] Jack Beatty, *The World According to Peter Drucker*, New York: The Free Press, 1998, p. 10.

This book, and others like it, illustrates that the business ethics movement has come a long way from compliance programs to a process of instilling values into organizations. An ailing patient, sorely in need of a healthy dose of ethical values, has been prescribed a wide range of cures, from codes of conduct and ethics audits, to widespread training and the continual reevaluation of programs and procedures. But in the past twenty-five years the focus on curing ethical malaise has mainly concentrated on reaching employees in far-flung facilities — the troops, not the generals.

While these efforts are obviously important, we also have to concentrate on the top levels of corporate governance. [1] We have hinted at this by selecting several stories in this book, where the issue of values resides at the board level. In our view, this is the right moment for such a focus. Attention to corporate governance is not new. For example, the National Association of Corporate Directors was founded at the same time (1976) as Bentley College's Center for Business Ethics. What is new, however, is the convergence of the two fields of corporate governance and business ethics. As the new millenium approaches, we have a clear message: incorporating integrity at the top of business institutions is critical for continued economic success.

As former chancellor William T. Allen of the influential Delaware chancery court said, "Governance contributes legitimacy to an enterprise." [2] We say, "Attention to ethics contributes

---

[1] This idea, and some of the material in this chapter, are expressed in an article for a special issue of *Business Ethics Quarterly* devoted to the challenges of the business ethics movement in the next millenium. This issue is scheduled to appear in January 2000.

[2] William T. Allen, "Independence, Integrity and the Governance of Institutions," *Director's Monthly*, January 1998, p. 13.

> **"A**s an article I read recently put it, business ethics comes down to personal responsibility and critical mass. We need plenty of both. Global business ethics is no longer just a matter of playing by the rules. It's a matter of making the rules to ensure that the global economy reaches its full potential and everyone gets a piece of the pie ... or sushi as the case may be. Enough business leaders must take personal responsibility to create the critical mass to get this job done."
>
> Dominic A. Tarantino
> chairman, Price Waterhouse World Firm,
> presentation to The Keidanren Subcommitttee on the Charter for
> Good Corporate Behavior, Caux Round Table, March 4, 1998

legitimacy to governance." We think the real success of efforts to implement values-driven management will occur when we are able to integrate considerations of ethics and values *up* in an organization, at the top levels of our global business institutions. Therefore encouraging a commitment to business ethics by those who govern institutions should be our charge. And to be perfectly frank, instilling values at that level can not be implemented by a ten-point program.

What's next?

Our attention today is necessarily focused on international global institutions, with concerns not just of garden-variety business ethics, but of public policy and human rights considerations. Our lives are intertwined around the world. As *New York Times* columnist Thomas L. Friedman reminds us, we are a community of one environment, one economy, and rapid communication through global technological systems.[3] The driving force of globalization is free market capitalism, but we need common ethical standards as well to guide the actions of all the world's econom-

---

[3] Thomas L. Friedman, *The Lexus and the Olive Tree*, New York: Farrar Straus & Giroux, 1999.

ic powers so that those with resources will be fair and responsible, and those without resources will be safe and secure.

There are mechanisms to hold governments accountable, but that's not the problem. "Today, the emerging issue is how do you hold private companies accountable for the treatment of their workers at a time when government control is ebbing all over the world, or governments themselves are going into business and can't be expected to play the watchdog or protection role?" Friedman asked. [4]

Will the next millenium be marked by a widening gap between the world's haves and have-nots or will more countries share in a millenium marked by economic prosperity? Will only a privileged few enjoy clean air and water and safe working conditions, or will we agree to a uniform set of global standards? It is not enough that the world be democratic and capitalistic. For globalization to succeed the business world must be ethical and its dealings based on a core set of values. Given that global megacorporations — particularly financial institutions — may have more influence on our future than governments, whether or not they operate with such values are of paramount importance. [5]

We can predict one thing with reasonable certainty. The result we desire will not come about if we pursue the business ethics movement in the same way we have before. Values must permeate every level of an organization, especially the top levels, to influence corporate policy.

What we see

We see global institutions that are lacking in values because the generals at the top don't think it's important. The effect is that the institution just "doesn't get it." Its leaders have a lack of awareness, missing the implications and current realities of how business should be conducted. Perhaps they have been shel-

---

[4] Thomas L. Friedman, "The New Human Rights," *The New York Times*, July 30, 1999, p. A23.

[5] See William Greider, *One World, Ready Or Not*, Simon & Schuster, 1997. For a specific discussion of the moral responsibility of corporations with regard to Burma, for example, see John R. Schermerhorn, Jr., "Terms of Global Business Engagement in Ethically Challenging Environments: Applications to Burma," *Business Ethics Quarterly*, Vol. 9, No. 3, July 1999, pp. 485-505.

tered; perhaps cultural considerations have overshadowed an appreciation of contemporary ethical standards. They don't see that their way of doing business (which usually brought them success) may ultimately be harmful to others.

Corporate leaders must be champions of universal values if economic prosperity and ethics in the next century are going to reach those who have lacked it in the last hundred years. For example, some believe that the economic crisis in Indonesia was as much caused by interlocking political and business connections as it was by the rapid movement of international capital.[6] The European Commission discovered it needed to rid itself of fraud and mismanagement if it was to retain any credibility in leading the European Union. An international anti-fraud unit reported that as much as a billion dollars had disappeared or was stolen from public monies, uncollected taxes and international aid directed to rebuild Bosnia, calling into question the willingness of world donors to continue to fund relief aid in the face of widespread corruption. In the next century those with economic prosperity will be the institutions that have a culture based on ethical boundaries, not just economic riches.

As an earlier chapter pointed out, one such global institution lacking values is the International Olympic Committee. (In fact, the scandal made a mockery of its values of "Faster — Higher — Stronger." Some cynics even suggested the motto applied to its members with their hands out.) It's the IOC today, where an opportunity (cities seeking to host the Games) met an opportunity (members seeking gifts and gratuities), with no controls or ethical culture. Will it be the International Red Cross, Catholic Charities, the United Nations or another important global non-governmental organization tomorrow?

We also see situations when an ethical issue stares an organization in the face but no one has the intellectual capacity to conceptualize it. Senior managers and board members are silent, despite overwhelming evidence that something is sorely amiss. "Maybe it will go away," they think, remaining voiceless and inactive.

---

[6] For further discussion, see the four part series by Nicholas Kristof with Edward Wyatt, "Global Contagion, a Narrative," *The New York Times*, February 15-18, 1999, p. A1.

We think "it" will not just go away. We've seen companies with ethics and values programs, infrastructure, web sites, booklets and awards on the shelf suddenly become dumb when presented with an ethical issue that doesn't fit a neat procedural model.

A glaring example is that of compensation given to top executives, clearly an issue that can only be dealt with by those who govern such institutions. The pay disparity between CEOs and United States workers is increasing.[7] In 1965 CEOs made 44 times the average factory worker's salary. Today, CEOs make 326 times the average factory worker's pay. If the minimum wage, enacted in 1960, had risen at the same rate as executive pay, it would stand at $41/hour.

Did CEOs earn it? Among 365 major United States companies, CEO pay climbed 35% in 1997. Corporate profits rose only one seventh that rate, at 5%. Factory employees' pay rose 2.6%.

Here is just one example. Richard Scrushy, chairman and chief executive officer of HealthSouth, took home nearly $107 million in 1997 in annual compensation and stock option exercises. He has another $216 million in unexercised stock options. Executive compensation expert Graef Crystal names Scrushy one of the most overpaid CEOs in 1996. In that year he took 36.9% of the total stock options granted to HealthSouth employees.

No one pockets a lot of cash and stock without some complicity. Among those on HealthSouth's board of directors is Dr. Philip C. Watkins, who owned property with Scrushy in the Florida Keys, and S. Sage Givens, a partner in a venture capital fund. HealthSouth has invested in Givens' firm, and the firm in turn invested in a managed care company that then secured a contract with HealthSouth. (HealthSouth's board members are not the only ones who have dealings with the company; Scrushy's mother Grace sold $12.9 million worth of computer equipment to HealthSouth.) Was all of this legal? Yes. Was it ethical? You be the judge.

We are not picking on highly paid CEOs, even those abetted by self-dealing boards. Rather, we are using the issue of executive compensation to illustrate a difficult ethical issue that

---

[7] Facts, figures and stories of runaway CEO pay can be found at the AFL-CIO's web site, www.afl-cio.org/paywatch.

resides at the top level of our institutions. At what point does compensation become so excessive that it becomes an ethical matter? Whose ethical problem is it? How does one address the issue and frame a response? The question of executive pay, like other topics, will not disappear, particularly as American companies merge with European organizations where such levels of pay are not commonplace.

Global issues — more difficult?

The admittedly extreme and complex case of Mobil Corporation's P.T.Arun, a liquefied natural gas producer in Indonesia's Aceh province, illustrates the problem of integrating a values-driven culture across global organizations. Mobil owns 35% of the company that is located in a province with a history of guerrilla uprisings against the military. Human rights organizations have uncovered evidence of massacres and mass graves, and allege that Mobil Oil Indonesia, a wholly owned subsidiary, provided crucial logistic support to the army that carried out the massacres. Furthermore, activists assert that representatives of Mobil's companies were aware of the torture going on in its backyard, as contractors told local Mobil managers that they had found human body parts. Rumors of the massacres were frequently discussed in the workplace. If everyone else in Aceh knew that that massacres were taking place, Mobil representatives surely did.

Mobil says that no managers were aware of the killings and that no reports exist to document that anyone had such information. The truth may never be known with certainty, but the entire discussion raises the question of the ethical responsibility of multinational corporations that do business in Third World dictatorships. They may have no legal responsibility to take action, but what is their ethical and moral responsibility? How do managers in the field, regional managers, corporate executives or the board of directors deal with such allegations and arrive at an ethical course of action for the corporation? Has the company's leadership developed a set of core values that it can then turn to for guidance?

Mobil is not the only global company to discover that tough moral issues complicate ongoing operations. Two consortia of oil companies operating in Colombia have been accused of complicity in killings, beatings and arrests committed by their private security forces. Similar allegations of killing, torture, rape and forced labor have been reported against Burmese forces providing security for the Yadana gas pipeline that runs from Burma to Thailand. Chevron has been sued for liability in human rights violations committed by Nigeria's military troops. Civilian massacres have been cited in the area of the Chad-Cameroon pipeline, as well as government corruption and a lack of environmental safeguards.

Corporations are clearly guilty when committing violations of human rights directly. Are they any less so when they fund, facilitate or participate in government human rights violations, or when they simply benefit from the failure of local government to enforce human rights standards? How will these global entities, many of them joint ventures involving several international companies, react to continued criticism of their passivity regarding human rights abuses? If, as in the case of Mobil's operations in the Aceh area, the company's presence is an economic benefit to otherwise impoverished citizens, the questions become more difficult. Because the generals at the top of organizations are often accomplished, well-known individuals of stature, we also see evidences of self-righteousness instead of values. These organizations believe they are acting ethically because of who they are and what they stand for. They believe their slogans. Would a "supermarket to the world" commit wrongdoing? Apparently yes. Archer Daniels Midland Corporation became famous not only for the guilty verdict against its senior executives for price-fixing, but for the conflicts of interest among the members of its board of directors.

We see ethical self-righteousness in other examples of corporate welfare. According to a *Boston Globe* study the U.S. federal government gives up about $70 billion each year through corporate tax breaks. Is it unethical for a company to take advantage of a provision of the tax code? Does it make a difference if the tax breaks are targeted or available to all? For example, three executives of C.R. Bard Inc. were convicted of concealing flaws in medical catheters, implicated in the deaths of two patients and 21 emergency surgeries. Bard paid a $61 million legal settlement with the government but took half the fine as a tax deduction.

Taxpayers are contributing $300,000 to help the Walt Disney Company improve its fireworks displays. Admittedly this is small change compared to the $110 million in government grants given to General Motors. But is it ethical? These may be questions for policy-makers rather than business leaders, but at the moment, it appears it is to no one's benefit to discontinue the pork barrel — except possibly the public.

Ethics scholars and practitioners could debate these examples, but that's not where the debate is apt to lead to a change.

A few ideas

We believe that we will not begin to instill values in the process of making corporate policy decisions until the group of business ethics advocates goes beyond academics and the current practitioners. Those who should think about ethics are the most influential individuals in the world: policy-makers, opinion leaders, the media, boards of directors, senior corporate leaders, leaders of business organizations and trade associations, lawyers, accountants, investment bankers, international economic experts, elected officials and global leaders. By any definition, they comprise the "International Club of Thinkers and Doers." Members of this Club, while often invisible to the man in the street, have considerable influence on one another.

We emphasize the word "international." As British Petroleum merges with Amoco, Daimler with Chrysler, Deutsche Bank with Bankers Trust, and so on, megacorporations will dominate national and international affairs and have a larger role in dictating policy and economic decisions. Discussions about employee ethics programs and programs to implement values-driven management will continue, but beyond that there will be tough issues of where corporate responsibility takes over from government responsibility. Open markets will continue to be a global goal, but only the leaders of the global giants themselves will determine the ethical framework within which they will operate.

Transparency is one idea

In this era of round-the-clock global communication, we know no better way to move ideas than disclosure and storytelling. For example, the Bank of Scotland, having decided to acquire the interests of Robertson Financial Services, decided to conduct a joint telephone banking venture with television evangelist Pat Robertson, founder of the Christian Coalition. The venture was to offer deposits to the televangelist's 50 million viewers and later pitch credit cards, loans and mortgages to them. Perhaps the senior executives in Edinburgh were not familiar with Robertson's social views when they proposed the deal, but it was not long before they cancelled it after a public outcry arose over Robertson's public comments about Scotland and homosexuals. Hundreds of bank customers cancelled their accounts and the West Lothian district council in Scotland said it would withdraw its $403 million account from the bank if the deal went forward. The bank's chief executive, Peter Burt, met with Robertson and announced the deal was dead because of changed external circumstances. In other words, while the financial concept may have been sound, dealing with an individual with Robertson's strongly held views did not correspond with the bank's values.

It is not just investigative journalists who keep the spotlight on global organizations. Watchdog organizations such as the National Labor Committee, Transparency International and Human Rights Watch play an important role in bringing corporate activity to light.

Training is another idea

Directors, trustees and senior managers are beginning to understand that setting an ethical tone and considering the ethical implications of major decisions play an important role and carry as much responsibility as financial oversight. But while many senior officers are comfortable and experienced analyzing financial statements, balance sheets and auditors' reports, it is the rare business leader who is equally facile discussing ethical principles openly and with candor.

And yet these "members of the club" must not wait until the ethical crisis hits to arrive at a consensus about the organization's moral values, as the International Olympic Committee story shows. They need to take the time to discuss ethics and hear each other's views. Thinkers and practitioners in the business ethics movement must help them do this. Business and global leaders cannot possibly demonstrate integrity without an ability to debate and resolve ethical concerns.

The importance of training has been emphasized earlier in this book, but it bears special mention for those at senior levels. Diligent boards of directors have set aside time at board meetings or retreats to learn more about business ethics and to discuss and debate both their own values and those of the corporation. These off-the-record sessions, many of which we have facilitated for directors, have been engaging and timely, underscored by an unmistakable note of urgency and concern. [8]

Global initiatives is a third idea

In Chapter 1 we saw that industry-wide initiatives to raise ethical standards in the United States can influence the business conduct and values of individual companies. Efforts to agree on common standards are not just restricted to this country. The Caux Round Table, comprised of international business leaders, created its first set of shared values in 1994 and has disseminated them widely. In the environmental area, the International Organization for Standardization, which consists of 112 countries, has promulgated ISO 14000, a series of 17 environmental management standards. The reach of such standards is great. For example, Asarco Mining company has agreed to conform to ISO 14001 (the one standard that is a requirements document) as part of a $61 million regulatory settlement with the Environmental Protection Agency. The attorney general of New York has strongly recommended that Brookhaven Laboratory conform to ISO 14001 before the facility can reopen.

But such standards are not used just to punish polluters. They also provide a roadmap for companies looking to conduct business the right way. Bristol-Meyers Squibb became the first multinational corporation to self-declare its overall environmental management system to conform to the requirements of ISO 14001, and Nissan Motor Manufacturing Corporation will be compliant worldwide by 1999. Aer Rianta, in Dublin, became the

---

[8] See Dawn-Marie Driscoll and W. Michael Hoffman, "Hark Corporate Director: 'Tis the Call of Ethical Leadership," *Ethics Today*, Vol. 3, No. 1, Winter 1998, p. 5.

world's first airport to register to ISO 14001 in 1996. The Canadian Government has adopted ISO 14001 as a government-wide policy, and Nova Scotia provides a twenty-five per cent tax credit on costs related to the implementation of environmental management systems.

In many ways ISO 14000 mirrors the notion of a comprehensive values-based ethics initiative with a philosophy that is based on managing the right way, not just reacting to regulations. As environmental consultant Faith Leavitt explained, "ISO 14001 is less about hugging trees and more about making good decisions for both the environment and business."

International organizations are beginning to attack other areas in which ethical problems disrupt the global economy. For example, the Organization for Economic Cooperation and Development and the Organization of American States have taken a first step by passing anti-bribery treaties, although some countries which have signed the treaties have been slow to change their tax laws which permit deductions for bribes. The International Monetary Fund and the World Bank plan to incorporate anti-corruption efforts into their lending policies, and Reverend Leon Sullivan, known for the anti-apartheid Sullivan Principles in South Africa, is working with the State Department to draw up a set of international voluntary principles that combat corruption. Business ethicists will watch with interest to see how many companies adopt these standards as their own.

Even religious scholars and theologians have attempted to draft common principles. *Declaration Toward a Global Ethic* emerged from a conference on world religions in 1993; *Interfaith Declaration and Mutual Responsibility: The Tie That Binds* are the result of two other similar meetings.[9]

Ethical capital required

Michael Milken, perhaps an unlikely character to be quoted near the end of a business ethics book, has said that a favorable fundamental shift has occurred in the business world as control of capital has moved from private institutions to public markets,

---

[9] See John Dalla Costa, *The Ethical Imperative*, Reading, MA: Perseus Books, 1998.

democratizing the availability of financing to individuals with ideas, rather than individuals with a pedigree. But public markets, he thinks, also look for the presence of "social capital" (such as education, police protection, religious freedom, community bonds, property rights, and financial reporting standards) before they invest. In his opinion inadequate social capital is the weak link that limits a country's prosperity. [10]

We agree and take his argument one step further. In our view, ethical capital is also a prerequisite for global economic success. Ethical capital includes universal agreement among a country's opinion leaders about fundamental values; evidence of a commitment to those values by "members of the club;" healthy debate and dialogue about complex, unresolved ethical issues; a willingness by all parties to work together to resolve disagreements by persuasion and negotiation; and a free and responsible press to investigate and report on activities of the country's major social and business institutions.

As international organizations, governments and global companies work together to develop fundamental principles of ethical capital while shunning investment in those countries that disdain their efforts, we expect the flow of capital, job creation and financial prosperity will underscore the importance of a values-driven economy.

Conclusion

Global corruption. Excessive executive pay and substandard working conditions. Environmental plunder. Complicity in human rights abuses. Corporate welfare. The list of challenges is endless, but we believe the prognosis for instilling values at the top of organizations is encouraging, despite the daunting nature of the task. The key is to develop a successful process and commitment to push values-driven leadership and governance to the top of our worldwide business organizations, with the goal of achieving ethics and values in every corner of the globe.

---

[10] Michael Milken, "Prosperity and Social Capital," *The Wall Street Journal,* June 23, 1999, p. A26.

INDEX

About the Authors

Dawn-Marie Driscoll is an executive fellow and advisory board member at the Center for Business Ethics and president of Driscoll Associates, a consulting firm. Formerly vice president of corporate affairs and general counsel of Filene's, the department store chain, and a corporate law partner at Palmer & Dodge, she is an independent trustee of several Scudder mutual funds and a director of several private companies. She is a member of the board of governors of the Investment Company Institute, the national association of mutual funds, and chairs its directors committee to advise the institute regarding issues for independent directors. She is a member of the Ethics Officer Association faculty and an advisory board member of the *Business and Society Review*. Ms. Driscoll has been appointed a visitor-in-residence at The Bunting Institute at Radcliffe College, a visiting scholar at the University of Montana School of Business and the visiting Aram Professor of Business Ethics at Gonzaga University.

W. Michael Hoffman, Ph.D, is the founder and executive director of the Center for Business Ethics and professor of philosophy at Bentley College in Waltham, Massachusetts. His work in business ethics includes the publishing of 15 books and over 50 articles, consulting for numerous organizations, including Fortune 500 companies, and serving as an expert witness in litigation. Dr. Hoffman was the first executive director of the Ethics Officer Association and currently is the advisor to its board of directors. He was a founder and president of the Society for Business Ethics, served on the advisory board of the U.S. Sentencing Commission, and is frequently sought out globally for professional lectures and media interviews.

Driscoll and **Hoffman** have published many written works together, including *The Ethical Edge: Tales of Organizations That Have Faced Moral Crises* (with Edward S. Petry, NY: MasterMedia, 1995).

Founded in 1976, the **Center for Business Ethics** at **Bentley College** is dedicated to promoting ethical business conduct in contemporary society. With a vast network of practitioners and scholars, an executive fellows program and an expansive multimedia library, the center provides an international forum for benchmarking and research in business ethics. The center helps corporations and other organizations strengthen their ethical cultures through educational programming and consulting.